Cornelius Nary in lay dress, by John Brooks.
(Courtesy of the National Library of Ireland.)

Dublin's Turbulent Priest

CORNELIUS NARY (1658–1738)

PATRICK FAGAN

ROYAL IRISH ACADEMY
DUBLIN 1991

Published by
Royal Irish Academy
19 Dawson Street
Dublin 2
Ireland

© Royal Irish Academy 1991
ISBN 0 901714 97 6

British Library Cataloguing in Publication Data
A catalogue record for this book is available from the British Library

By the same author:

View from Mount Pelier (a collection of verse)

Three one-act plays

The last citadel (a three-act play)

Bíonn an fhírinne searbh (a collection of short stories in Irish)

Fíon an ghrá (three one-act plays in Irish)

Éigse na hIarmhí (Gaelic poets from Westmeath)

The Second City: portrait of Dublin 1700–1760

A Georgian celebration: Irish poets of the eighteenth century

Cover design: Philip Quested
Printed by Dundalgan Press (W. Tempest) Ltd.

CONTENTS

ACKNOWLEDGEMENTS

My sincere thanks are due to Dr Patrick Kelly, Dean of the Faculty of Arts (Humanities), Trinity College, Dublin, for reading the original manuscript and for his advice and help in revising it. For the use of material from the Stuart Papers in the Royal Archives at Windsor Castle the permission of Her Majesty, Queen Elizabeth II, is gratefully acknowledged. I should also like specially to acknowledge the permission of His Grace the Archbishop of Dublin, the Most Reverend Desmond Connell, D.D., for the use of material from the Dublin diocesan archives; of Lord Talbot of Malahide, Hook Manor, Donhead St Andrew, Shaftesbury, for access to and use of correspondence (in his possession) of Cornelius Nary with Sir Richard Bellings; of the Reverend Mother, Poor Clares Convent, Harold's Cross, Dublin, for the use of material from the Annals of the Poor Clares; of Father Benignus Millett, O.F.M., editor, *Collectanea Hibernica,* for the use of material from the Vatican Archives edited or calendared in that journal by the late Father Cathaldus Giblin, O.F.M.; and of Father Christopher Twomey, P.P., for the use of material from St Michan's parish register.

I am also indebted to the staff of the following institutions for their help and cooperation in my research work: Royal Irish Academy, Dublin; National Library of Ireland; Gilbert Library (a branch of the Dublin Public Libraries); National Archives, Dublin; Representative Church Body Library, Dublin; Dublin Diocesan Library, Clonliffe, Dublin; King's Inns Library, Dublin; Central Catholic Library, Dublin; British Library, London; Registry of Deeds, Dublin; Franciscan House of Studies, Killiney, Dublin; Discalced Carmelites Library, Morehampton Road, Dublin; and the libraries of Trinity College, Dublin, University College, Dublin, and St Patrick's College, Maynooth.

FOREWORD

The late Mary Alice McNeill was the author of a number of elegant and well-received biographical studies: *Mary Ann McCracken, Little Tom Drennan—Portrait of a Georgian childhood* and *Vere Foster 1819–1900, an Irish benefactor*. In 1984 she left a sum of money to the Royal Irish Academy to endow a literary award which would take the form of assistance in the publication of a work of scholarship relating to Ireland. She expressed two wishes: that preference should be given to 'historical studies in the broadest sense' and that particular encouragement should be given to 'persons who are not necessarily professionally engaged in academic study either in a university or elsewhere'.

The first competition was held in 1990 and was judged, in accordance with the instructions of Miss McNeill, by a panel of representatives from the National University of Ireland, Queen's University, Belfast, the Linen Hall Library, Trinity College Dublin, and the Academy. There was a large entry of good quality and the panel was pleased to be able to recommend with full confidence the publication of the work on Cornelius Nary submitted by Patrick Fagan. Although Mr Fagan has already made valuable contributions to our knowledge of eighteenth-century Dublin, he is not a scholar by profession, so that the first publication funded from the request meets Miss McNeill's wishes with fitting precision.

Aidan Clarke
President, Royal Irish Academy

vii

Chapter 1

CHILD OF THE RESTORATION

A great ash tree shades the southern corner of the graveyard. All around it are the tombstones of the long-departed, many dating from the early eighteenth century. A little to the north are the ruins of an old church, and beside it a stone cross, believed to be a memorial to the Delahyde family, with the date 1616 engraved upon it. The part of the graveyard beyond the church to the north is completely devoid of tombstones, perhaps indicating that this was where the poorer class of people, who could not afford the luxury of tombstones, were buried.

As in everything else, there is a kind of snobbery evident in graveyards. Here at Tipper the south-west corner, around the great ash tree, was clearly the area favoured by the 'better sort' of family, for it is well supplied with tombstones. But we search in vain for the grave of Father Cornelius Nary although it may be safely assumed that he was buried here on a March day in 1738. For had he not directed in his will that he should 'be interred in the churchyard at Tipper, at the foot of an ash tree, south side of the churchyard, where my father and mother were buried'?[1] The absence of a tombstone is not surprising, however, since he had further directed that nothing costly be laid out on his funeral, and this was probably interpreted as meaning also that he desired no monument to mark his resting-place.

Evidently, then, it was here in Tipper that the saga of Cornelius Nary ended. But it was here, too, in Tipper that that saga began. . .

He was a child of the Restoration. In 1658,[2] two years before Charles Stuart returned from his travels to ascend the throne of the Three Kingdoms as Charles II, Cornelius Nary

1

was born in the parish of Tipper,[3] one or two miles from Naas, Co. Kildare, on the Blessington road. There are six townlands in the civil parish of Tipper—Tipper itself, Baltracey, Craddockstown, Bullock Park, Kingsfurze and Newtown, any one of which could have been his birthplace. The total area of the parish is 3,182 acres. In 1640 Nicholas Sutton, 'Irish Papist', owned 700 'profitable acres' in the townland of Tipper, but he lost it all to one Thomas Piggott under the Act of Settlement. William Eustace, 'Irish Papist', held 715 acres in Craddockstown, 625 acres of which were retained by his son, Christopher, under readjustments made after the Restoration.[4] These were the landowning class, and underneath them were the tenant farmers, who leased farms of varying sizes from the landlords, and further down the scale were the cottagers to whom the landlords or the tenant farmers let little patches of ground of sufficient size to accommodate a cabin and a potato patch.

I have been unable to discover any information about the occupation of Cornelius Nary's father. One can detect a certain smugness or snobbishness in some of his letters and pamphlets, which would imply that he himself came from a well-to-do background. Given the limited opportunities available at that time in a rural economy, the only occupation his father could have followed and remained affluent, apart perhaps from that of miller, was that of large tenant farmer. One source which would have given us at least his father's name and some idea of the type of house the family lived in is the Hearth Money Returns, but unfortunately these were all destroyed in the fire in the Public Record Office in 1922 and, as far as I can discover, they had not been previously extracted for County Kildare as they had been for neighbouring County Dublin. Under the Hearth Tax the occupant of each house paid a tax of two shillings per annum in respect of each hearth in his house. An examination of the Hearth Money Returns for 1664 for County Dublin[5] (and the situation in north Kildare cannot have been much different) shows that over 90% of all houses had only one hearth, and this can only mean that the houses of some substantial tenant farmers had only one hearth. Indeed, an inspector-general of Hearth Money stated that the occupier of a one-hearth house might be a substantial farmer, a small shopkeeper, or a skilled artisan with a comfortable standard of living.[6]

A statistical survey of County Kildare, published in 1807, tells us that 'the farmhouses in general consist of a long thatched building of one story, containing a large kitchen and fire-place in the centre, and lodging rooms at either end', and that 'farms generally rise from ten acres to one or two hundred'.[7] The situation was probably much the same in the latter half of the seventeenth century.

The probability, therefore, is that Cornelius Nary's father was a substantial tenant farmer, living in a large thatched house. Large families were then the rule, and the Narys were no exception. The beneficiaries under Cornelius Nary's will, executed on the day of his death, were his brother Walter, who apparently survived him, and the children of his brother Denis and of his sisters Mary, Joan and Anne. All of these shared between them the not very large sum of thirty pounds.[8] He may have had other brothers and sisters who predeceased him but did not leave any children. The family name does not appear to have survived for very long around Tipper for there is no mention of it in the Tithe Applotment Books of the 1820s, nor in Griffith's Valuation of the 1850s.

MacLysaght tells us that the name Nary is a variation of the more common Neary.[9] In the eighteenth century the form 'Nary' appears to have been in use mainly in Connaught, while the more common 'Neary' was to be found mainly in County Louth.

The period of Nary's youth and early manhood was a period of great revival, great development and relative prosperity in Ireland. After ten years of devastating war, the recovery had begun in the 1650s and continued, apart from one or two setbacks, until the country was again plunged into war with the 'Glorious Revolution' of 1688. There was thus a period of over thirty years of relative peace and prosperity. It was a period of great changes in the ownership of land. The pattern of land ownership in certain Leinster counties, which had not changed since the Norman Invasion nearly five hundred years before, was rudely disrupted by the Cromwellian Settlement. In the counties of the Pale—Dublin, Meath, Westmeath, Louth and Kildare—this meant that the Anglo-Norman lords and minor gentry, whose ancestors had acquired these lands by right of conquest in the twelfth century, were to a large extent deprived of their estates and condemned to try their luck in the province of Connaught. These people entertained great hopes of repossessing their estates with the return of the monarchy in 1660. After all, they, like the king, had fought and lost against Cromwell and the Parliamentary forces, with the consequent

3

appropriation of their estates by ex-soldiers and adventurers. But their hopes were only to a small extent fulfilled under the Act of Settlement and Explanation. Charles II did not have the political will to uproot the Cromwellian settlers and perhaps precipitate another bloody struggle. He had no desire to risk going on his travels again, and so the settlers largely remained put and only a minority of the old landowners regained their estates. Thus in his own neighbourhood Cornelius Nary was to see the Suttons in Tipper lose out to the Piggotts, but the Eustaces remain in possession in Craddockstown.

It is necessary, however, to distinguish between the ownership of land and the occupancy of it. While the owners (largely landlords) changed to an overwhelming extent, the indications are that the tenant farmers, who leased their farms from the landlords, did not change to anything like the same extent. A substantial proportion of land continued to be occupied by Catholic tenant farmers, and through all the vicissitudes of the eighteenth and nineteenth centuries this remained the case.

In the highly fertile land of north Kildare the young Nary grew up in a prosperous farming community. During the Restoration period and into the early years of the eighteenth century there was in this area and in neighbouring County Dublin a great emphasis on tillage, which must have made for a much more prosperous economy, with a much greater employment potential, than the alternative of cattle- and sheep-raising. We find Archbishop King of Dublin early in the eighteenth century bemoaning the passing of tillage in the neighbourhood of Dublin, and the effect this had on the tithes of the clergymen of his Church: 'When the great ploughing in the Kingdom was about or near Dublin, the clergy had a comfortable maintenance from their tithes; and the pasturage of bullocks and dry cattle was so insignificant that clergy commonly threw them into the bargains they made for the tithes of grain. But of late the plough is everywhere laid aside, and generally in the leases the landlords have obliged the tenants not to plough; one consequence of which is that all manner of grain is dearer in Dublin than in London'.[10]

Thus the strong tenant farmer achieved a degree of comfort and civilised living during the Restoration period which might appear surprising to us today. Laurence Whyte, born about 1680, as a teacher of mathematics in Dublin remembered such a home in Westmeath and described it minutely in verse. His long

4

poem *The parting cup, or The humours of Deoch an Doruis*[11] brings one such strong tenant farmer, known affectionately as Deoch an Doruis, vividly to life, and tells us what he ate and drank, how he was clothed, how he reared his children, the games and pastimes. We can envisage the Nary home at Tipper as being not very different.

The farmer in Laurence Whyte's poem 'stood at a moderate, easy rent', a situation which was to change some thirty or so years later when, Whyte tells us, he was rack-rented into ruin. This farmer, however, in the days of prosperity, 'kept a harp and pair of Tables,/good oats and hay in barns and stables,/and all extravagance to shun,/he wore the cloth his wife had spun. . ./And nothing foreign, she would tell you/should clothe her back or fill her belly'. The sons engaged in a wide variety of games and pastimes, but eschewed hunting and racing because these were apt to prove too expensive: 'They seldom did refuse a summons/to play at football or at Commons,/to pitch the bar or throw a sledge,/to vault or take a ditch or hedge;/at leisure hours to unfold a riddle,/or play the bagpipes, or fiddle'.

The farmer's wife was no less busy with the training and upbringing of the daughters of the house. Proper deportment, apparently, was considered a very desirable attainment for the strong farmer's daughter with matrimonial ambitions: 'Walk smooth and straight, keep out your toes, and see to manage well your clothes./To be good house-wives you must learn/to make and mend, to wash and darn, . . ./If you be handy, 'twill support you,/and bring industrious lads to court you'. At the more practical level, she trained them to be good cooks and house-keepers, and also 'to use the needle, read and write,/and dance the Irish Trot at night'. At the patrons and the country dances the daughters were expected to give a good account of themselves: 'At Patrons dance a Jig or Hornpipe,/played on a fiddle or a corn-pipe,/such country dances as they play/on Salt Box or the Tongs or Key. . ./With mein above the common sort,/they mimicked those that came from Court,/and walked a Minuet, smooth and straight,/according to the Figure Eight,/and that with better grace and airs,/than some who dance at the Lord Mayor's./Though never bred in town or city,/with repartee or pun could fit ye,/and as their heels denote them dancers,/their heads were turned for witty answers./And when at work, could sweetly chime/their Irish songs in tune and time'. It is apparent from this poem that education and training

5

could be, and was, handed down from father to son, and from mother to daughter, with little benefit of teachers or tutors.

The majority of the people among whom the young Nary grew up were undoubtedly poor cottagers, that class of people whom he was fond of describing in later years as 'the little people'. But the lives of such people, in a prosperous area like north Kildare at any rate, as depicted in the prose and verse of the period, were not ones of unrelieved gloom. Despite the long hours of work required from them, they found time, particularly on Sundays and holydays, of which there were no less than 33 in a year, for a great deal of merriment and celebration, which found expression in dancing, singing, drinking, and a wide variety of games and pastimes. As regards games, football and more particularly hurling, or 'Commons' as it is called in Laurence Whyte's poem, were widely played in Kildare in Nary's youth.

An Englishman, John Dunton, passed through this area of north Kildare in 1683, and left us the following description of the lives of ordinary people:

> The Irish have another custom, to plant an ash or some other tree, which will grow big in the middle of a village, though I never observed them to be planters of them anywhere else. In some towns these trees are old and very great, and here all the people resort on Sundays or Holydays in the afternoon, where the young folks dance till the cows come home. I have seen a short, truss young woman tire five lusty fellows, who thereby gets a husband. . . The elder people sit spectators telling stories of their own like feats in days of yore, and now and then divert themselves with a quill full of sneezing or a whiff of tobacco. . . If in the dance the woman be tired, the man throws her to the piper, whose fee is half a penny, and he, if tired, is served after the same manner. Their games within doors are Backgammon and Five Cards, as common here as All Fours in England.[12]

As to the degree of religious toleration afforded to Catholics during this period, there are conflicting views even from contemporaries who ought to have known the situation well. This is how John Brenan, bishop of Waterford and later archbishop of Cashel, describes conditions in a report to Rome in 1672: 'Many of the pastors have no mass-house and celebrate on the mountains or in the open country, spreading some tent or covering over the altar. This is occasioned, not only by the poverty of the pastor, but by the fact that all the land is held by heretics, who will not allow a mass-house to be built'.[13] And again, in the same report for 1672, Brenan states that 'the Protestant magistrate, under pain of imprisonment and other arbitrary penalties, prohibits anyone to walk the streets [of Waterford] on Sundays while the heretics are assembling for service in the Cathedral or other churches, so that in our oratories Mass must be over and all celebrations before they go to Church'.[14] Brenan's report for the year 1675 states that 'the Catholic youth of this country is deprived to a great extent of good learning and instruction, for in virtue of the Penal Laws no Catholic is allowed to be a schoolmaster, and thus our young people have to be taught by Protestant masters, a most sad condition of things which cannot but be very prejudicial as time goes on'.[15]

But how are we to square views such as these with the provision in the Articles of Limerick that 'Roman Catholics shall enjoy such privileges in the exercise of their religion as are consistent with the laws of Ireland or as they did enjoy in the reign of Charles II'? If there had been widespread persecution in the reign of Charles II, is it likely that the Articles would have been framed in such misleading terms? Clearly, the perception of the negotiators must have been that Irish Catholics enjoyed a fair degree of toleration throughout that period.

Nor is it easy to square Brenan's reports with Cornelius Nary's view of the period as set out in his *The case of the Roman Catholics of Ireland,* when, he tells us, it was 'manifest the Roman Catholics had Bishops, Dignitaries, priests and Religious Orders of their own Communion to instruct and govern them in religious matters'. He goes on further to state that in the reign of Charles II it was

> manifest that all the Roman Catholic peers and gentlemen of Ireland and all others who would or could purchase them, carried arms; and that some of them were in posts of honour, as that of Sheriff, Justice of the Peace and other posts of profit and trust; that their lawyers, attornies and solicitors practised their respective callings with the same freedom and liberty as the Protestants. As also that the Roman Catholic merchants, dealers and tradesmen were Aldermen and Burgesses in cities and Freemen in towns and corporations over all the Kingdom.[16]

How are we to reconcile these conflicting views of the period? It must be said at once that Brenan was writing about a particular period (1672–5) and place. Nary's comments, on the other hand, are an overview of the period of almost twenty-five years of Charles II's reign, written many years afterwards on mature consideration. What the negotiators at Limerick had in mind was also an overview of the treatment of Catholics over

7

the entire reign. It appears that the only logical conclusion we can come to, then, is that, while it cannot be gainsaid that there were periods of very active persecution of Catholics during the reign of Charles II, these must have appeared in hindsight as exceptions in a period with a reasonable degree of toleration, taken as a whole.

The principal laws which affected Catholics during this period were the Acts of Supremacy and Uniformity, both of which dated from Elizabeth's reign. The oath required under the Act of Supremacy acknowledged the king's authority in spiritual matters, and was required of members of parliament as well as holders of public office. The form of religious rites to be used was prescribed under the Act of Uniformity, and penalties were laid down for any other form of 'open' prayers. But, as will be seen to have been the case with much of the penal legislation of William's and Anne's reigns, the letter of the law was one thing, but how and when and where it was applied was another.

Given its propinquity to the capital, it is safe to assume that north Kildare was one of the areas of the country which early succumbed to Anglicisation. It is quite probable that the Irish language had disappeared early on, as it had in north County Dublin, where it was never the language of the Norman and English settlers of that area. In north Kildare it may in Nary's youth have lingered with the elderly, but it is quite possible that he never learned it. He never mentions the Irish language, as far as I can discover, in any of his writings or correspondence.

Harris, in his updating of Ware's *Writers of Ireland,* tells us that Nary was 'educated in book learning in the town of Naas'.[17] It is quite possible that the school he attended there was one of the Protestant schools mentioned in Bishop Brenan's report above. It is of interest that Archbishop Synge in his controversy with Nary in the 1720s mentions that Nary was supposed to have lived for many years among Protestants.[18] I feel that this can only refer to his early life, since at no time following his ordination in 1682 could he have lived for *many years* among Protestants—his sojourn of two to three years in London could not be described as 'many years'. It is possible that the pupils of the school he attended in Naas were predominantly Protestant or that the particular area he came from had a high proportion of Protestants. It is known that, when Nary was a boy, a Mr England kept a school in Naas, for it is on record that in 1671 England paid a rent of thirty shillings per year in respect of the schoolhouse. It is quite likely that Nary got his early education in Mr England's school.[19]

We have no definite information as to his further education after he left the school in Naas. We know that from the early 1660s onwards the Jesuits were active in setting up schools in various towns throughout the country. These schools had such a high reputation that some Protestant children attended. A school in New Ross run by two Jesuit fathers, Rice and Jelosse, was so successful that it attracted the attention of the local Puritans, and was forced to close down in 1670. Jelosse subsequently opened a school near Dublin which was still operating in 1677; it appears to have struggled on until 1685 when James II came to the throne and, with the increased toleration for Roman Catholics, it was able to open up inside the city in Lucy Lane (now Chancery Place). The Father Rice mentioned above later went to Drogheda to take charge of a new school which had just been established by the primate, Oliver Plunket. Before long the Drogheda school was catering for 175 students, 40 of whom were Protestants. It was, however, forced to close in 1673.[20]

These Jesuit schools included a proportion of clerical students who were given lectures in theology and in methods of preaching and catechising. It seems likely that the young Nary attended such a school but we have no information as to where it was located. Since he belonged to the diocese of Dublin, it would be natural for him to attend the school founded by Father Jelosse. It is also possible that he attended a similar Jesuit school in the diocese of Ossory, which, it is known, enjoyed a higher degree of toleration than other parts of the country. It had a very active bishop in the person of James Phelan and it would be surprising if he did not have some kind of seminary in operation for the training of priests. At all events, when Cornelius Nary was ready for ordination in 1682 it was Bishop James Phelan of Ossory who performed that function in Kilkenny city, there being no archbishop in Dublin at that time.

We know something of the character of Bishop Phelan from the reports of his contemporary, John Brenan, who states that Phelan was 'a prelate of excellent zeal, wholly devoted to his duties; throughout evil times he was perhaps more among his people than any other, a discreet and peaceful man, well regarded by his own and even by the others'. Or again, Brenan tells us:

> The Bishop of Ossory invited me to accompany him in visiting his diocese and to learn how ecclesiastical matters fare in his diocese. I

9

confess I witnessed this with great pleasure, having seen the wise administration of that diocese where the clergy are numerous and exemplary, and assist at the functions with zeal and earnestness; and the ecclesiastical functions are performed there with greater decorum than in any other diocese I have seen here, and they enjoy greater liberty than in any other part of the Kingdom. Moreover I find that the Bishop of Ossory is a most vigilant prelate and obeyed promptly by everyone.[21]

Because of the unsatisfactory level of education available in the Jesuit colleges, priests at the time of their ordination did not have a satisfactory level of competence in such subjects as theology, philosophy and Scripture studies. Hence it was the custom in the seventeenth and eighteenth centuries to send young priests, following ordination, to one of the Irish Colleges on the Continent for further study. And so in 1683 young Father Nary was entered as a student in the Irish College in Paris.

Notes

1. Nicholas Donnelly, *Short histories of Dublin parishes* (Dublin, issued in parts, various dates), part XI, 55. This work was originally titled *A short history of some Dublin parishes* but, as the work became more comprehensive, later editions were titled *Short histories of Dublin parishes.*

2 I have seen no direct evidence as to the year of Nary's birth. However, he was forty-six at the time of the registration of priests in July 1704, and this would indicate that he was born in either 1657 or 1658. According to Harris he was in the twenty-fourth year of his age (i.e. he was twenty-three) when he was ordained in 1682, and this would indicate that he was born in 1658 or 1659. Since 1658 is common to both sets of data, it should follow that he was born in that year.

3. I am relying on Donnelly as regards the place of birth. Nicholas Donnelly (1837–1920) was auxiliary bishop in the Dublin archdiocese from 1883 to 1920. As indicated in note 1, he was the author of *Short histories of Dublin parishes.* As auxiliary bishop he was in a position to get sound information, although he does not cite any authorities. Furthermore, the fact that Nary's father and mother were buried in Tipper graveyard, and that he himself asked to be buried there, would indicate that he came from that neighbourhood. I am assuming that Donnelly meant the civil parish of Tipper and not the Catholic parish, which would be larger and has been known as Eadestown since 1884. If Donnelly had been referring to the Catholic parish he would presumably have called it Eadestown.

4. *Books of Survey and Distribution for County Kildare,* Tipper parish, microfilm Pos. 3764, National Library of Ireland.

5. Captain G. S. Cary (ed.), 'Hearth money roll for County Dublin 1664', *Journal of the Kildare Archaeological Society* 11 (1930–3), 386 ff.

6. R. B. McDowell, 'Ireland in 1800', in T. W. Moody and W. E. Vaughan (eds), *A new history of Ireland IV . . . 1691–1800* (Oxford, 1986), 670.

7. Thomas Rawson, *A statistical survey of County Kildare* (Dublin, 1807), 14.

8. Donnelly, *op. cit.* in note 1, 55.

9. Edward MacLysaght, *More Irish families* (Dublin, 1960), 189.

10. Gilbert Library, Dublin, MS 28, p. 347.

11. Laurence Whyte, *Original poems on various subjects* (Dublin, 1740), *passim*. The 'pair of Tables' referred to in the poem were backgammon tables.

12. Quoted in Edward MacLysaght, *Irish life in the seventeenth century* (Dublin, 1939), 354.

13. Quoted in Emmanuel Curtis, *Blessed Oliver Plunket* (Dublin, 1963), 206.

14. *Ibid.,* 209.

15. *Ibid.,* 212.

16. Cornelius Nary, 'The case of the Roman Catholics of Ireland', in Hugh Reily, *Genuine history of Ireland* (1762 edition), 127. In this connection it is of interest that records in the library of Trinity College, Dublin, for the borough of Naas, a town with which Nary would be familiar, show that the number of freemen increased as follows during the period in question: 1672, 76; 1681, 284; 1683, 342; 1684, 455. It would be difficult to explain these substantial increases otherwise than by the admission of growing numbers of Catholics as freemen during the years mentioned.

17. Walter Harris, *Writers of Ireland* (Dublin, 1746), 299.

18. Edward Synge, *The archbishop of Tuam's defence of his charitable address* (Dublin, 1729), 283.

19. Thomas J. de Burgh, 'Ancient Naas', *Journal of the Kildare Archaeological Society* 1 (1891–5), 273.

20. Emmanuel Curtis, *op. cit., passim.*

21. Quoted in P. Power, *A bishop in the Penal times* (Cork, 1932), 25. Some years later, in September 1686, Phelan was instrumental in having a college set up in Kilkenny city 'to teach the liberal arts'. This college enjoyed the status of a university for a few months in 1690, before having to close down on the defeat of the Jacobite cause. (See article by John Lennon in *Archivium Hibernicum* 43 (1988), 79.)

Chapter 2

THE PARIS AND LONDON YEARS: A FIRST TASTE OF CONTROVERSY

Paris

THE Irish College in Paris[1] was established towards the end of the sixteenth century by Father John Lee. In 1677 it entered upon an entirely new phase of its existence when two Irish priests, Dr Malachy Kelly of Cashel and Dr Patrick McGinn of Down, secured premises in the Rue des Carmes known as the Collège des Lombards because it had previously been a college for Italian students. These two priests rebuilt the old college from the foundations at their own expense and presented it to their compatriots, together with eleven small burses which had been attached to the old Italian College.

Under the original rules of 1679, this new Irish College was to be governed by two provisors, one from Ulster and one from Munster, presumably because the founders, Kelly and McGinn, came from those provinces. They were not to live long enough to see their ideas come to fruition, for McGinn died in 1683 and Kelly in 1684. Following the demise of the two founders, there was a reorganisation in 1685, under which four provisors were provided for, one from each of the four provinces.

The original policy of the college was to accept students who were already ordained priests. There were sound arguments in favour of this policy. Firstly, such students could earn a little money for themselves through Mass offerings and so ease the burden of their upkeep. Secondly, they were already committed to the priesthood and to returning to Ireland to minister there when they had finished their course of studies in Paris, whereas students who were not priests often forsook the clerical calling for some other profession or, even if they succeeded in being ordained priests, often secured posts for themselves in France or elsewhere and did not return to Ireland. Thirdly, it was possible for students already ordained to live a more sheltered life at the Lombard College; they would not have to attend courses in the University of Paris to the same extent as would unordained students, and were thus much less integrated into the French way of life and less subject to the temptations of a great city.

It was not found feasible, however, to adhere strictly to this policy. Unordained students attached to the Irish College had their own house in the Rue Traversine from 1694 onwards. In 1707 it was decided that they should also be admitted to the Lombard College, and although the number of such students increased as the century advanced, the number of ordained students remained in the majority. For example, in 1776 there were 100 ordained students as against sixty who were not ordained. In the early years of the century, at least, the failure rate among the unordained students was high. In the forty years from 1694 to 1734, it was said that such students had not provided more than twenty-five priests for the Irish Mission.

From about 1680 onwards the Lombard College became more formally a university college. The archbishop of Paris appointed the superior-major, to whom the four provisors rendered an account of their administration when required, although in other respects they still had full spiritual and temporal control of the college. The archbishop also exercised the right of visitation. The college was also subject to the University of Paris, whose rector possessed and exercised the right of visitation.

In 1769 the college moved to new premises in what was then the Rue de Cheval Vert but has long since been the Rue des Irlandais. But the old Lombard College continued to be used as part of the Irish College down to French Revolutionary times. It had gained early on a great reputation as a seminary. Dr Patrick Plunket, himself a superior of the college and subsequently bishop of Meath, claimed that almost alone among the Irish Colleges on the Continent it turned out properly educated priests. Indeed, according to Plunket, the other colleges regarded them with a jaundiced eye, and dubbed them sarcastically the Jesuits of the secular clergy.

Thus when Cornelius Nary arrived in the Lombard College in 1683 the college buildings would have been quite new. There

13

were then only thirty students in the college, all of them already ordained.

While the students led relatively sheltered lives in the college, they could not be unaware of, and uninfluenced by, the great events which were taking place all around them. Louis XIV was then at the height of his power in France. He had two relatively successful wars behind him, and France and the rest of Europe were enjoying a few years of peace before the Sun King's reckless thirst for glory was to plunge the Continent again into war. In the meantime he used the years of peace to settle a few internal matters. Louis was determined that Catholicism, and none other, should be the religion of France, but he was equally determined that it was he and not the pope who would be in control of the French Church. In line with this policy he suppressed the Jansenists, and later, in 1710, he rased to the ground their main power-base, the convent at Port Royal just outside Paris.

By the Gallican Articles of 1682, agreed by the assembly of the French clergy, it was affirmed, *inter alia,* that the pope had no power to depose princes nor to release their subjects from their oaths of allegiance. Louis ordered in particular that these articles were to be observed by all teachers and professors of universities and all candidates for theological degrees. In 1685, in accordance with his policy of one state religion in France, he revoked the Edict of Nantes, resulting in the flight of Protestant Huguenots from France.

The young Nary's time in France thus coincided with a period of great controversy and upheaval. That he came under the influence of Gallican principles is certain, and until the end of his life he openly opposed the pope's assumed power to depose kings and to dispense subjects from their allegiance. It was a stance which in later life may have cost him a mitre. On the other hand, the expulsion of the Huguenots from France he profoundly disagreed with, since it offended against his ideas of toleration for all religions and, at the pragmatic level, he could see that a persecution of Protestants in France was likely to be matched by a persecution of Catholics in Ireland.

Although Jansenism had been suppressed, its influence lingered on for more than a century among the French clergy. Some, like Bishop Colbert of Montpellier, openly favoured it. Others, like Louis Noailles, later (from 1700) to be cardinal archbishop of Paris, were quite ambivalent about Jansenism. Noailles did not formally accept *Unigenitus,* the papal bull against the heresy, until 1728, some 15 years after it was first promulgated. The Jesuits, the most resolute opponents of Jansenism, he regarded with particular disfavour, and forbade them to preach or hear confessions in the archdiocese of Paris.[2]

The kernel of Jansenism was the proposition that man was so totally corrupted by original sin that he could do nothing by himself to gain salvation; he had to receive God's grace, which he was not free to accept or reject, and which was given by God only to those who had been predestined to be saved. To what extent, if any, Cornelius Nary came to be influenced by Jansenism is unclear. Certainly he was accused on more than one occasion of having Jansenist leanings in his writings. But to have spent eleven or twelve of one's formative years in the Paris of those times was probably sufficient, in some men's eyes, to be tarred for life with the Jansenist brush.

The Paris Nary knew was thus an exciting, challenging, invigorating, alarming hotbed of controversy, the unchallenged centre of literature and the arts, the capital not only of Europe but of a steadily expanding world. But in the midst of all this the young men of the Lombard College had to get on with their studies with a view to acquiring worthwhile degrees from the University of Paris. The more brilliant students, among whom Cornelius Nary was numbered, were allowed to remain in the college beyond the customary six years, with the goal of a doctorate in mind. The university was divided into four great faculties—theology (*Sacra Facultas*), law (*Consultissima Facultas*), medicine and arts.

Nary went on to follow a highly successful course of studies, culminating, it would appear, in a doctorate in both canon law and civil law (*Consultissimae Facultatis Parisiensis Doctor*) from the College of Cambrai. There is some confusion, however, as to Nary's actual academic qualifications. According to Brockliss and Ferté[3] the only degrees conferred on him were bachelor of canon law (1688) and licentiate in canon law (1689). The same authorities go on to state that 'biographical dictionaries erroneously call him Doctor of Theology'.

With regard to Nary's qualifications in canon law, the catalogue of the Bibliothèque Nationale, Paris, shows that he submitted theses in May 1694 for a doctorate in canon law. In the *approbatio*s from John Farely and Michael Fogarty which preface Nary's translation of the New Testament, both these divines, who were themselves doctors of theology of the

15

University of Paris, describe Nary as 'Consultissimae Facultatis Parisiensis Doctor', in other words doctor of law. A third *approbatio* on the same occasion—that from Michael Morris of the College of Navarre, University of Paris—is considerably more revealing when it describes Nary as a doctor of Paris University *juris utriusque,* a phrase used in the university meaning a degree in canon *and* civil law.[4] The fact that in a legal document signed by him in 1737 the letters L.L.D. appear after his name is further evidence of his doctorate in civil law. We can conclude, then, that Nary was a doctor of both canon and civil law but not a doctor of theology. If he had been a doctor of theology it would have been quite inexplicable not to so describe him in the *approbatio*s mentioned above.

Nary does not appear to have spent all his time in Paris, nor indeed in France, for he was to boast in his first reply to Archbishop Synge (1728) (see Chapter 11) that he 'had an opportunity of consulting some of the best of the libraries of Europe'.[5]

The arts faculty of the University of Paris was divided into four Nations—France, Picardy, Normandy and Germany. These Nations were subdivided into tribes, that of Germany into the tribe of the Continentals and the tribe of the Islanders, i.e. the Irish, the English and the Scots. To become a member of a Nation it was necessary to have taken the M.A. degree at the university, but the number of members was restricted to twenty. Throughout the seventeenth century a high proportion of the members of the German Nation were Irish, and indeed there is extant a document dated October 1651 accusing Irish members of clubbing together and ganging up on the other members.

In 1684 as many as eighteen out of twenty members of the German Nation were Irish. The most important office in a Nation was that of procurator. He held office for four months at a time and was a member of the council of the rector of the university. In view of their numerical superiority, it is not surprising that Irishmen figured to a large extent in the list of procurators of the German Nation. Thus we find that 'M. Cornelius Nary of Kildare, priest' was appointed procurator in 1691. Nary was appointed procurator again in 1693, when he is described as 'Licentiate of Laws, Paris, and Provisor of the Lombard College'.[6] He appears to have been appointed to the post of provisor (Leinster) earlier in 1693.

Nary cannot have looked upon appointment to the post of provisor as any great challenge, since he was merely one of four

16

such provisors in a college of about forty students. Once he had obtained his doctorate in 1694, he probably saw no compelling reason for remaining on in Paris. He had come there to be educated for the Irish Mission and he knew that it was to Ireland he must eventually return, although his journey thither was to be broken by a sojourn of a few years in London.

It was an Ireland vastly different from the one he had left in 1683. The Ireland he had left was a relatively peaceful, prosperous country where Catholics were accorded a certain degree of toleration. Catholic hopes were heightened with the accession of James II, and indeed there were a few years in which they enjoyed a supremacy. That had all been turned on its head by the 'Glorious Revolution' and the victory of William of Orange over James. From his standpoint in Paris Nary could see that this had been no war of religion, as it was perceived in Ireland, but just another manifestation of the principle of the balance of power in operation in Europe. If it was a war of religion then the pope was on the wrong side, for the papacy throughout the conflict had been notoriously hostile to Louis XIV and, by extension, to his ally, James II. Clearly, then, one had to distinguish between the pope *qua* spiritual leader and the pope *qua* politician. Cornelius Nary would have to make up his mind where he stood in regard to these two separate personae. While in later life there would be no more loyal adherent of the pope as spiritual leader, he would at the same time be resolute and outspoken in his opposition to papal pretensions in the sphere of temporal powers.

London

Harris in his *Writers of Ireland* gives the year and place of publication of Nary's *Chief points in controversy between Roman Catholics and Protestants* as London and Antwerp 1699. The only copy I have been able to discover in the Dublin libraries is dated Antwerp 1705. In the *Archbishop of Tuam's answer to Nary's rejoinder* (1731),[7] Archbishop Synge mentions that *Chief points in controversy* was published in 1696 and again in 1705. Nary later, in reply to Synge,[8] confirms this 1696 date. This is also the date in the British Library Catalogue. The date of first publication of this book must therefore be taken as 1696, not 1699. Incidentally, this is not the only mistake of this kind made by Harris; his many errors in regard to dates of publication of Nary's works are detailed in Chapter 10.

17

It is stated by Harris and others (who may only have been repeating Harris) that Nary arrived in London in 1696. However, given that his *Chief points in controversy* was published in that year, he must have arrived in London earlier than 1696, for it seems almost certain that this book was written in London rather than in Paris. He mentions in the preface to the book that the proximate reason for writing it was his meeting with a certain 'Roman Catholic gentlewoman'. This lady, he tells us, 'was very much solicited by one, to whom she had some special obligations, to read Dr Tillotson's sermons as the most effectual means to see the truth of the Protestant religion and the errors of her own'.[9] He thus wrote the book for the benefit of this apparently English lady, to stave off the possibility of her defecting to the Established Church. It was a book which, even for a man of Nary's learning, required a good deal of research, and for all this research and the writing of the book to be accomplished in London, the probability is that he arrived there early in 1695.

Harris tells us that while in London Nary was engaged as governor in the house of the earl of Antrim, a prominent Catholic peer. This means that he was engaged as a tutor for the earl's son, then a youth of fifteen or sixteen. Alexander MacDonnell, third earl of Antrim, was born in 1615. His family owned vast estates in County Antrim. He commanded a regiment of the Confederate Army until the final surrender to Cromwell in 1652. His lands were confiscated under the Cromwellian Settlement, but following the Restoration he was fortunate to have 35,000 acres in County Antrim restored to him. In 1685 he was admitted a member of the Privy Council of James II and given command of an infantry regiment. In the subsequent war between William III and James, his chief claim to fame was that the Apprentice Boys of Derry shut the gates of that city in his face in 1689. He was later outlawed as an adherent of James II but he was successful in having his outlawry reversed, as far as Ireland was concerned, under the Articles of Limerick. His outlawry in England, however, remained in force, a point on which he was so sensitive that he spent the last years of his life in efforts to have it reversed. In May 1695 he came to England to petition King William in council, and although William was disposed to grant the petition nothing could be done before William's departure the same month to join his army in Flanders. The earl came to England again in 1696 on a similar mission.[10]

The youth whom Nary was engaged to tutor was the child of the earl's second marriage, to Helena, daughter of Sir John Burke of County Galway, and had been born in 1680 when the earl was already sixty-five years of age. Considering Nary's qualifications and learning, it seems unlikely that his sole purpose in coming to London was to tutor a youth of fifteen or sixteen, even if he was the heir to an important Catholic earldom. The post of tutor, one feels, must be seen as a cover for other activities.

In view of Nary's legal qualifications, it would be only reasonable to assume that he made some contribution (perhaps tenuous, because he was a French-trained lawyer) to the earl's petition for reversal of his outlawry in England. As already stated, the earl first came to England in May 1695 for this purpose, and this would tie in with the suggested date of Nary's arrival in England also. The earl returned to Ireland that year, and the probability is that, as tutor to the young heir, Nary accompanied him, for, as will be seen later, he left England for a time after the writing of his book *Chief points in controversy*.

When the earl returned again to England in 1696, presumably Nary returned with him, and it is probable that he had some part in the writing of *Thesis of the earl of Antrim's case*, dated October 1696. The petition for the reversal of the outlawry eventually succeeded but, ironically, the earl was by then already dead.

The other important activity upon which Nary was engaged in 1695, and perhaps the early months of 1696, was, as already suggested, the writing of his book *The chief points in controversy* or, to give it its full title, *A modest and true account of the chief points in controversy between Roman Catholics and Protestants together with some considerations upon the sermons of a divine of the Church of England* by N. C., a book of 302 octavo pages. It will be seen that Nary wrote under his initials as reversed and this led to some doubt as to the identity of the author. Thus the British Library Catalogue ascribes the book to either Nicholas Colson or Cornelius Nary but with a preference for Nary. However, it is made quite clear in the published pamphlets of Nary's controversy with Prebendary Clayton (see Chapter 3) that Cornelius Nary was the author of this book. As pointed out by Nary in the preface, the book was written as a rejoinder to the published sermons of John Tillotson, archbishop of Canterbury.

19

John Tillotson (1630–94), archbishop of Canterbury, by J. Houbraken. (Courtesy of the National Library of Ireland.)

Tillotson was born in Halifax in 1630 and was originally a Non-Conformist. Ordained an Anglican priest about 1661, he quickly gained a great reputation as a preacher. He was appointed a chaplain to Charles II, and in 1664, rather improbably, he married Elizabeth French, a niece of Oliver Cromwell. When he was appointed archbishop of Canterbury in 1691, he stipulated that his wife should have a large apartment at Lambeth Palace, although no wife of an archbishop had been seen at Lambeth since 1570. His primacy was brief and uneventful, and he died penniless in 1694. However, his sermons were afterwards sold for 2,500 guineas, equivalent to perhaps a quarter of a million pounds today.

In person Tillotson was of middle height, with fresh complexion, brown hair and large, 'speaking' eyes; when young he was very thin, but became corpulent as he advanced in years. He was perhaps the only primate who took first rank in his day as a preacher. He thoroughly believed in the religious efficacy of the pulpit. 'Good preaching and good living', he told a colleague in 1661, 'will gain upon people'. There are 255 of his sermons in the definitive edition published in 1752.[11]

Nary was not unappreciative of the hardihood of a mere priest such as himself daring to cross swords with the head of the Anglican Church, particularly as Catholics in England as well as in Ireland at that time were expected to be docile and grateful for the small mercies shown them by the government and the Established Church. The idea of a popish priest answering back must have appeared impudent and presumptuous. But answer back Nary certainly did and, in doing so, he showed scant regard for the status and dignity of his opponent, although in the preface to his book he was at pains to explain his hardihood. He says that in answering the books of an archbishop it might seem to need some apology that he does not treat him with the civility and respect due to his person and character. But he believed that it was not possible to manage a controversy of this nature and at the same time show the respect that might be expected on other occasions without betraying the cause; he had, indeed, on purpose forborne to give Tillotson any other title than that of Doctor, because his 'dispute with him is not, as he was an Archbishop, but as a Doctor of Divinity; and because I conceived I might with less disrespect use the necessary freedom of speech under that notion'.[12]

Nary is also aware that 'it may seem very hardy and bold for a R. Catholic (*sic*) to engage in a controversy which must needs offend many especially at this time of day, when the most innocent of our actions are liable to sinister constructions'. To this he answers that he 'never intended to provoke or exasperate any man; much less would I provoke any of the worthy members of the Church of England, whom I am in duty bound to honour and respect'. If he wrote anything that looked that way, it was the necessity of the subject and not his inclination that forced him that way.[13]

Nary goes on to mention the existence of many liberally minded Protestants, a constant theme in his writings:

> I am not ignorant that our lives and fortunes are at the mercy of the law; and shall be deprived of both when it shall please our magistrates to put them into execution, but such is their lenity and goodness that they overlook us and suffer us to live. . . The Better Sort (which, blessed be God, is also the greater) are sensible that our only crime is our conscience, which we cannot help and which, I trust in God, we shall ever prefer to all that is most dear to us in this world. They desire our conversion, because they think us in error; and we likewise desire and earnestly pray for theirs, because we are persuaded they are in the wrong. . . We are not, therefore, insensible of the clemency and good nature of the worthy men of the Church of England, nor are we so dull as not to take notice of the connivance and liberty they are pleased to allow us; but we think we cannot make them a more suitable return (a more charitable, I am sure we cannot), than to lay before them the dangerous consequences of their errors and the desperate state of their souls.[14]

As well as a preface, Nary's book has an introductory chapter in which he makes some general remarks on how he proposes to manage his reply to Tillotson. He tells us:

> It is commonly said, and our own experience teacheth us, that good language goes far in gaining credit to whatever is said; and that a smooth, polished discourse, when gravely delivered seems to carry the face of truth, though it should happen to be otherwise. Words, when handsomely laid together, have I know not what of charming in them, and do challenge the attention of the most obstinate, especially when delivered by a man in a high station. This, with some other considerations, moved me to examine the sermons of Dr Tillotson, late Archbishop of Canterbury, to see if the intrinsic value of his coin be answerable to the lustre and outward appearance of it.

Nary goes on:

> This ingenious man has taken a great deal of pains to convince the world of his skill in controversy, and has delivered his thoughts in such fine, smooth language, that, in my opinion, very few of his Brethren can equal him in the elegancy of his style. . . In handling then of this important piece of controversy, I shall, with God's assistance, observe these methods; First, I will lay down what the Roman

22

Catholics believe as of faith concerning these points. Secondly, I will prove their tenets with reason, Scripture and authority of the Fathers. Thirdly, I will answer all the material objections which Dr Tillotson brings against the said tenets.[15]

Nary goes on to claim that Tillotson's fundamental principle is this: 'Whatever is plain and evident to our senses and reason is to be believed, though all the Churches and men in the World should persuade us to the contrary'.[16] Nary, in the succeeding chapters, goes on to deal with the different points of controversy, viz. infallibility; the pope's supremacy; Transubstantiation; Communion in one kind; prayers in an unknown tongue; invocation of saints; images; purgatory; indulgences.

The topics covered by Nary in *Chief points in controversy* are treated of also in his two books, published in 1728 and 1730, in reply to Archbishop Synge (see Chapter 11). To avoid repetition, and as it appears more equitable to set down in juxta-position the arguments put forward by Nary on the Catholic side with the replies by Synge on the Protestant side (as has been attempted in Chapter 11), it is not proposed to go into any great detail in this chapter on specific points at issue. It is proposed to content ourselves with how, in general, Nary managed the controversy and the tenor of his replies.

Despite all Nary's protestations as to his hardihood in tackling an archbishop, the first thing that has to be noted is his habit of personal, vindictive and quite outrageous attack upon Tillotson. The following are a few examples.

When dealing with the question of Transubstantiation, Nary states:

> Never Roman Conqueror sang more paeans after victory, or exulted more over his enemies with more ostentation than Dr Tillotson has upon this subject over the Roman Catholics and the Church of Rome; and (to complete the parallel) if his railing eloquence and unChristian contumelies (I am sorry he extorts such words from me) were of equal force to bind with that of Roman chains, no barbarous captives were ever worse used by their insulting conquerors, than the sons of that mother, whose piety and zeal brought forth, in Christ, his ancestors, have the fortune to be treated by the unChristian slanders and calumnies of his bitter tongue and pen.[17]

Nor was Nary above indulging in what might be termed ecclesiastical muck-raking:

> Luther tells us in his book *De Missa Angulari* that what he wrote about the Mass was suggested by the Devil. This book was printed and published by his own reformed Doctors of Wittenberg; but because it looks now something scandalous to pious reformed ears, it must pass for an imposture. Bolsec, a Protestant writer, tells us that

Calvin agreed to give a certain man named Bruleus a sum of money on condition that he would feign himself dead, that he might come and resuscitate him; and when all things were prepared for this farce, the new Apostle had no sooner commanded the living to rise, when his words had that strange efficacy as to strike him dead, but Bruleus' poor wife, who lost both her husband and the hopes of her money, reviled the imposter and discovered the imposture. But this is still so offensive to the Reformation, that it is meet it should likewise pass as a fable.[18]

With regard to Tillotson's *Discourse against Transubstantiation* Nary writes:

In this piece I meet with as copious a collection of scurrilous, injurious language; of notorious and manifest impositions; and such disingenuity in citing of authors, and managing their authorities, as I believe was ever possible for any man who had never so little esteem for his credit, to bring within so narrow a compass.[19]

And here is Nary in full flight on page 190:

But, Good God! what may not men undertake, who have the confidence to give out such calumnies of truth? 'Tis a vulgar observation, but a true one, that when mountebanks pretend most to infallible cures, they are then furthest from them; just so it is with these gentlemen (for there are mountebanks in Religion as well as in Physic) when they pretend most to evidence and demonstration, in matters of Religion, then they have the least colour of reasonable pretence to it.

The following are examples of the pat, didactic, triumphalist style often adopted by Nary:

Now all the societies of Christians who, with any colour of reason, can pretend to the name of Catholic, are these: 1. The Nestorians and Euthycians; 2. The Greek Church; 3. The Church of England; and lastly, the Roman Catholics. I have on purpose omitted the Waldenses, Socinians, Hussites, Lutherans, Calvinists and all those almost innumerable sects continually shooting out on the trunk of the Reformation, and spreading far and near over our own unfortunate islands, as Anabaptists, Independents, Quakers, Mugoltonians, Seekers, Familists, Philadelphians etc., because all of these are destitute of even the least pretence to the name of Catholic Church; having neither lawful pastors, lawful mission, nor right of ordination, which as all the Christian world before the Reformation, and as the Church of England still grants, cannot be given without imposition of hands performed by Bishops.[20]

Or again:

To prove that the Church of England is both heretical and schismatical (I am heartily sorry I must use such hard expressions to so many ingenious and great men, whose learning and other good qualities I very much honour and respect) I shall make use of no arguments but

24

such as are grounded on the clear light of natural reason, upon the consent of mankind and the concession of our adversaries; and upon such known and evident matters of fact, as the most impudent wrangler would be ashamed to deny. As to the first, that the Church of England is heretical, I prove thus: Whatsoever society of Christians obstinately denies any doctrine believed by the Catholic Church to be of faith, is heretical; But the Church of England denies obstinately some doctrines believed by the Catholic Church to be of faith. Therefore, the Church of England is heretical. . . Touching the Second viz. that the Church of England is schismatical, this is no less evident than the former, for, if Schism be wilful separation from the Church, as it is defined by all mankind, as well Protestants as Catholics, the Church of England is doubly guilty of this crime. First, for separating from the Pope and their own immediate Heads, the Bishops of England. Secondly, for separating from the Communion of all other Bishops in the world besides.[21]

On the other hand, Nary can be quite persuasive and reasonable, as he is when arguing for the Latin Mass, where he makes the following points. Firstly, Latin was the language universally used in the liturgy from the earliest times. Secondly, it ensures a uniformity in faith and practice throughout the Church. Thirdly, there is no great loss to 'the vulgar people' through having Latin used in the Mass, because, firstly, they have prayer-books where they can read in their own language what the priest is saying, and, secondly, if the priest was using their own language the vast majority, in a large church, would not be able to hear him anyway. Fourthly, there is a difficulty in translating the liturgy into vernacular languages and preserving it in its purity. Furthermore, vernacular languages change so markedly with the passage of time that new translations would have to be made at regular intervals.[22]

The modern reader will find a few surprising disclosures in the course of this book. For example, with regard to literacy among ordinary people Nary tells us (and it should be noted that this was written in England towards the end of the seventeenth century): 'The most part of the common people are taught at least to read in their own language; and, if we except some of the commonalty of Ireland and the Highlands of Scotland [i.e. areas where Gaelic was spoken], who are industriously barred from all sort of education, there is not one in a hundred, even of the meanest of the common sort, who want this help'.[23]

It is surprising too that Nary was rather lukewarm on the rosary: 'Touching the Rosary or Beads, in which the Doctor [Tillotson] reproaches us for saying ten *Ave Marias* for one *Pater Noster,* I believe everyone knows the Church obliges

25

nobody to say it; I am sure there are millions of Roman Catholics who never do'.[24]

He gives us a rather startling description of the practical reasons for discontinuing Communion under the form of wine:

> She [the Church] saw that as the piety and devotion of the people diminished, so their negligence to receive the Sacred Cup, in such a manner as to secure it from spilling, abounded. She found from experience that many infirm and old, and even folks in perfect health, what with coughing and other convulsions, as they received the Sacred Cup, gave up their stomachs into the Chalice, or shed the Precious Blood, to the great horror of the spectators and their own greater confusion; that others, what with trembling and quaking, did very often, notwithstanding all their care, spill some drops of the Sacred Blood; in fine, that in cities, where some thousands use to communicate at a time, crowds of people pressing upon the priest, have sometimes spilt the Sacred Chalice in his hands, and (what I cannot mention without horror) trod upon that Precious Blood, by which they were redeemed. These, and the like considerations, moved the Church, or rather the people (for the Church did only confirm the custom which was introduced for many years before) to abstain from the Sacred Cup; and to content themselves with the Body and Blood of Christ, under the form of Bread.[25]

Apart from a general comment already mentioned, Nary did not essay any rebuttal of Tillotson's *Discourse against Transubstantiation,* and when years later Archbishop Synge taxed him with this in the course of their controversy he had this to say:

> Your Grace observes that a certain author [i.e. Nary himself] in a book which he published in the year 1696, and again in the year 1705, promised to answer Archbishop Tillotson's discourse concerning Transubstantiation, but had not as yet performed his promise. All this, My Lord, is very true; and the reason why the author did not perform his promise was that, soon after, the said author was necessitated to leave England for a time; and before he could well settle anywhere, there was published at Louvain in Flanders, by Doctor Martin, a book in Latin entitled *Scutum Fidei* [The Shield of Faith]; in which Archbishop Tillotson's chief objections were, as well as in the said Discourse as in the rest of his writings against the Church of Rome, sufficiently answered. Dr Martin, in his Preface, promised to cause his book to be put into English; and therefore the author Your Grace speaks of [Nary] did not think fit to answer Archbishop Tillotson's Discourse: But possibly Your Grace may soon hear of an answer to it. If Your Grace has not seen Dr Martin's book in Latin, I have it by me and will be proud of Your Grace's commands to send it to you.[26]

Like much of his subsequent theological writing, Nary's *Chief points in controversy* did not escape the watchful eyes of the censors. Dr Martin, an Irishman on the staff of the

26

University of Louvain, and the author of *Scutum fidei* already mentioned, wrote to the internuncio in Brussels in April 1707 concerning a book written by one Nary, 'an Irish missionary', which he thought might have been denounced to the Holy See. While the name of the book is not stated, it must have been *Chief points in controversy* since this was the only one of Nary's books to have been published at that date. Dr Martin forwarded to the internuncio the opinions of some of the doctors at Louvain on the book and the retractions made by Nary when he was advised to correct certain points in it.[27]

This Dr Martin was Father Francis Martin (1652–1722), a native of Galway city. He was a secular priest and not an Augustinian, as stated in the *Dictionary of national biography*. As a youth he went to the Continent and entered Louvain University, whence he obtained a doctorate in theology in 1688. He later became regius professor of Holy Scripture at Louvain and, *inter alia,* censor of books and a member of the Strict Faculty of Louvain.

It is ironic that within a few years of his complaint about Nary's book Martin was to find himself in serious trouble with Rome because of 'two provocative works' he had published. In a long battle with Rome he was suspended several times and was in danger of losing his chair at Louvain University.[28]

Nary's reply to Tillotson was to launch him on a life of controversy during which he was to cross swords with the vicar of Saint Michan's, the vicar of Naas and Archbishop Edward Synge. His *History of the world* was published, he tells us, as a corrective to the ideas in that field of atheists and free-thinkers. His translation of the New Testament, which he published without any intention of provoking anyone, was to be the cause of bitter recriminations between him and members of his own Church.

Nary's role as a controversialist may account in some degree for the rather charmed life he was to lead and his apparent immunity even when, as in the case of Tillotson, he treated his opponents to a considerable degree of verbal abuse. An aspect of religious controversy that should not be overlooked is that the opposing controversialists, like prize-fighters, need each other and can not function to any meaning-ful degree without each other. If the Catholic divines were to be silenced or removed from the scene, the Protestant divines would be left with no one to argue with but themselves. It will be seen that, while Nary and Archbishop Synge could be quite sharp and abusive to each other in the throes of their long-drawn-out controversy, they were at the back of it all apparently good friends.

The second half of the seventeenth century, and in particular James II's short reign, was a period of great religious debate in England and Nary's reply to Tillotson in 1696 can be viewed as a part of this continuing discussion. The Church of England has at no time produced so many great divines as during the second half of the seventeenth century, when, in addition to Tillotson, the Church was served by men like Isaac Barrow, the erudite Cambridge scholar; Edward Stillingfleet, the great defender of Protestantism during James II's reign, when Catholicism was briefly in the ascendant; Thomas Spratt, bishop of Rochester, who lived to regret his dalliance with King James but managed to hold on to his see; and Henry Moore, who devoted his life to study and religious meditation at Cambridge and refused to leave the peace and quiet of that 'paradise', as he termed it, for a bishopric. The Catholic Church was served during this period by such men as the Benedictine James Corker, the son of a Church of England vicar who became a convert to Catholicism; the Jesuit Andrew Pulton, who gained considerable fame through his controversy with Thomas Tenison, who was to succeed Tillotson as archbishop of Canterbury; and the aforementioned Irishman, Francis Martin, in Louvain.

These controversialists were not simply indulging in a high-minded, academic argument among themselves; they had a vast audience and readership among the laity. For example, Corker's *Catholic principles in reference to God and King* ran to numerous editions. But it is apparent that some, at any rate, of the laity remained unaffected by the '*furor theologicus*' of the controversialists. The poet Alexander Pope, a Catholic, in a letter dated 20 November 1717 to the bishop of Rochester, who was trying to convert him to the Established Church, has left us this wise, penetrating and witty comment on the religious controversies of his time:

> Your Lordship has formerly advised me to read the best controversies between the churches. Shall I tell you a secret? I did so at fourteen years old, for I loved reading, and my father had no other books; there was a collection of all that had been written on both sides in the reign of James II. I warmed my head with them, and the consequence was that I found myself a Papist and protestant by turns, according to the last book I read. And I'm afraid most seekers are in the same case, and when they stop, they are not so properly converted as outwitted. You see how little glory you would gain by

28

my conversion. And after all, I verily believe your Lordship and I are both of the same religion, if we were thoroughly understood by one another; and that all honest and reasonable christians would be so, if they did but talk enough together each day, and had nothing to do together but to serve God, and live in peace with their neighbour.[29]

Notes

1. For information on the Irish College in Paris I am indebted mainly to Patrick Boyle, *The Irish College in Paris from 1578 to 1901* (Dublin, 1901). I am also indebted to Patrick Boyle, 'A plea for the Irish College in Paris', *Irish Ecclesiastical Record* 21 (Jan.–June 1907), 285–99, and to Liam Swords, 'Collège des Lombards', in Liam Swords (ed.), *The Irish/French connection, 1578–1978* (Paris, 1978), 44–62.

2. *New Catholic Encyclopaedia* (Washington, D.C., 1967), vol. 10, 476.

3. L. W. B. Brockliss and P. Ferté, 'A prosopography of Irish clerics who studied in France in the seventeenth and eighteenth centuries, in particular in the universities of Paris and Toulouse', deposited in the library of the Royal Irish Academy (see *Proc. R. Ir. Acad.* 87C (1987), 527–72).

4. C. N. [Cornelius Nary], *The New Testament of Our Lord and Saviour Jesus Christ* (1719), 11 f.

5. Cornelius Nary, *A letter to his Grace Edward Lord Archbishop of Tuam in answer to his charitable address* (Dublin, 1728), 147.

6. Patrick Boyle, 'Irishmen in the university of Paris in the seventeenth and eighteenth centuries', *Irish Ecclesiastical Record* 14 (July–Dec. 1903), 42.

7. Edward Synge, *The archbishop of Tuam's defence of his charitable address* (Dublin, 1729), 2.

8. Cornelius Nary, *A rejoinder to the reply to the answer to the charitable address* (Dublin, 1730), 129.

9. N. C. [Cornelius Nary], *A modest and true account of the chief points in controversy between Roman Catholics and Protestants. . .* (Antwerp, 1705), preface. Authors sometimes wrote, as here, under reversed initials.

10. *Dictionary of national biography* (London, 1895).

11. *Ibid.*

12. Cornelius Nary, *op. cit.* in note 9, 7.

13. *Ibid.*, 6.

14. *Ibid.*, 10.

15. *Ibid.*, introduction.

16. *Ibid.*, introduction.

17. *Ibid.*, 130.

18. *Ibid.*, 32.

19. *Ibid.*, 131. Nary makes only a general comment on Transubstantiation at this point. He promised to return to that subject in greater detail at a later date.

20. *Ibid.*, 49.
21. *Ibid.*, 54.
22. *Ibid.*, chapter 6, *passim.*
23. *Ibid.*, 202.
24. *Ibid.*, 233.
25. *Ibid.*, 197.
26. Cornelius Nary, *op. cit.* in note 8, 129.
27. Cathaldus Giblin, 'Catalogue of material of Irish interest in the collection Nunziatura di Fiandra, Vatican Archives', *Collectanea Hibernica,* no. 4 (1961), 88.
28. *Dictionary of national biography* (London, 1895).
29. James Aitken (ed.), *English letters of the eighteenth century* (Harmondsworth, 1946), 12.

Chapter 3

THE PARISH PRIEST

THE Dublin parish of St Michan's is of considerable antiquity. The original church of St Michan, dating from the eleventh century,[1] was built for the colony of Ostmen, or 'Foreigners', which had grown up outside the city walls on the north side of the Liffey. By the seventeenth century the parish encompassed the entire stretch of country north of the Liffey from present-day Phoenix Park eastward to the sea. There was just one bridge, known for centuries as Dublin Bridge, connecting the walled city on the south side with St Michan's parish and the north county. Until well into the seventeenth century there was little expansion north of the Liffey. Speed's map (1610) shows only a few streets centred around Church Street and Mary's Abbey. From Strafford's time onwards, however, there was steady expansion in this area, so that in 1685 Phillips's map shows a considerable network of streets from Liffey Street across to Queen Street, and along the river Bachelor's Walk, Ormond Quay and Arran Quay were already in place. This expansion was accompanied by the building of four new bridges over the Liffey during the short period from 1670 to 1685.

It is of interest that at this period and for nearly a century afterwards the people of Oxmantown, as it came to be known, did not regard themselves as part of Dublin. Instead, they looked on their area as being very much a suburb of the city, and were wont to make such remarks as 'Are you going into Dublin?' or 'Are you going into town?'[2]

By the later 1690s the population had grown to nearly 10,000,[3] at which point (1697) Archbishop Marsh authorised the reconstitution of St Michan's as three Church of Ireland (and civil) parishes, St Paul's to the west, St Mary's to the east, and

31

the new St Michan's occupying the middle ground between the two.

Although the Catholic authorities, under the Act of 1704, assigned parish priests to each of these civil parishes, this was merely a ploy for taking advantage of the Act to the extent that it allowed one priest to be registered for each civil parish even though there was canonically only one Catholic parish. Although legally the priests registered for the parishes of St Paul's and St Mary's were parish priests, canonically their status continued to be that of curates of St Michan's.

Following his appointment as archbishop, Edmond Byrne in 1707 effected a similar carve-up of the old parish, but with somewhat different boundaries to those of the civil parishes. However, St Michan's and St Mary's appear to have continued to operate as one parish down to 1729 when the new chapel for St Mary's parish was opened in Liffey Street.

There is some confusion as to the date on which Cornelius Nary took over as parish priest of St Michan's. An article in *The Irish Builder*[4] gives the date as 1702, but Donnelly in his *Short histories of Dublin parishes*[5] prefers the date 1700 for the reason that in a document dated early in 1729 Nary is stated to have already been parish priest for twenty-eight years. A note with a crucifix which once belonged to Nary in the present St Michan's Church, Halston Street, gives the date as 1699. It will be seen later in this chapter that a conference between Nary and Clayton, the Church of Ireland rector of St Michan's, must have taken place early in 1700, and to have become involved in that debate Nary must necessarily have been in the parish for some time. This, I feel, points to the year 1699 as the more likely year of his arrival, though not necessarily of his appointment as parish priest, and indeed he could possibly have arrived in 1698. There is extant a list of priests resident in Dublin city towards the end of 1697 in which he does not figure, indicating that the earliest possible date of his arrival in the parish was 1698.

This 1697 list is of sufficient interest to warrant reproducing it here in so far as it relates to St Michan's (Catholic) parish. The list is headed 'A particular account of the Romish clergy, Secular and Regular, in every parish of the Diocese of Dublin'.[6]

Saint Michan's [Civil] Parish: 6 Secular viz.

William Dalton, Parish Priest, lodging at Figham Bramham's, Barb. [barber?] in Smithfield.
James Gibbons, priest, assistant to William Dalton, at the chapel in Channel Row, lodging at Mr Elliston's in Channel Row.
John Linegar, priest, lodging at the Widow Linegar's in Church Street.

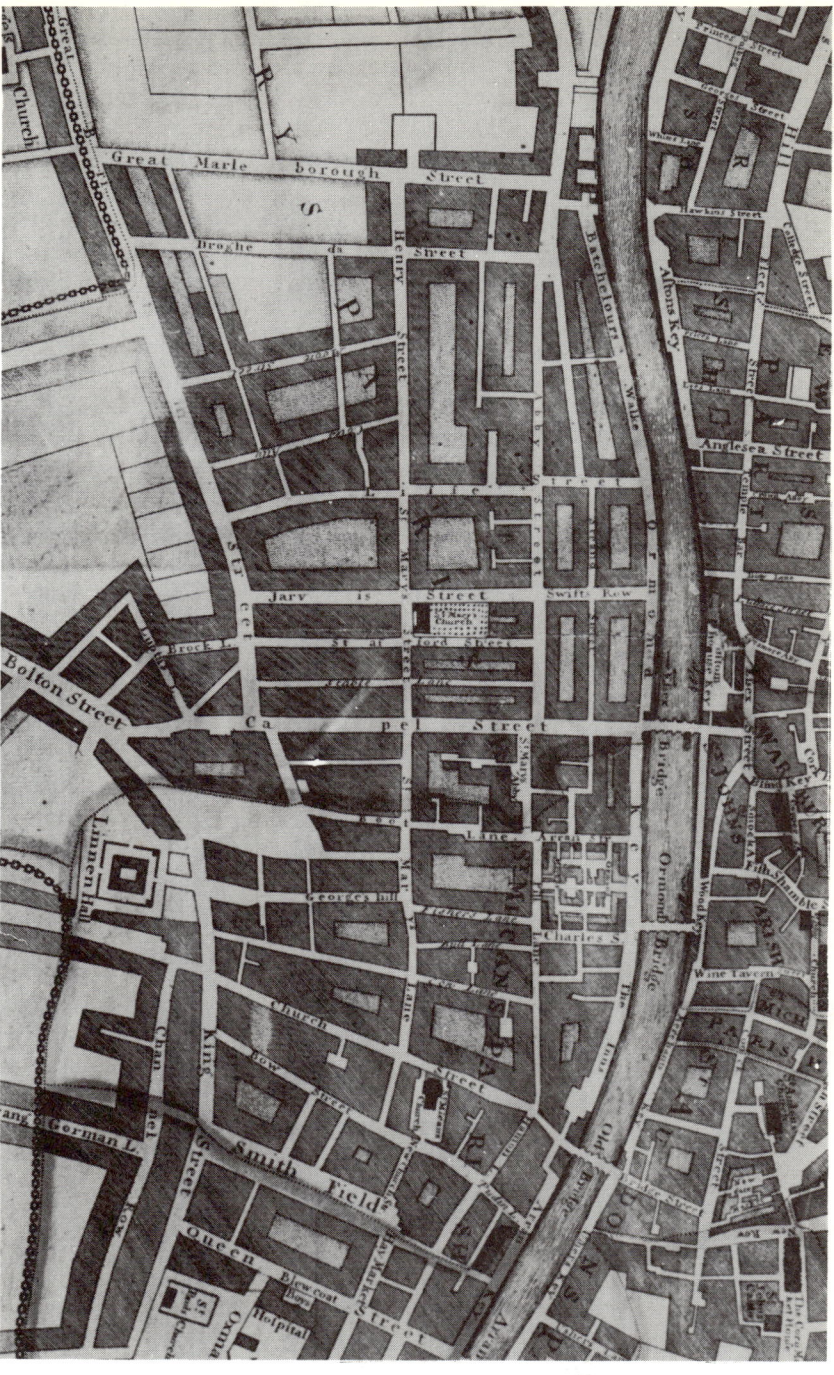

St Michan's parish and surrounding area, from Charles Brooking's Map of the City and Suburbs of Dublin, 1728. (Photo: John Kennedy, The Green Studio.)

Lawrence Dowdall lodging at Matthias Burgess's in Church Street.
Richard Murphy, priest, lodging at Edmond Reynolds in Smithfield.
William Dardis, P.P. of Abbeylara, lodging at Matthew Barrett's in Smithfield.

Regular:
John Weldon, Capuchin Friar, lodging at Luke Dowdall's in Smithfield.

Saint Paul's [civil] Parish:

Secular:
Father Dempsey, Parish Priest of Saint Michan's, is said to be a titular Bishop and lodges at My Lady Clanmalura's [Clanmalier's] in the said parish.
Father Gibbons, said to be a Jesuit, but calls himself Assistant to Father Dalton, who is but an Assistant himself to Father Dempsey.
Richard Murphy, calls himself a secular priest, lodging now in Bridge Street.

Regular:
Father John Meldon, Capuchin Friar, now lodging in Smithfield.
Father Netterville, a Jesuit, lodges on the Key in Dr Cruise's house.
Father Berminghame, sometimes in the parish of Saint Paul, sometimes in Cook Street.

Saint Mary's [civil] Parish:

Secular:
Fergus Farrell, priest, chaplain to the Lady Castlehaven, who lives in Capel Street, near the Mint.

If we exclude the 'titular bishop' and the parish priest of Abbeylara, there would have been twelve priests between the three civil parishes, which, as we have seen, formed one Catholic parish. There is some confusion as to who was actually parish priest, since it will be noted that two are described as such in the list above. Donnelly was of the opinion, however, that John Dempsey was both bishop of Kildare and parish priest of St Michan's.[7] But since he was also vicar-general of Dublin, where there was then no archbishop, he could have had very little time to devote to his duties as parish priest and it is likely that he held that post only in a nominal sense. The man actually carrying out the duties of parish priest was apparently Father Dalton. At the date of Nary's arrival in Dublin Dalton may have been in poor health, necessitating his replacement by Nary. Dempsey, as vicar-general, would have been the man to take that decision. In the pamphlet that he published in 1703 on his controversy with Clayton, Nary says of Dalton, about whom Clayton had made some disparaging remarks: 'Father Dalton is a man of good sense and parts, but sickly and infirm; and, though he were such as is represented in your paper, yet you need not fear to put others in the same predicament with him, so long as you have the management of their answers'.[8] Nary, therefore, found himself in charge of a large parish with perhaps eight secular priests under him. Any regulars who remained following the Banishment Act of 1698 would presumably have been operating independently of him.

The Englishman John Dunton (already mentioned in Chapter 1) visited Dublin in 1698 and left us a contemporary assessment of the position of the Catholics in the city at that time:

> Our Red Lettered Gentlemen were never under such circumstances here, as now; for all their bishops and regular clergy are banished by Act of Parliament, which makes it death to find any of them returned again. So that they are now wholly depending on the seculars, and every parish is allowed its priest; but when he dies, there being none to ordain a new one, it must remain without; and this will be the state of the whole Kingdom in a little time when the present set of priests shall be extinct. There is also another law that no Papist shall keep a school, nor any one native of a foreign education be admitted to dwell in the Kingdom; so that by these Acts it will appear plain enough that the Romish religion is on its last legs in Ireland; and the present Romanists, who survive their priests, must conform to the Protestant religion, or live and die without the exercise of their own. . . These ghostly Fathers were to render themselves on the first day of May for transportation at Dublin, Cork etc. where their names were entered with the Magistrate of the Town; You may guess at the lamentations which were made at parting with such precious jewels; and masses were said and money begged for them, besides what the people voluntarily gave without asking. One old Friar, called Father Keveen, who had been a famous exorcist, and excellent good at helping cattle that were overlooked or bewitched, (for some of the vulgar are so superstitious as to believe this) made sale of good store of holy water, which had helped to cast out devils, and of several other consecrated Trinckams, by which it is said he acquired such a sum of money as might suffice for his support all his days.[9]

The actual position of the Catholic clergy up to the end of 1697 cannot, however, have been very critical. The comprehensive lists of their names, addresses and ranks made by the authorities for that year is evidence that they had been living and officiating quite openly in the city. This official list was compiled for the purposes of the Banishment Act of 1698, mentioned by Dunton (above). The extent to which the regulars fled the country as a result of that Act is arguable. That many remained and went underground, some in the houses of wealthy Catholic patrons, is certain. The secular clergy (the bishops excepted) were untouched by the Act of 1698 and the indications are that they continued to operate openly. It will be seen later in this chapter that from 1700 onwards Cornelius Nary was carrying on quite a controversy with the local Church of Ireland rector, Clayton. He had a conference with him and wrote a hard-hitting pamphlet against him. It will be seen, too, that Clayton had at the same time a second controversy in hand with another priest, Father Burn, and it is apparent that Clayton welcomed such jousts with the Catholic clergy.

Such activity is scarcely compatible with a downtrodden, persecuted existence. Granted, it was all too easy for a priest to land himself in jail and it will be seen later that Father Burn was imprisoned about 1700. Imprisonment, however, has to be seen as a relatively light form of punishment in an era when people were hanged for stealing as little as a shilling and when, as punishment for what we today would regard as quite minor offences, people were whipped through the streets or clapped in the pillory, there to be pelted by the populace with rotten eggs, sometimes resulting in blinding. The *Dictionary of national biography* (London, 1895) states that Nary 'was arrested and imprisoned for his religion in 1702'. While he may have been in prison at some stage in his career I do not think it can have been in 1702, for he was busily engaged in his controversy with Clayton throughout that year. We do know that his name appears on a list of Dublin Catholic clergy prepared by a priest-hunter or other type of informer about this time.[10]

But Nary was not, apparently, the kind of man to worry about such inconveniences. The indications are that he pressed on with the building up and administration of his large parish. As to where he lived in these early years in the parish, Myles Ronan tells us that it was in Viscountess Clanmalier's house in Church Street.[11] Church Street is indeed the address given by Nary in the return required under the Act of 1704 for the Registration of the Popish Clergy.

Viscountess Clanmalier was a widowed lady whose husband, Maximilian O'Dempsey, Viscount Clanmalier, had sat in King James's parliament in 1689 and had died in 1691. Her maiden name was Anne Bermingham and, like Nary, she was a native of north Kildare (townland of Dunfierth). She had no children but she had an unruly nephew, Richard, Lord Bellew, who was very anxious to get hold of her estate—so anxious indeed that in August 1705, when the viscountess was living in Kildare, he sent Cornelius Nary and another priest, John Tyrell, to her with the warning that he would turn Protestant if she did not settle her estate on him.[12] Lord Bellew conformed shortly afterwards, and in 1707 Nary is said to have undergone an examination of some length before a committee of the Irish House of Commons on the validity of some deeds regarding property which was the subject of litigation between the viscountess and Bellew. She died in 1708.[13]

It must have been apparent to Cornelius Nary that the most urgent need of his large parish was a chapel. Up to this the chapel of the Benedictine nuns in Channel Row had been in use as a place of worship for the parish. These nuns had been forced to flee the country in the early 1690s following the failure of the Jacobite cause. About 1702 Nary secured an old building at the corner of Bull Lane and Mary's Lane and, with the aid of funds that he collected, transformed it into a substantial, albeit severely functional, chapel. From Rocque's map of 1756, which was claimed to be meticulously drawn to scale, this chapel appears to have covered an area of 36 feet by 72 feet approximately. It would then have been about four-fifths of the size of the chapel in Francis Street, which was at that time the largest in the city with dimensions of 40 feet by 80 feet. A memorial in the Registry of Deeds, Dublin, in regard to the lease of a house in Bull Lane dated August 1728 states that this house was bounded on the north by 'the passage into the Popish Chapell'.[14] The passage is clearly shown on Rocque's map, from which it would appear that there was access to the chapel also by a passage from Cow Lane. In accord with the usual practice of the times in regard to Catholic chapels, there would have been no direct access to the chapel either from Mary's Lane or Bull Lane.

Myles Ronan tells us that the Mary's Lane chapel became one of the most popular chapels in the city because of the learned and eloquent preachers who frequented it. Chief amongst these were the Jesuits, who previously had a chapel in the parish in Mass Lane but were forced to close it down in 1690.[15]

Nary went to live in Bull Lane in 1705 and remained there until his death. According to a report in 1722 by Garzia, the priest-hunter, Nary's lodgings were next door to the chapel. This was apparently the house already mentioned above as being bounded on the north by 'the passage to the Popish Chapell'.[16]

The parish had, of course, the usual cycle of marriages, christenings and funerals, but there are no parochial records of such events prior to 1726. Records of the Church of Ireland parish of St Michan's are, however, available, and these show that occasionally a couple, having been married by the Catholic priest, went along to the Protestant church to register their marriage before a justice of the peace, so as to put the legality of their union beyond all question. Thus the Church of Ireland register records that on 11 August 1712 Thomas Butler, clothier, and Alice Sullivan, spinster, were married by 'a Roman priest'; likewise Hugh McVeigh, chirurgeon, and Mary Walsh, spinster, on 17 September 1712, and one Clark, baker, and Elizabeth Butterly, spinster, on 12 July 1713.[17]

As long as they complied with the provisions of the Act for Registering Popish Clergy (1704) it was intended that Catholic secular priests should live and officiate unmolested, but they could not officiate outside the civil parish for which they were registered nor hold any office involving ecclesiastical jurisdiction such as the office of vicar-general. Since only one priest could be registered for each civil parish, only three priests could be registered for the Catholic parish of St Michan's, where in 1697, as we have seen, there was a total of eight secular priests. The return made under the 1704 Act in respect of Cornelius Nary shows that he was then (1704) living in Church Street, was 46 years of age, and had been ordained in 1682 at Kilkenny by James, bishop of Ossory; he had as sureties Nicholas Lincoln, merchant, Capel Street, and John Butler, Ormond Quay. Registered for St Mary's parish was John Linegar, living at the Widow Linegar's in Church Street, aged 33, ordained in 1694 in Lisbon, and having as sureties Nicholas Drumgoold, gentleman, Church Street, and James White, gentleman, Mary Street. Father William Dalton, who was registered for St Paul's civil parish, was aged 48, was ordained in 1679, and had as sureties Roger Coughlan, brewer, High Street, and Patrick Purcel, saddler, Christchurch Yard.[18]

Bishop Dempsey of Kildare, who, as we have already seen, was vicar-general of the Dublin archdiocese, died about 1703. There was a hiatus then until 1707 when Edmond Byrne was appointed archbishop. The following document from the Dublin diocesan archives is undated but it apparently refers to a period when there was no archbishop in the diocese. It is worth quoting in full for the light it throws on what is a sparsely documented period in the history of the Catholic Church in Ireland.

We, the under-named Parish Priests of Dublin, observing the many irregularities and disorders committed in this city and city liberties by several clergymen that flock hither from other parts, and other unknown clergymen who do not apply themselves as they ought to the pastors of the town to receive their approbation, without which they cannot administer the Sacraments or do any sacerdotal function without sacrilege, to the great detriment of their own souls, the disedifying of the people and great scandal to religion.

Moreover, the said libertines for want of observing the directions given and inculcated from time to time by the pastors to proceed cautiously, discreetly and prudently lest any offence may be given to ye Government or any provocation given to put ye laws strictly in execution, whereby the exercise of our holy religion might be entirely suppressed, do gather great congregations in stables, yards and waste houses and other places, having rather some sordid lucre in view than the honour and glory of God and good of souls, whereby they bring the indignation of the Government upon the whole body of the Catholics, who take a handle at our own indiscretion to execute the laws against us.

We then the said pastors, meeting and concerting together to remedy the said evils and prevent the like disorders for ye future, do order as follows.

Imprimis, that no priest, whether regular or secular he be, of what degree or circumstance whatsoever, do presume to celebrate Mass after the hour of ten inclusive in any public chapel, waste house or backside in the city or city liberties of Dublin.

Secondly, that no priest, whether regular or secular, shall presume to administer any Sacraments, especially the holy Sacraments of Baptism, Penance, Extreme Unction or Matrimony without the approbation of two at least of the undernamed pastors, and that so approved they shall not administer the Sacraments of Baptism, or Matrimony or Extreme Unction without the parish priest's leave.

Thirdly, that no secular priest of any other diocese shall be employed or seconded (?) by any Parish Priest of this city without a recommendation from his proper superior, but such of other dioceses as are actually employed by any of the pastors of the town shall have a month's time to procure such a recommendation, and the month being expired, which shall commence the 1st of February, without producing it, the said priests shall be dismissed and natives taken in their place.

And in regard it is our intention as well to punish as to prevent the disorders aforesaid, we declare that all and every transgression of the aforesaid directions shall be published in every chapel of this town at the end of every mass and we hope and desire that all good Catholics for the honour and glory of God, the good of their souls and in obedience to the word of God (intimating to us to beware of false prophets that come in sheep's skins but are ravenous wolves; for such are all those that come not in by the gate, that is, that are not authorised by the pastors of the Church; since Saint Paul says how will they preach if they be not such;) will reject and not look upon such clergymen as true ministers of the Gospel but rather as mercenary devourers of the flock.[19]

The names of the parish priests who issued the foregoing instructions are not appended to the document in the Dublin diocesan archives. However, on the assumption that the instructions refer to the early years of the century, there were at that time only five parish priests in Dublin city and liberties, their names at the time of the registration of priests in 1704 being Cornelius Nary, St Michan's; Edmond Byrne (later archbishop), St Nicholas's Without; Edward Murphy (later archbishop), St Audoen's; James Russell (for many years dean of the chapter), Ss Michael and John's; and James Brohy, St Catherine's and St James's.[20]

Population

The population of the three civil parishes of St Paul, New St Michan and St Mary increased by leaps and bounds in the early years of the eighteenth century. The number of houses more than doubled from 1,101 in 1695 to 2,414 in 1718. Since the average number of persons per house also increased from about eight in 1695 to about ten in 1718, the population would have increased from 9,000 in 1695 to 24,000 in 1718.

As regards the denominational make-up of the three parishes, a survey undertaken *c.* 1715, endorsed by Archbishop King, of the number of men in the city capable of bearing arms showed that in St Paul's 40% of such men were Catholics, in New St Michan's 38%, and in St Mary's 21%, figures which one would think could be taken as approximating to the percentage of the total populations in these parishes who were Catholics. However, a radically different situation was disclosed in New St Michan's civil parish in 1723, when a survey showed that only one-third of the population belonged to the Established Church. When Protestant Dissenters are taken into account, the total Protestant population could on this reckoning have amounted to no more than about 40%, with Catholics accounting for the remaining 60%. That this was the more likely scenario is borne out by the number of baptisms (which would broadly equate with live births) in St Michan's Catholic parish for 1726—records commenced on 25 February 1726—which can be estimated at 240. When this is related to a probable birth rate of around 35 per 1,000, a figure of approximately 6,800 emerges as the Catholic population of the parish in 1726. But since St Michan's Catholic parish comprised about four-fifths of St Michan's civil parish (the missing one-fifth being in St Paul's), the Catholic population of St Michan's *civil*

40

parish can be estimated at about 8,500. The total population of St Michan's civil parish in 1726 was about 14,000 (i.e. 1,150 houses at an average of twelve persons per house, this being the average disclosed by the 1723 survey), and accordingly the proportion of Catholics on this estimation also emerges as just 60%.

Although there are no baptism figures on which to make a projection, it seems probable that the proportion of Catholics in St Paul's was much the same as in St Michan's; according to the 1715 survey the proportion of Catholics in St Paul's was marginally higher than in St Michan's. St Mary's parish appears to have been mainly Protestant, although the proportion of 21% disclosed by the 1715 survey may also be an underestimate. On the basis of the number of baptisms for the parish, estimated at 148 for 1726, and a probable birth rate of 35 per 1,000, the Catholic population can be calculated to be about 4,200, and when this is related to a total population of about 12,000 the Catholic proportion is seen to be 35%. However, in this case the possibility cannot be ruled out that the Catholic proportion moved from 21% in *c.* 1715 to 35% in 1726 as a result of Catholic infiltration of the parish.

The total population of Dublin city and liberties was around 85,000 in 1715, but only about one-third of these were Catholics. Nary's life and labours have therefore to be viewed against the background of a city which, at least in the early years of the century, was nearly as Protestant as Belfast is today.

Education
While there is little specific information available in regard to Catholic education in the parish in the early years of the century, it can be assumed that there were several schoolteachers operating clandestinely at the rudimentary level of the 'Three Rs'. The position generally in the country at this time can be gleaned from the preamble to a bill, never passed into law, which stated that 'great numbers of papists do continue to keep public schools and are entertained to teach children in private houses to the great detriment of the true protestant religion, notwithstanding many good laws made and now in force to the contrary', and that 'most parishes in this kingdom, except in cities or great towns, are either wholly destitute of [protestant] schools or privately entertain popish schoolmasters for want of due encouragement to protestants to

Copy of a painting of St Francis Xavier which hung in Nary's chapel in Mary's Lane (now in St Michan's Church, Halston St.). (Photo: John Kennedy, The Green Studio.)

keep schools'. The purpose of this bill was to set up Protestant parish schools throughout the country. It appears to have evolved from the recommendations of a committee headed by Thomas Parnell, archdeacon of Clogher and a poet of some note.[26]

As was mentioned in Chapter 1, the Jesuits operated a classical school and seminary in the parish in Lucy Lane during the reign of James II. While this school was scattered following the Jacobite defeat in 1691, it may have regrouped later. This may account for the presence of two Jesuits, Gibbons and Netterville, in the parish according to the list of priests for 1697 already mentioned.

A Jesuit presence was to be a continued feature of life in the parish. Two members of the order, Fathers Milo Byrne and Michael Murphy, set up a classical school there about 1712. Murphy was one of the priests arrested in 1718 on the word of the priest-hunter Garzia, who in evidence at the trial stated that it was well known that Murphy conducted a school in which he taught grammar and philosophy. Murphy was sentenced to deportation, but it is not clear whether this sentence was ever carried out. In any event, he returned later to St Michan's and laboured there until his death in 1736.[27] Where the school was located in those early years is unclear. It may well be that the chapel served also as a school.

Another Jesuit connected with the parish in the early years of the century was the saintly Englishman Thomas Tasburgh. He died there in 1727 and—such are the incongruities of the times—was buried in the vaults of St Michan's Protestant Church. A relic of this saintly man (one of his fingers, in fact) was preserved in the Presentation Convent, George's Hill, until the 1960s when the church authorities ordered all such relics to be disposed of.[28]

At present there hangs in St Michan's Church, Halston Street, a painting of St Francis Xavier, one of the founders of the Society of Jesus. It is stated to be a copy of the painting of that saint 'which hung in Mary's Lane chapel in 1712'. The painting is said to be 'set up in recognition of the services of the Jesuit fathers in the parish in penal times'.

The house in Capel Street

Nary's ownership of a house in Capel Street, then a superior residential and emerging business quarter, comes as a somewhat surprising discovery to anyone researching his life and times. How he came to own this house is unclear. It is probable that it was left to him, in trust for the parish, by a previous Catholic owner. When it was leased by Nary to Patrick Meyler, probably a brewer, for a term of thirty years from September 1718 at a yearly rent of £10, it was mentioned in the lease that it had lately been inhabited by one William Warren. The deed of lease in favour of Meyler was witnessed by Anthony Hay, a prominent merchant, and by Francis White, a victualler. Eight years later, in December 1726, a new lease was entered into between the same parties for a term of thirty-one years at a yearly rent of £9. 10s.[29] It is not possible to identify the location of the house in Capel Street from the information given in the memorials of these leases in the Registry of Deeds, Dublin. I can find no record in the Registry of Deeds of the transfer of ownership of this house to Nary, or of any lease between Nary and William Warren, the tenant previous to Meyler. This would seem to indicate that Nary came into possession of the house at some date prior to the setting up of the Registry of Deeds in 1708.

The house is not mentioned at all in Nary's will—probably because it had already been transferred at that stage to Denis Byrne, Nary's successor as parish priest. The house is mentioned in Father Byrne's will, which was admitted to probate in 1744, where he provides that 'the candlesticks left to Dr Nary and by him to me, for the same use and intent, together with the house in Capel Street for the same use and purpose left to me, to my Executor'.

The controversy with Prebendary Clayton

Cornelius Nary had barely settled into St Michan's parish when he found himself involved in a controversy with the local Church of Ireland rector, John Clayton. Nary must have come to the parish with quite a reputation as a Catholic apologist and divine, and the fact that he had lately published a book which sought to refute Anglican doctrine, as outlined in the sermons of Archbishop Tillotson, must have marked him out to Clayton as an adversary worthy of his steel. Clayton appears to have been well versed in all the controversies, heresies, popes and antipopes of the Christian Church and, as Nary was to remind him, had an itch for controversy.

Clayton was born in Lancashire in 1657 and studied at Oxford under Narcissus Marsh, afterwards archbishop of Dublin. We find him mentioned as rector of Crofton near Wakefield in 1687. He later spent some years on missionary work in Virginia, where, in a revealing sidelight on the early Episcopalian Church there, he recalls that

> when sometime I was Minister of James City in Virginia, I settled the service of our church very regularly. I was the first that wore a surplice there, and by expounding the Common Prayer in the afternoon, I had the happiness to give great satisfaction to many sorts of Sectaries, and I brought over many Dissenters to be very affectionate to our Church services. I received also and baptised

some Anabaptists and Quakers; I baptised many Negroes who had been there lamentably neglected. But I got my brother, who was a most eminent lawyer, to take off one grand obstruction that had obtained viz. a notion that a Negro, being baptised, was immediately free. For their masters would rather hazard their salvation, trusting God Almighty with their souls in the other world, than lose the benefit of their services in this; as they would often too profanely express it.[30]

Clayton came to Dublin in 1697 with Charles, second duke of Bolton, on the latter's appointment as a lord justice. In 1698 he was appointed rector of St Michan's, Church Street, a post which traditionally carried with it the additional distinction of prebendary of Christ Church. He became a canon of Kildare in 1705 and dean in 1708, while continuing, of course, as rector of St Michan's. While he appears to have been well thought of by Archbishop Marsh, he was not held in high regard by Marsh's successor, King, who had his doubts about Clayton's orthodoxy and rectitude of character. Swift did not think too highly of him either, for he is on record as describing Clayton as 'a most malicious, ignorant and headstrong creature'.[31]

Clayton inherited considerable wealth when his brother died in 1715. He himself died in 1725 and is buried in the vaults of St Michan's Church, where presumably his body still enjoys (if that is the word) some degree of preservation, owing to the unique preservative properties of that resting-place. He was the father of Robert Clayton, who was successively bishop of Killala, Cork and Clogher.

Clayton has his own special claim to fame as the reputed discoverer of gas lighting, and indeed, as recently as 1926, a short and poorly researched booklet was written about him by Walter T. Layton. He probably saw his appointment to St Michan's in 1698 as a stepping-stone to a bishopric, since some of his predecessors in that parish had become bishops. Clayton may have seen a joust of theological argument with this newly arrived papist divine, who was probably living in the same street (for the earliest address we have for Nary is the Viscountess Clanmalier's house in Church Street), as a means of drawing attention to himself and advancing his claims to preferment.

The proximate cause, however, of the controversy between Nary and Clayton was a Mrs Rose O'Neill, who appears to have been one of Nary's upper-class parishioners, and whom he describes as 'a lady of quality'.[32] Evidently she was being pressurised by Clayton to conform to the Established Church, and she brought the two divines together so that she could hear both sides of the question.[33] There is internal evidence in the two extant pamphlets on the controversy that the meeting between the two churchmen took place in Mrs O'Neill's house some time in the year 1700.

According to Nary the meeting lasted only forty-five minutes. Also present with Clayton was a Mr Davis, who may have been a clerical colleague of his. Some eighteen months after this conference Clayton wrote and published a pamphlet which purported to be a true account of what transpired between himself and Nary, the arguments which Nary had put forward and how he (Clayton) had dealt with those arguments. This pamphlet does not appear to have survived.

The next shot in this battle of words came when Mrs O'Neill placed an advertisement in *Dublin Intelligence* stating that Clayton's pamphlet on the conference misrepresented the position. Clayton's response to this was to get Mr Davis to write to both Mrs O'Neill and Nary. Davis's letter to Mrs O'Neill is quite civil, indeed more in sorrow than in anger:

> You have been pleased lately to give your attention in a matter (wherein you and I were the only witnesses) after such a manner that either I do not understand what you mean by falsehoods and foul representing, or I am afraid our judgments concerning matters of fact are likely to be as opposite as they are concerning points of religion.[34]

Davis's letter to Nary is, on the other hand, quite lengthy (three quarto pages) and abusive. For example, he writes:

> There are two things more wherein you were favoured in the printed account and they both related to your learning, if a body may be so bold as to touch a thing so celebrated. And for certain reasons, I chose rather to begin with you at the top and so come downwards, chiefly because my opinion of it (which was very high while I had it only from hearsay) by some misfortune or other, the longer we were acquainted, sank lower and lower.

He ridicules Nary's 'positiveness' about having seen some expression in Greek, when, Davis contends, there was no such thing in Greek and continues:

> But you solemnly swear you had seen it in Greek in some place or other, in some book or other and in some edition or other, but what you can't remember. This puts me in mind of a gentleman who, coming to a certain College [no doubt Trinity College] to enquire for a friend that was a Scholar there, could get no other satisfaction from the porter, who had an impediment in his speech, but that he lodged over against what d'ye call 'um, in the same room with what d'ye call 'um, in what d'ye call 'us buildings'.[35]

Davis goes on to question Nary's knowledge of the Greek versions of the Scriptures, refers scathingly to Nary's translation of a Latin phrase for Mrs O'Neill, and pronounces that 'a schoolboy would be whipt if he were guilty of such mistakes'. He dismisses Nary's book *Chief points in controversy between Roman Catholics and Protestants*:

> The book, which you are so fond of being reputed the author of, is a new collection of old arguments which have been so long ago sifted and refuted that the bringing of them thus over and over again carries some semblance of chewing the cud. But to repeat them without giving the least notice of the answers that have been given to them is such an intolerable piece either of ignorance or impudence that one would think the man that would be guilty of it, must either have no forehead or no brains. To conclude . . . if there be any argument left out [in Clayton's pamphlet], which you brought at the time for the proof of any one of these three points, let me see you at the Coffee House at the time mentioned in last Tuesday's Intelligence, for I find that all private conferences with you are dangerous.[36]

The advertisement referred to appeared in the *Dublin Intelligence* in October 1702 and read as follows:

> Whereas there has of late been published an advertisement, wherein a lady has affirmed that Mr Clayton in his relation of the Conference between him and Mr Nary, lately printed, has misrepresented the case. This is to give notice that Mr Davis (who was the only other witness besides the said lady) desires it may be made appear to him that any material thing is wanting or superfluous; and that he will be at the Oxmantown Coffee House from 6 to 7 every night till Saturday in expectation thereof; and that then he will deliver his opinion thereupon. This not being a dispute of Church or State he hopes that the vain, common excuse of fear of the law, may not pass as reasonable.[37]

Apparently, there was no appearance by either Mrs O'Neill or Nary in response to the advertisement. Accordingly, a second advertisement appeared in *Dublin Intelligence* on 20 October, stating that Mr Davis had waited at the coffee-house as proposed, but neither Nary nor the lady had turned up. Davis, therefore, felt himself obliged to deliver himself of his judgement on Clayton's report of the conference, to wit, 'that it is a modest, candid and true account of the matter of fact'.[38]

If Nary had been incensed by Clayton's untrue and biased report of their conference, Davis's public confirmation that Clayton's report was a true account must have angered him further and made the publication of a pamphlet setting out his side of the story all the more necessary. At all events, Nary's pamphlet in reply to Clayton duly appeared. It is dated 1703 and appears to have been published early that year.

47

Nary is highly contemptuous of Clayton's claim to recall in any detail what was said at a conference which had taken place eighteen months previous to his recording it, particularly as he did not take any notes of what was said. He maintains that the arguments put forward on both sides have been fabricated by Clayton to suit his own purposes: 'Mr Clayton's surprising memory furnishes him with my words and his own, or, to speak truth, his fruitful invention puts such words in my mouth as he thought most proper to suit his own answers, which is so bold a stroke as to be fit only for men of Mr Clayton's size'.[39]

We gather from Nary's pamphlet that the subjects debated with Clayton at the conference were (a) Doctor Hammond's treatise on schism, (b) whether Communion should be taken in two kinds (i.e. bread and wine) and whether fasting was necessary before Communion, and (c) the primacy of the bishop of Rome.

The argument between Clayton and Nary as to what the Fathers of the Church said about schism could be narrowed down to a difference in the translation into English of one word in the original Greek of St Irenaeus, a second-century Father of the Church. With regard to schism Irenaeus, according to the Catholic translation, had said: 'It is *impossible* to receive such a provocation from the Governors of the Church as may make a separation excusable'. In elaboration of this, Nary pointed out: 'And the reason is plain, because when a man separates from the Church, he exposes himself to eternal damnation; and the crime of Schism is besides attended with so many dismal consequences and carries so many horrible aggravations along with it, that no other crime can be greater'.[40]

According to Doctor Hammond's treatise, the word 'impossible' should read 'very hard, if not impossible', thus softening somewhat the effect of Irenaeus's pronouncement in line with Protestant susceptibilities, since the Protestant Reformation was in effect another Great Schism of the Church.[41]

The decree of the Council of Constance about fasting before Communion and on whether Communion should be taken in two kinds (bread and wine) also gave rise to some disagreement between Clayton and Nary. While they were *ad idem* on what the council had decreed about fasting before Communion, they disagreed as to how the decree was to be interpreted with regard to Communion in two kinds. Nary maintained that the decree provided that the laity should receive Communion in the form of bread only, while Clayton argued that the decree did not

48

prohibit Communion by the laity under the forms of both bread and wine.[42]

On the third point, the primacy of the bishop of Rome, Clayton maintained that what the councils of Nice and Chalcydon had in mind were 'prerogatives of precedency' and not a supremacy of the bishop of Rome over all other bishops. Nary argued that what these councils decreed was no less than the primacy of the bishop of Rome over all others. Furthermore, this was a declaration of the faith by the Fathers of the Church, which had been received from their ancestors; these councils did not purport to make new articles of faith.[43]

The foregoing is a broad summary of the issues debated by the two churchmen. However, the principal value of Nary's pamphlet to a biographer must be the light it throws on his character, on the relations between Catholics and Protestants at the time, and the degree of toleration afforded to Catholics.

Nary comes across as a fearless and formidable controversialist who was quite prepared to give as good as he got. Indeed, his language at times could only be called provocative, particularly having regard to the very uncertain position of Catholics at the time *vis-à-vis* the law. He also appears to have had great faith (perhaps too much faith) in the liberality of a high proportion of Protestants in the Dublin and the Ireland of the time, and the fact that he could engage at all (and that publicly) in such a controversy in itself points to a considerable degree of *de facto* toleration. Nary remarks:

> Thus much concerning the first point, which I would have had very willingly omitted, as also all other disputes in religion if I could help it; for having a great deal of civility shown to me by some of the nobility and gentry and even by some of the clergy of the Church of England (*sic*) since my coming to this country, 'twas no little trouble to me to be put upon anything that should give them any sort of dissatisfaction. And the lady in whose presence I had the conference with Mr Clayton can bear witness that I refused to have any dispute with him till she assured me he had promised upon his word it should not be made known. But since he has been pleased to publish it and to treat me as if I had been an Impostor, I hope no honest man will take it ill that I make a natural and necessary defence and keeping within bounds of good manners and respect.[44]

Nary goes on:

> And here I shall desire the reader to observe how improbable it is that I should be so sheepish and dull as to hear Mr Clayton treat me with the fine language he sets down in his paper and make him no manner of return; or that the lady who is very nice of the respect due to one of her birth and quality, should suffer any man in her presence

to use such language and yet take no notice of it. In very deed, if Mr Clayton did utter such injurious words, it was never in the lady's nor my hearing, bating, I think, one or two words all in a breath, for which the lady gave him, as I thought, sufficient reprimand. . . I confess that if he had given me ill language a second time, I would not return his words but make a leg and withdraw. Secondly, how unlikely it is that a man of common sense should answer after so sneaking and so silly a manner as he makes me speak in his paper.[45]

With regard to the discussion on the primacy of the bishop of Rome, Nary is at his most provocative:

I do not think that what he says or makes me to say in his paper was ever spoken in our conference. As to his Billingsgate Sharper and the rest of his Billingsgate language, I positively aver I heard nothing of it upon this head. And, indeed, it is so rank and coarse that, if I may be allowed to judge of the man's company by his behaviour, he seems to be no stranger to the scolds of that famous place.[46]

According to Nary, the conference ended abruptly when Clayton suddenly excused himself, because (Nary maintains) he realised he had no answer to the translation into English of the decree of the Council of Constance on Communion in two kinds which Nary was asked to make by Mrs O'Neill.[47]

It should be mentioned that, as a kind of sub-plot (some might call it comic relief) to the main thrust of the controversy between Nary and Clayton, we are treated to the problems of a married couple, rather quirkily named Joy. Mrs Joy had been converted to Protestantism, while her husband remained a Catholic. Mrs Joy's conversion, to say the least, did not help relations between Nary and Clayton. In any event, it appears that Clayton had included in his report of the conference with Nary an account of Mrs Joy's ill-usage at the hands of her husband; he went on to complain of being scurrilously treated himself by several of the 'Romans' and of his being constrained to print his report of the conference because it was said that he (Clayton) 'preaches against Father Nary's book but dare not print anything whereto he [Nary] may make a fair reply'.[48] The book referred to here is undoubtedly Nary's *Chief points in controversy between Roman Catholics and Protestants.*

With regard to the relations between Mr and Mrs Joy, Nary in his pamphlet states:

As to Mrs Joy's ill-usage, I can only say that the woman in whose house she lodged at that time and two other grave women told me they were ready to make an oath if required, that Mr Joy was bloody all over his face by the blows given him by his wife; and one of those three who was present when the quarrel happened, says that Mrs Joy struck her husband first in the face, and made him bleed before he gave her any ill-usage. And they all further add that Mrs Joy will not deny this to be true. But however that matter was, methinks Mr Clayton's reflections upon it savours but very little of the apostolic spirit, whose tenderness and compassion ought rather to be a barrier for the defence of his fellow Christians than a means to exasperate the Magistrates and people against them; as if the ill-usage of one man to his wife were a sufficient reason for him to involve all the rest of this man's persuasion in the same fact, or to suppose they would do the like if they were in his circumstances. But, blessed be God, our Magistrates and the rest of the Protestant clergy are not of Mr Clayton's complexion.[49]

Clayton now felt it necessary to issue a further pamphlet in reply to Nary's. It includes Davis's letters to Mrs O'Neill and Nary, as well as the text of the two advertisements which appeared in *Dublin Intelligence* in October 1702. Clayton adopts a superior attitude to Nary's style of English when he says: 'Nor shall I in return sum up his false English, his Irish and Scotch expressions, his blunders and gross ignorances',[50] although it is patently obvious that Nary is far superior to Clayton as a writer of English.

He vouchsafes some further information regarding Mr and Mrs Joy, which is reminiscent of a chapter from Defoe:

The first time I set seriously to read this pamphlet, Mrs Joy came accidentally to my house, whereupon I read this passage to her, who admired at [i.e. wondered at] such confidence and gave this account thereof. [Note: The pamphlet referred to above is apparently Nary's.] After her husband had lain abroad several nights without allowing her anything to support her family, when they met he was very furious against her turning Protestant and denied his marriage and said he had two men who would swear she was only his whore, not his wife, to whom he said he had given two guineas and gave her a kick in the breech. This, says she, was such a provocation that I confess I was enraged so far as to give him a slap in the face. This was not the natural temper of her husband, but the instigations of their wicked cabals, who took viler methods to make her return, or ruin her. And she has given under her hand that a gentleman unknown came to her lodgings and pretended to be a Justice of the Peace, or one sent by a Justice of the Peace, to take her examination, hearing that her husband had abused her since her conversion to the Protestant religion. Whereupon he asked several questions and writ something down. After that he pulled her to his knee and said that her husband had very much abused her though she was a pretty woman. But he loved a pretty woman in his heart and clapping his hand on her breast and belly and so forth, said that if she would go with him, she would want for nothing and that he would be kinder to her than her husband, and said and offered many more things than she can well remember or is it fit for her to tell. The same man she since knows to be Father Adams, for he came several times after to

51

her lodging, dined with her husband and drew him abroad, who generally returned in a bad humour. And the same Father Adams took away several books that Mr Clayton gave her, which she could never get again. This she has signed by way of deposition.[51]

Clayton goes on to take Nary to task for his interpretation of the decree on schism:

> The rest of Mr Nary's discourse on this head is very extravagant, running it up to that pitch that no crime nor no error, nor both in conjunction can justify a separation . . . that, therefore, the Protestants must all be damned for their separation from the Church of Rome, that there is no salvation for them outside that Church. . . But the same argument brings Christianity itself in consequence to be a damnable sin, being a separation from the Jewish Church, which was once the Established Church of God, and makes all the Apostles guilty, according to his principles, of as great a sin as that of the Holy Ghost, and this learned man knows what that sin is positively. [Nary had suggested in his pamphlet that the sin against the Holy Ghost was idolatry.] . . . But if idolatry be the sin against the Holy Ghost, I'm sure they, that would be saved, must separate from the Church of Rome, that is most grossly guilty of idolatry.[52]

Clayton devotes the remainder of his pamphlet to further arguments against the primacy of the bishop of Rome and to arguments in favour of Communion in two kinds.

Clayton's controversy with Nary was not the only one which he (Clayton) had in hand with the Catholic clergy at this time. On 23 February 1701, in St Michan's Church, in the presence of Archbishop Marsh, he preached a sermon, in rabid, uncompromising style, against papal infallibility. The occasion was the reception into the Established Church of two converts from the Catholic Church, Sir Terence MacMahon and Christopher Dunn. In the course of this sermon Clayton referred scathingly to correspondence which he had had with the Catholic clergy in Dublin on the question of papal infallibility. The reply which he got from the Catholic side he dubs 'a most tedious answer, which I could never get a copy of' and ends his diatribe with the remark: 'They [the Catholic clergy] only vomit out their own shame'.[53] 'B.B.', one of the Catholic clergy, took Clayton up on what he had said in his sermon, and Clayton reproduced a good deal of B.B.'s rejoinder in a further lengthy pamphlet entitled *The defence of a sermon,* printed in 1701. Clayton, in this pamphlet, identifies B.B. as a Dr Burn, in all probability (although the initials do not correspond) Dr Edmond Byrne (alias Burn), who at this time was parish priest of St Nicholas Without and was later archbishop of Dublin.

It appears that Dr Burn was imprisoned by the authorities at about this time, a development in which the Catholics, rightly or wrongly, believed Clayton to have had a hand. This Clayton denies in the course of the pamphlet: 'But they spread a false report that I got the Government to clap up one Dr Burn upon account of his answer; to which I declare, I was neither directly nor indirectly privy; and I am told it was because some letters were found in the Posthouse, subscribed with his name, of treasonable consequence'.[54]

Burn's imprisonment and Clayton's suspected part in it would account to some extent for Nary's obvious contempt for Clayton. In any event, in some comments in his pamphlet already discussed, apparently directed at *The defence of a sermon,* we find Nary at his vituperative best. He first of all refers to Clayton's statement that he had shown in *The defence of a sermon* what sort of scholar Burn was and that he challenged Burn 'and the whole tribe' to answer him. Nary continues:

> And so you may ad Kalendas Graecas, but never find any to answer your challenge. For who would be at pains of answering a paper that has so many scurrilous and injurious expressions in it? The best answer a man can make to such Billingsgate language is to contemn it. As to what you say of me, I should likewise have passed it by with the same contempt, if I had not thought it may perhaps contribute to cure you of your itch for controversy and serve to disabuse the meaner sort of people, to show the world (to use your own phrase) what sort of scholar you are and how little of that sincerity whereof you so much boast, and whose want in others you so highly reproach, is to be met with in your paper.[55]

Whether the bickering between Clayton and Nary ended there we do not know, and little light can be shed on the future relations of these two clerics, who perforce had to live cheek by jowl with each other for a quarter of a century. There is just one little clue that they may have mellowed with the years and learned to tolerate each other. In 1724, when it was proposed to erect a new organ in St Michan's (Protestant) Church, a contribution of a pistole (a Spanish coin then in circulation worth 18s. 6d.) is on record as having been received from 'Dr Nairy, registered priest of ye parish'.[56] It was a generous contribution, in the region of £100 in today's money. Clayton lived only three months after the new organ was installed. The organ is still in place in St Michan's. However, the keyboard on which Handel is reputed to have played in 1743 has had to be replaced and is now on view in the vestibule of the Church.

As to the identity of the Mrs Rose O'Neill who was the primary cause of the controversy between Clayton and Nary, she was almost certainly the same lady who, together with her maid, spent some years as a parlour-boarder in the Dominican Convent, Channel Row, before her death in January 1727, and who figures in the records of that convent as Mrs Rose O'Neill and Madam R. O'Neill. Nary is recorded as having paid £14. 5s. 'for the expense of both Mrs O'Neill's offices' (i.e. Requiem Mass etc.), indicating that they remained to the end close friends.[57] We gather from Nary's pamphlet that she was a highly-connected 'lady of quality'. It can be deduced from *Betham's abstracts of prerogative wills* in the National Archives, Dublin,[58] and from other sources that the lady in question was Rose, daughter of Sir Henry O'Neill of Killyleagh, Co. Down, widow of Captain Con O'Neill of the Fews and niece of Richard Talbot, duke of Tyrconnell.

Notes

1. The accepted date of foundation of this church appears to be 1096.
2. Nathaniel Burton, *Oxmantown and its environs* (Dublin, 1845), 2.
3. Sir John Gilbert (ed.), *Calendar of ancient records of Dublin* (Dublin, various dates), vol. 6, 580. Captain John South's enumeration for 1695 gives the number of houses in St Michan's parish (i.e. the entire north side of the city) as 1,101 and the population as 8,894.
4. Anon. (believed to be Edward Evans), 'History of the Roman Catholic church and parish of St Michan', *The Irish Builder* 34 (1892), 175.
5. Nicholas Donnelly, *Short histories of Dublin parishes* (Dublin, issued in parts, various dates), part XI, 51.
6. The list is printed in *The Irish Builder* 34 (1892), 174 ff, from a MS in Marsh's Library.
7. Donnelly, *op. cit.,* part XI, 50.
8. Crofton collection of manuscripts in the library of Trinity College, Dublin, no. 96.16, 2.
9. John Dunton, *The Dublin scuffle* (London, 1699), 332–3.
10. W. P. Burke, *Irish priests of the penal times* (Waterford, 1914), 150.
11. Myles Ronan, 'The story of a Dublin parish', *The Irish Rosary* 8 (April, 1904), 256.
12. National Library of Ireland, microfilm Pos. 4034.
13. T. R. England, *The life of Revd Arthur O'Leary* (London, 1822), 22.
14. Registry of Deeds, Dublin ref. 22–137.
15. Ronan, *op. cit.,* 249–57. Bull Lane, which ran parallel with present-day Greek Street, was, together with Fisher Lane, taken down to make room for the Corporation Fruit and Vegetable Market. The Mary's Lane chapel

also appears to have been the venue for debates on religious topics by Catholic priests. For example, Garzia, the priest-hunter, in his report to Archbishop King dated 2 February 1722, included a document (in Latin): 'Conclusions defended publicly by the papist priests in the chapel of Doctor Nary in the city of Dublin'. These 'conclusions' related to the supremacy of the pope and other matters which had been publicly defended by Father John Curry, with Father John Herald presiding. Father Herald is described in a postulation by Dublin clergy to Rome in 1729 as doctor of theology and professor of sacred theology.

16. Kevin McGrath, 'John Garzia, a noted priest-catcher and his activities', *Irish Ecclesiastical Record* 72 (July–Dec. 1949), 512 ff.

17. *Journal of Irish Memorials Association* 11 (1921–5), 1–66.

18. Official publication entitled *A list of the names of popish parish priests* (Dublin, 1705), in King's Inns Library, Dublin.

19. Dublin diocesan archives, item 19.

20. Nicholas Donnelly, 'The diocese of Dublin in the eighteenth century', *Irish Ecclesiastical Record* 9 (1888), 837–49.

21. Sir John Gilbert, *op. cit.,* vol. 7, 577.

22. George T. Stokes, *Some worthies of the Irish church* (Dublin, 1899), 246 ff.

23. Sir John Gilbert, *op. cit.,* vol. 6, 578.

24. Monck Mason MS in Gilbert Library, Dublin, part 3, 155.

25. Sir John Gilbert, *op. cit.,* vol. 7, 577. The figure of 85,000 is arrived at on the basis of an average of nine persons per house.

26. National Library of Ireland, microfilm Pos. 1946, p. 219.

27. Kevin McGrath, *op. cit.,* 499.

28. Leon O Broin, *Miss Cruikshank agus coirp eile* (Dublin, 1951), *passim.*

29. Registry of Deeds, Dublin refs 25–178 and 53–207. Nary is described in these documents simply as 'gent'.

30. Crofton collection of manuscripts in library of Trinity College, Dublin, no. 96.19, preface, p. 1.

31. F. Elrington Ball (ed.), *The correspondence of Jonathan Swift* (London, 1910), vol. 1, 48. It is of interest that, on the occasion of the selection of a successor to Clayton in 1725, King wrote to Radcliffe, vicar of Naas: 'I pray God send us a good man in it [St Michan's] for I have known it fifty-eight years and never rightly supplied'. (See N.L.I., microfilm Pos. 1116.)

32. Crofton 96.16, 3.

33. Crofton 96.19, preface, p. 2.

34. Crofton 96.17, 2.

35. *Ibid.,* 4.

36. *Ibid.,* 5.

37. *Ibid.,* 6. Since the Oxmantown coffee-house is referred to as 'the coffee-house', it was probably the only one on the north side of the Liffey at this period. It may have been one and the same as the Grecian coffee-house which was located in Capel Street (Registry of Deeds ref. 8–315) in the early decades of the century.

38. *Ibid.*, 6.
39. Crofton 96.16, 1.
40. *Ibid.*, 12.
41. *Ibid.*, 10.
42. *Ibid.*, 15.
43. *Ibid.*, 20.
44. *Ibid.*, 12–13. The liberality of some Protestants, highlighted by Nary, has to be seen in juxtaposition with the extreme illiberality of others. For instance, the arch-bigot John Whalley (later to be publisher of *Whalley's Newsletter*), in his *Humble address to the Irish Houses of Parliament*, must have had Nary particularly in mind when he proposed that authors of Catholic pamphlets ('as some have lately done in opposition to some things published by Dr Clayton and others') should, 'if of the clergy, be gelt and banished, and if of the laity, fined and imprisoned'. (See R. R. Madden, *The history of Irish periodical literature* (London, 1867), vol. 1, 247.)
45. Crofton 96.16, 4.
46. *Ibid.*, 18.
47. *Ibid.*, 13.
48. *Ibid.*, 2.
49. *Ibid.*, 2.
50. Crofton 96.17, 1.
51. *Ibid.*, 7–8.
52. *Ibid.*, 12–13.
53. Crofton 96.18, 17.
54. Crofton 96.19, 3.
55. Crofton 96.17, 3–4.
56. John Meagher, 'Glimpses of eighteenth century priests', *Reportorium Novum* 2, no. 1 (1958), 132.
57. National Library of Ireland, microfilm Pos. 3787.
58. National Archives, Dublin, BET-1-53, 52, and BET-1-53, 58. See also John Lodge, *The peerage of Ireland* (London, 1789), vol. 3, 256, and *Burke's Peerage* (1970 edition), 2032, 2nd column.

Chapter 4

THE BELLINGS CORRESPONDENCE

APART from the letter to Bishop Michael MacDonagh included in Chapter 9, this is the only private correspondence of Nary's which I have been able to trace. It is in the possession of Lord Talbot of Malahide, Hook Manor, Donhead St Andrew, Wiltshire. Lord Talbot was previously Mr Arundell and only in recent years succeeded to the title. There are ten letters in all, the first dated April 1706 and the last dated September 1718. Eight of the letters were written by Nary, six to Sir Richard Bellings and two to Sir Richard's son. The two remaining letters are from Sir Richard to Nary. Sir Richard's address is given as St James's Square, London.

Sir Richard Bellings was born about 1632. He is usually styled 'the younger' since his father was also named Richard. His father took a very active part in the Confederation of Kilkenny and was secretary to the Supreme Council of that body. He retired to France in 1649, but following the Restoration he returned to Ireland and succeeded in having some of his confiscated estates restored to him. He died in 1677. Richard, the younger, left Ireland in 1643 and apparently never returned. His only claim to fame is that he was secretary to Charles II's queen, Catherine of Braganza. He married Frances, heiress of Sir John Arundell. Their son assumed the name of Arundell and his only child married Henry, Lord Arundell of Wardour in Wiltshire, from whom the present Lord Talbot of Malahide is descended.[1] It is clear, then, how the Nary correspondence comes to be in his possession.

Nary's letters are written in a clear hand, although there is the occasional illegible word. In all cases he signs himself simply 'C. Nary'. The purpose of the correspondence, as far as

Nary was concerned, was to secure financial assistance for various people who had known better days, some of them Sir Richard's relations. Another family for whom assistance was sought were the Farrells, who were descended from a foster-brother of Sir Richard. The practice of a well-to-do family putting their children out to fosterage with families of modest means persisted up to the end of the eighteenth century, and quite strong ties were built up between the wealthy child and his poorer foster-brothers and sisters. It will be seen that the Farrells were for turning to advantage these ties and were threatening to call on Sir Richard in London.

Nary's first letter to Sir Richard, although lengthy, is of sufficient interest to be quoted in full.

Dublin, April 27th, 1706

Sir,

Though I have not the honour to be personally acquainted with your Honour, yet I am no stranger to the great charities you have lately done in this Kingdom, which indeed give me some assurance that you will not take amiss I should recommend a poor relation of yours (as she tells me) to your charity. Her name is Elizabeth Beling, daughter of Patrick Beling and sister of Ismay Beling, with whom your Honour was very well acquainted, as I am informed. This poor woman is about seventy years old and was for many years past subsisted by Alderman Gardiner, but since his death was forced to beg, though a very sweet, venerable, old gentle-woman; and now her sight beginning to fail her, she is like to be reduced to greater straights. I need not tell you, Sir, your duty in this case, being persuaded you are very sensible you are only a steward of your substance, which Almighty God was pleased to entrust you with, and that no article of your account in the Last Day will be more agreeable to your great Master than that divine item 'So much laid out for the relief of the poor', since this alone determines Him to pronounce the agreeable sentence 'Come ye blessed of my Father'. I should not, upon my word, trouble your Honour at this distance with such a business, had I not discovered something in this old gentle-woman that distinguishes her from the common sort of beggars. Sweetness of humour, gentleness of behaviour, a godly, mortified countenance, accompanied by a great deal of patience and resignation to God's Holy Will, are graces which urge (?) very much, nay, and seem to extort, what they ask. All which seem to be, in my opinion, very happily concentred in the person of this poor widow. In short, Sir, she earnestly desired me to recommend her to your Honour's charity, only to allow her bare bread for the few days she has to live. I have herein obeyed her prayers, though not my own inclination, because of the presumption which attends writing to a person of quality by a man of my meanness and (what is more) by a stranger to your Honour. But 'Charity beareth all things'. If your Honour is writing to grant her petition, you will give me cause to rejoice and glorify God, who gave you that goodwill, and you will also inherit the blessing of the widow and the reward of Him, who is the judge of widows and the father of orphans. If you are not willing, I shall find no fault, being content to have freed my own soul.

And now that I have with so much freedom shot the bolt of my presumption, it is but reasonable that I should discover my own meanness, if I have not already done it too much. As to my person, I need not tell you that I am a poor miserable man, a vessel of wrath fitted for destruction, but by God's mercy designed to carry a precious treasure, viz. the Grace of the Holy Ghost, which yet by my rashness and folly I have often split and dashed in pieces on the rocks and shelves of this wicked world. As to my character, great indeed, though very unworthy of it, viz. a priest and what is more dreadful to me, Parish Priest of Oxmantown, by consequence so much the more miserable, and by how much my charge is the greater and my insufficiency to carry so great a burden, the more apparent. More I will not say, because if I should say truth, as I resolve I never will do otherwise, I should discover too much of my nakedness and offend your modesty. But such as I am, a miserable sinner, I hope I shall sincerely dispense to the poor widow your earthly blessing (if you please to send it to me) that Jesus Christ may ratify the blessing of your widow to you in Heaven. If your Honour will think fit to favour me with an answer, please to address your letter to Dr. Nary at Captain Usher's house in Church Street who (if a sinner's praise be of any value) shall always reckon your Honour among his clients and shall be very glad to be styled, if your Honour will please to permit him, Sir, your Honour's most humble and obedient servant,

C. Nary

Sir Richard Bellings was, at the date of this first letter from Nary, already well into his seventies. It is interesting that Nary describes himself in this letter as parish priest of Oxmantown. This description was presumably a means of getting around the difficulty (discussed in Chapter 3) that, while he was legally registered as parish priest of the *civil* parish of St Michan's, he was at this time, canonically speaking, parish priest of the much larger *Catholic* parish of St Michan's, which embraced the entire north side of the city and was known collectively as Oxmantown.

The Captain Usher whom Nary uses as a convenience address belonged to a Catholic branch of the Usshers, a family which was predominantly Protestant. He was the father of George Usher, described as 'an eminent merchant', who in turn was father of the Jesuit Stephen Usher.[2]

Sir Richard replied to Nary in the following letter, dated London, September 1706:

Sir,

I should not this long have deferred answering your obliging letter but that having received it in the country, I had not there an

59

opportunity of taking that notice I ought to do of a particular, which with so much zeal you recommended to my consideration. I do now return you many hearty, humble thanks for your many kind admonitions and other expressions which, though I cannot but be very sensible of, I must own not to deserve. I send you here enclosed a Bill for thirty pounds drawn upon . . . which though oppressed with pastoral duties, I make no question your charity will move you to undergo the trouble of distributing to the persons hereafter named.

To Elizabeth Belings £8

To an ancient gentle-woman, who signs herself Hellen Butler, and says that she is my nearest relation, and heretofore received some assistance from me, which I do not well remember—£8

To Dr Oliver Doyle, Priviledged Parish Priest of Castleknock £5

To Mr Cruise, who lives on the farm called Bussardstown, fifty shillings.

There are in Dublin or near it two brothers and sisters, named Farrells, descended as they say from a foster-brother of mine, who lived many years on a farm of mine in the County Kildare and received some assistance from me, but they themselves thinking it time to disperse, desired I would continue my bounty for the last time, which I did, and I wish you could find means to distribute £5 amongst them. Mary Farrell, the eldest sister, has of late got someone to write for her, that having served in Dublin, she thinks she may be useful to me and my family, and adds that her brother, John, is likewise ready to come along with her. But the Queen, my Mistress, being dead, it is not to be imagined I should have any thoughts of enlarging my family or turn out any of my servants here, to make them room, and that I desire you will tell them you would not have had this perplexted additional trouble, but that Mary Farrell in her paper, begged that I would in my letter to you give her an answer to her petition. I left Ireland in 1643, and I have a confused remembrance of Ismay Belings, but know nothing of any sister she had, and as for Mrs Hellen Butler, I presume she must be descended from My Lord Mountgarret, whose daughter was my mother, if we be so near a kind. What little remains of the thirty pounds I desire you will lay out in your own chapel on prayers for the Captain whose funeral you took so much care of. I should add much to this letter, already too long, if I did enlarge as I might do upon the different character you deserve, confirmed by universal approbation and good works, which still are the best proofs, but I will end with assuring you that I am very really and with much esteem etc

The Dr Oliver Doyle mentioned in Sir Richard's letter was registered as parish priest of Castleknock under the Act of 1704. He was then aged thirty-nine and had been ordained in Salamanca in 1687.[3] In 1706 he was living with a retired priest, Walter Cruise, at Bussardstown, Mulhuddart. In the period between June 1705 and March 1708 Dr Doyle was also engaged in writing begging letters to Sir Richard or to Lady Bellings, and some half-dozen of these survive in the archives of Lord

Talbot of Malahide. Sir Richard had estates in the Mulhuddart area and on this basis Dr Doyle saw fit to style himself chaplain to Sir Richard, although the latter had not apparently set foot in Ireland since he was a youth.

As regards the reference to 'the Queen, my Mistress', Catherine of Braganza had died the previous year (1705). It can be inferred that Sir Richard continued as her secretary until her death, although she had returned to her native Portugal in 1692. However, her residence in London, Somerset House, remained her property and was a focus for Catholic affairs for many years after her departure.[4]

The Captain referred to towards the end of the letter appears to be Captain James Bellings who, according to a letter from Dr Doyle to Sir Richard, died in 1705 and was buried in Mulhuddart, following, apparently, a funeral service in Nary's chapel in Mary's Lane.

The House of Mountgarret (i.e. the Viscount Mountgarret) was one of the branches of the Butler family in County Kilkenny. The Mountgarrets were still Catholic at this date although they conformed to the Established Church later on in the century. It later transpires that Hellen Butler, one of the ladies in reduced circumstances, was a first cousin ('cousin german') of Sir Richard. She thus shared with him a common grandfather in the person of the third Viscount Mountgarret, president of the Supreme Council of the Irish Confederation (of Kilkenny), and a common great-grandfather in the person of Hugh (the Great) O'Neill.[5]

Nary wrote again to Sir Richard in October 1706:

> Honoured Sir,
> I had the favour of your Honour's letter with the enclosed Bill, which I would have sooner answered but that all the people, except Hellen Butler, were in the country, to whom you desired your charity should be distributed; and indeed it came very seasonably, for the poor folks for whom it was given stood in very great need of the same, especially the poor old gentle-woman whom I have been obliged these many days to supply myself. So that I was well pleased to have money sent for their relief as if it had been sent to myself. Hellen Butler is of the House of Mountgarret, as your Honour observes, and, as she tells me, your cousin german, but I do believe neither she nor Mrs Beling will ever trouble your Honour more, being both very old and infirm. All the four Farrells are very poor but I charged them they should not go over to trouble you. There is one of the sisters, who is a sensible, gentile, young woman, being now these six or seven years here in town, but being lately out of service she went to the country to her sister, who is extreme poor, till I had

61

sent for them all. There are two Parish Priests in the County Kildare, one Father Heilan and Molloy, who are indeed the most learned and zealous priests in all that county, and withal the poorest without exception in all Leinster, even to the degree that none that I know of but men of their piety and virtue would remain or continue with such poor people as they take care of, who are not able to give them ordinary Raggs. One of them is Parish Priest of Killussy and the other bordering upon him, and both indeed extreme poor. I beg, dear Sir, if it may be done, you may please to remember them whenever you make your charity in this country next. This I take the liberty to remind your Honour of because you were pleased to remember the Parish Priest of Killussy in your charity you sent by Mr Molloy about four years ago. And I can with a good conscience assure your Honour that it cannot be better bestowed on any two clergymen in Ireland. The enclosed are the acquittances [receipts] for the £25-10-0, distributed as you ordered, and the other £4-10-0 shall be given for to pray for Captain Beling's soul. God in his mercy bless and preserve your Household and family and give you the reward of your charity among His own elect, which is the sincere and hearty prayer of etc.

C. Nary

It will be noted from the foregoing letter that Father Heilan was parish priest of Killussy (Killashee), Co. Kildare,[6] which adjoined Nary's native parish of Tipper. Sir Richard owned land in Killussy and the request for financial assistance for Fathers Heilan and Molloy was no doubt prompted by the fact that Sir Richard was landlord for the area.

There is a further, undated, letter from Sir Richard, which was apparently written in June 1709. He states that he has directed his agent, Mr Thornton, to pay Nary £50 and requests the latter to distribute this amount to the persons named in the letter. Sir Richard says that he has one request to make, i.e. 'that if you cannot conceal from whom you have this commission, you will not send me any acquittances [receipts] and it will be abundantly enough to tell me you have received the letter of such a date'. In a reply dated January 1710 Nary mentions that one of the old gentlewomen, Helen Butler, has died and he has given her share to 'one Richard Belings, heir, as he tells me, to Belingstown, and your Honour's relation, and to my proper knowledge a very honest virtuous gentleman, who has lived till of late by the industry of a very careful, stirring (?) wife, whom God was pleased to call unto Himself about a twelve month ago. So that the poor gentleman being bred to no Manner of a calling, is very helpless and worthy of your Honour's consideration . . .'.

In a letter dated September 1716, Nary acknowledges further assistance from Sir Richard's son, also named Richard, who, as already stated, assumed the name of Arundell. With regard to the Farrells Nary states that

> they are really very poor, but then they have so little industry that to give them any considerable sum at once, would only relieve them for a time, but when that were spent they would be as before, because they do not know how to improve anything otherwise than to lay it out for their present necessity. So that to continue your annual charity to them, which pays their rent and gets them from time to time some cloaths is as much as they are well able to manage right for want of industry. One of them hath a pretty boy and girl both fit to be bound prentices. If Your Honour would think fit to bestow a little money to that purpose, I believe it would be well placed. For by this means these two may come to have some more knowledge of the world and learn trades that may in time enable to assist their parents in their old age.

On 18 December 1716 Nary writes again to Richard Arundell, this time to offer his condolences on the recent death of his father, Sir Richard Bellings. Nary is profuse in his praise of Sir Richard:

> I have been in the country for a fit of sickness from Michaelmas [29 September] till the day before yesterday; else I should have written to your Honour to let you know how much a part I take in your loss of so good and so pious a father . . . His piety toward God and his extraordinary charity to the poor afford you a well-grounded hope that he has only changed his condition and is translated from a mortal state to an immortal bliss, where he shall from henceforth for all eternity receive with joy the glorious fruits of his piety and charity. Long life, riches and wealth are no doubt great blessings and proceed from the hands of God. This the holy man was sensible of and withal (which was more to his advantage) wisely considered that whatever portion of these God was pleased to bestow on him, he was only steward thereof and, therefore, took care to dispense the same faithfully as his Lord and Master had prescribed unto him. Hence I say we may justly conclude he is only translated, is happy and will be so for all eternity, which, that he may be (if not so already), I do assure your Honour I will not miss a day during my life to move the Father of Light in my poor prayers; as also to grant your Honour the grace to succeed him in his piety and good works as you do in his estate and fortune.

Nary went on, however, to avail of the opportunity to raise with the new landlord a very important matter with regard to the leasing of his lands:

> I wrote to him [Sir Richard] some years ago to let him know how cruelly the poor natives of this country were dealt with by their Protestant landlords, who very rarely suffer any of the little people to have as much as cabbins upon their land, but keep all under stock, so that there are few of the native little people but such as are on land held by Catholics, and therefore recommended to him very earnestly

that he would please to let his lands in this country to Catholics as they would fall out of lease.[7] This I find he has partly executed, which is no small example (?) of his piety and love for his country, and I understand that your Honour has happily finished the work in the power you have given to Counsellor Weldon, lately arrived here, of setting the rest.

Nary concluded his letter with a request that a friend of his be accommodated with a good farm on the estate:

Now, dear Sir, I should be ever obliged to you if you would please to recommend to Mr Weldon to let a friend of mine, Mr Richard Westbye of Newabbey,[8] have a good farm. He is, I assure your Honour, a very worthy gentleman, a pious Catholic and one who will faithfully answer the pious ends of your father of blessed memory, that is, relieve the poor natives and afford them conveniences of life. Mr Weldon is acquainted with him and knows he is well able to pay his rent. I might say a great many other good things of this gentleman that would recommend him to your Honour's esteem but shall at present forbear them.

In September 1718 Nary wrote to Richard Arundell reminding him of the need for continued charity to the poor. With regard to the Farrells he states: 'The three remaining Farrells (for your last charity has settled the other two, so that they shall no more be a burden to your Honour) have promised they would not be troubling you with their impertinent petitions, as they used to do, any more, upon my promising them that I would put your Honour in mind of them at proper season'. This is the final letter in the correspondence.

The correspondence between Sir Richard and Dr Oliver Doyle, parish priest of Castleknock and Mulhuddert, already mentioned, is of considerable interest but hardly of much relevance in a biography of Cornelius Nary. However, the last letter from Dr Doyle, dated 30 March 1708 and written while he was a prisoner in Kilmainham Jail, is of sufficient general interest to warrant quoting in full:

Upon a report that the Prince of Wales [i.e. the Pretender] is to land in Scotland, all the registered clergy of this Kingdom and all persons having commissions from King James, his father, are taken into custody and are committed into the several jails of this Kingdom without bail or mainprise. Amongst whom Father Walter Cruise and I are committed here, which is the common jail for this county, where we are to continue during Government's pleasure, which in all probability will be whilst the differences in Scotland continue. I writ to you, Sir, twice within these fifteen months earnestly requesting your charity for Mr Cruise and myself who are in great scarcity of some little subsistence by reason of the great poverty of the people, but was not so successful as to receive an answer to either of those letters, which made me once of the opinion not to trouble your Honour further, preferring ease from my importunity before our satisfaction and necessity. But this hardship and confinement of ours obliges us both to address ourselves once more to your Honour as to our landlord, patron and benefactor, who, I thank God, is able to extend your charity and relieve us poor prisoners, with what will do us the greatest of good, prevent us starving in jail and doing yourself no prejudice. May it therefore please your Honour to order something for our relief either by Alderman Lincoln, Doctor Nary, Mr Thornton or somebody who will not fail to give us what your Honour shall think fit. Assuring yourself you will herein extremely exert your charity, goodness and a work of mercy to your chaplain in confinement, whilst we shall forever pray for the prosperity and happiness of you and your family.

It might appear from this that, while priests generally were interned consequent on the Jacobite invasion scare of 1708, Nary remained free, since he is named by Father Doyle as one of those to whom Sir Richard might send money for passing on to Father Doyle. However, the likely explanation for this apparent immunity from arrest may be found in a report in the *Flying Post* for 24 March 1708, which stated that 'yesterday [22 March] our Lord Mayor put out a proclamation with the names of 31 Popish priests of this city, who have withdrawn themselves from their usual places of abode, requiring them to appear this day'. Presumably, then, Nary went into hiding, the same as the other priests in Dublin, and so escaped arrest. It would still have been possible to contact him through an accommodation address, perhaps Captain Usher's house in Church Street, mentioned in one of his letters to Sir Richard Bellings.

Notes

1. *Dictionary of national biography* (London, 1895).
2. William Ball Wright, *Ussher Memoirs* (Dublin, 1889), 32–3. (The Catholic branch used the spelling Usher, while the Protestant branch used Ussher.)
3. Official publication entitled *A list of the names of the popish parish priests* (Dublin, 1705), in King's Inns Library.
4. Patrick Kelly, ' "A light to the blind": The voice of the dispossessed elite in the generation after the defeat at Limerick', *Irish Historical Studies* 24, no. 96 (November 1985), 440–2.
5. See *Burke's Peerage* under appropriate headings.
6. Ainsworth Report no. 316, National Library of Ireland.

7. With regard to Nary's comments on the leasing of land by landlords, it is no harm to point out that diametrically opposite views were expressed by Protestant commentators. Archbishop King, in a letter dated 2 June 1717 to the archbishop of Canterbury, states: 'The landlords set up their farms to be disposed of by cant and the Papists, who live in a miserable and sordid manner, will always outbid a Protestant. . . By these means most of the farms of Ireland are got into their [Catholic] hands; and as leases expire, it is probable that the rest will go the same way'. (See MS 28, p. 327, Gilbert Library, Dublin.) Stephen Radcliffe, vicar of Naas, had in 1727 the following to say: 'However, I am, I hope, at liberty to give my opinion, as freely as you do, and it is this, that as far as I have observed, though Protestant landlords do, for the sake of advancing the price of their land, encourage too many Popish tenants; yet Popish landlords generally admit few, or none, but of their own sort'. (See Stephen Radcliffe, *A reply to the Revd. Edward Synge . . . wherein his sermon . . . is further considered* (Dublin, 1726), 195.

8. Probably New Abbey near Kilcullen, County Kildare.

Chapter 5

THE COMING OF THE NUNS

BETWEEN 1712 and 1729 three different orders of nuns—
the Poor Clares, the Dominicans and the Carmelites—were
established on the north side of Dublin, all, as it happened, in
the Catholic parish of St Paul, just outside the boundaries of St
Michan's. The nuns were concentrated in this part of the city
mainly, one feels, because it was a fast-developing Catholic
area. Another attraction was the availability of a large disused
convent in Channel Row (now Brunswick Street). This convent
had been built for the Benedictine nuns in the reign of King
James, but they were forced to flee the country following the
overthrow of that monarch.[1] While Cornelius Nary played a
major part in bringing the Poor Clare nuns to Dublin, the part he
played in bringing the other two orders to the city may have
been rather minor.

The Poor Clares
According to the Annals of the Poor Clares,[2] there was an
attempt very early in the eighteenth century to found a convent
of that order in Ship Street. This was right under the nose of
Dublin Castle and seems a most unlikely place to found a
convent, given the circumstances of the time. We are told that it
was suppressed and that the sisters fled to Athlone and established a convent there. Mrs Concannon, in her book *The Poor
Clares in Ireland* (Dublin, 1929), ignores this story altogether,
but she points out in her book *Irish nuns in penal days* that a
convent of Benedictine nuns was established in Ship Street by
the Duchess of Tyrconnell in King James's time, when, of
course, conditions were favourable for such an enterprise. Like
the Benedictine convent in Channel Row, these Ship Street nuns
were also forced to flee the country in the early 1690s.[3] This

seems a much more likely story than the version found in the Annals.

The Annals go on to tell us that Dr Nary, whose 'whole life was dedicated to the promotion of the glory of God', was extremely desirous of procuring a 'colony' of Poor Clares for Dublin, and to this effect he applied to the then archbishop, Edmond Byrne. In 1712 the provincial of the Franciscan Order in Ireland (of which the Poor Clares are a part), Revd John Burke, came to an agreement with Dr Byrne and the clergy of Dublin to have six members of the community in Galway sent to Dublin, and, as the Annals put it, 'consigned to the auspices of Dr Nary'. Notwithstanding certain apprehensions and objections from the Poor Clares about a transfer to Dublin, Nary continued to press for the opening of a convent there, and in a letter to the abbess he assured her that, 'if she gave her consent and influenced the Sisters to this effect, he would become their most steadfast patron, protector and friend'.

The Annals state that it was at the instigation of the duchess of Tyrconnell that Nary first sought to bring the Poor Clares to Dublin, and indeed a manuscript written in 1749 about the Catholic chapels in Dublin states that the Poor Clares settled themselves there 'by the encouragement and invitation of the Duchess of Tyrconnell'.[4] A more contemporary source, the report of the trial of Father Francis Moor in 1718, states that Father Moor had celebrated Mass very often 'for the nuns of the Duchess of Tyrconnell', which at the time in question could only mean the Poor Clares.[5] On the other hand, Mrs Concannon believes that it was the countess of Antrim who influenced Nary in that direction, and she cites a letter from the abbess to the countess in the archives of the order in Galway in support of this view.[6] It is possible, of course, that Nary was influenced by both these good ladies.

A word about Frances Jennings, duchess of Tyrconnell, will not be out of place here, since she figures a good deal not only in the saga of the Poor Clares but also in that of the Dominican nuns, of whom we treat later. Almost alone among the maids of honour of the court of Charles II, the beautiful, witty and vivacious Miss Jennings maintained a reputation for chastity. Her prank of going to the playhouse dressed 'as an orange wench' in February 1665 is narrated by Pepys. In 1681 she married Richard Talbot, who was to be created duke of Tyrconnell and appointed lord lieutenant by James II. It was a second marriage for both of them. The duke died of apoplexy at

Frances Jennings, duchess of Tyrconnell. (Courtesy of the National Library of Ireland.)

Limerick in 1691. Following the defeat of King James, the duchess lived for many years at King James's court at St Germains. However, since her sister, Sarah, was married to the duke of Marlborough, she was able, through the influence of that worthy, not only to be allowed to return to Ireland but to obtain a small portion of her husband's property. She finally returned to Ireland in 1708 and she died, aged 82, in 1731 in, some sources say, the Poor Clares' convent in North King Street.[7]

But to return to the coming of the Poor Clares to Dublin in 1712. It was judged imprudent, the Annals state, for the nuns to proceed to Dublin in a body lest they should attract the notice of ill-disposed persons. Consequently, only four nuns initially made the journey—the future reverend mother, Mary Augustine Lynch, one professed sister and two lay sisters. They arrived in Dublin on 7 June 1712 and were conducted to Dr Nary's lodgings in Bull Lane. The Annals tell us that he received them with every demonstration of joy and had lodgings taken for them in nearby Phrapper Lane, in the house of a widowed lady named Ambrose. They remained there for three weeks until the old convent in Channel Row had been fitted up for them. On their removal there, Archbishop Byrne appointed Dr Nary as their confessor and a Father Redmond as their chaplain. In doing so, however, he neglected to consult the reverend mother beforehand, and she saw fit to make objections to these arrangements on the grounds that she could not remove her community from the jurisdiction of the superior of the Franciscan Order. In order to resolve these difficulties, Archbishop Byrne put a case to Rome, which in due course produced a compromise solution under which the confessor and chaplain were to be appointed by the Franciscan Order but were to be approved by the archbishop. These difficulties with the archbishop were the cause of a good deal of opposition to the nuns from the Catholic laity of Dublin. The Annals tell us that while the case was pending in Rome the inhabitants of Dublin were not willing to countenance the nuns, lest it should appear that they opposed their archbishop, and no person could be expected to join them in community nor could they expect to get pensioners (i.e. paying guests).

These difficulties were scarcely resolved when the officers of the law pounced on the convent one morning 'precisely as Mass was ended'. Two sisters were arrested, but the reverend mother, since she was not wearing the habit of the order, escaped the attentions of the officers. The latter proceeded to search the house and seized papers and books, amongst which was the order given by Archbishop Byrne, at the solicitation of Dr Nary, for the transfer of members of the order to Dublin. When the officers proceeded to make fun of the ceremony book of the order, the reverend mother was so incensed that she informed them that 'it was shameful for them to come thus to torment virtuous, harmless women whilst they suffered the city to be over-run with vice and houses of ill-fame'. The books and papers, together with some of the habits, were packed in a box, which the officers took away with them. However, Mr Francis

Lynch, a Catholic merchant, agreed to go bail for the two sisters, thus securing their release.

Some time after this, a proclamation was issued by the government against Dr Byrne, Dr Nary and Father Burke, based on the incriminating papers found in the convent. It read as follows:

> Whereas upon information given to us the Lords Justices, that an unlawful society of Popish persons calling themselves nuns, was lately translated from the town of Galway to the city of Dublin, to be there settled and established by the pretended order of a person calling himself Brother John Burke of the Order of Saint Francis and Provincial of Ireland, testified under his hand and seal, we, the Lords Justices, gave immediate directions for the apprehension of the said pretended Nuns and the said John Burke, and divers of the said nuns have since been taken in the habits of their pretended order; but the said John Burke hath absconded himself and fled from justice: And whereas upon perusal of divers papers it appeared to this Board, that there are divers Popish regulars in several parts of this Kingdom, and that Doctor Byrne and Dr Nary of the city of Dublin, Popish priests, have pretended to exercise Ecclesiastical Jurisdiction contrary to the laws of this Kingdom, or have respectively aided and assisted in the exercise thereof, whereupon we the Lords Justices and Council gave directions for apprehending them in order to their being examined, and further proceeded against according to law; but the said persons have withdrawn themselves from their usual places of abode, that they cannot be apprehended. To the end therefore that the good laws made against Popish Archbishops and Bishops, and persons using and exercising and pretending to use and exercise Ecclesiastical Jurisdiction and Popish Regulars, may be put in due execution, and to prevent the above named persons from escaping the hands of justice, we the Lords Justices and Council do think fit by this our Proclamation, strictly to charge and command, and we do hereby strictly charge and command the Lord Mayor of the city of Dublin, and all Justices of the Peace, Mayors, Sovereigns and other Magistrates, Sheriffs, Bailiffs, High and Petty Constables, and all Her Majesty's Officers and Ministers of Justice, within the limits of their respective jurisdictions and powers, to use the utmost endeavours to take and apprehend the said John Burke, Dr Byrne and Dr Nary, and to commit them and every of them to safe custody, and to give speedy notice thereof to the Clerk of the Council, in order to their being prosecuted according to law.[8]

The Annals tell us that 'there followed great persecution and disturbance throughout the Kingdom'. The order's house in Galway was rifled and the nuns turned out of doors. However, after a short period the persecution subsided and the nuns were able to return to their house in Channel Row once more. But two of them, Mrs Kirwan and Mrs Daly, were obliged for a period to appear at the King's Bench and have bail entered for them every term.

Meanwhile, in anticipation of action by the authorities, Archbishop Byrne and Dr Nary had gone to ground in their native heaths, the archbishop to Borris in County Carlow and Nary to Yeomanstown, near Naas, to the house of Captain James Eustace. Acting apparently on a tip-off, an officer of the law duly came looking for Nary, and reported on 25 September 1712 as follows:

> This day I received from the Subsheriff of Kildare a proclamation for the taking and apprehending of John Burke, Dr Byrne and Dr Nary, and immediately I went to the house of Captain James Eustace of Yeomanstown in this neighbourhood, where Dr Nary had been for three or four months past, and made diligent search for the said Doctor but could not find him but was told the Doctor had gone this day to surrender himself to the Government, and that the search should have been made yesterday for the said Doctor.[9]

The Captain James Eustace in whose house Nary spent three months 'on the run' in the summer of 1712 was one of those Catholics who were licensed to carry arms in accordance with a list published in 1704.[10] Following the search for him in Captain Eustace's house, it seems likely that Nary lay low for a further period until the uproar caused by the proclamation had died down, and did not in fact stand trial. W. P. Burke, in his *Irish priests in penal times,* without stating his authority, tells us that 'if Dr Nary went to surrender himself, he changed his mind on the way, for he took excellent care to keep out of the hands of the authorities'.[11]

In 1717 Nary persuaded the Poor Clares to vacate the convent in Channel Row. The reason given in the Annals for this move was that they were liable to meet with disturbance from the authorities if they remained in the old Benedictine convent, since it was well known to be a convent in the past. However, since Dominican nuns moved in there almost immediately, it is difficult to accept this as the real reason. The most likely explanation for the move was that the old Benedictine convent, which was too large for the Poor Clares, was required by the Dominican nuns to set up a boarding school. In any event, the Poor Clares did not have to move very far, only to the other side of the street in fact, for, as Donnelly points out, their new abode was in Channel Row although the address was always given as King Street, since the main entrance was from that street.[12]

The Poor Clares were not fated to enjoy peace and tranquillity in their new convent for long, for on 14 June 1718, at four o'clock in the morning, the house was surrounded by officers of the lord mayor. But before they could gain admittance, the reverend mother gave orders that the sisters should change into lay apparel. She did not eventually open the door until the officers of the law were on the point of breaking it open. Since the officers were afraid of being attacked by the mob, they requisitioned three carriages into which they crammed the sisters along with themselves. 'Thus equipped', the Annals tell us, 'they were conducted to Judge Caulfield's where, to ascertain they wore no badge of religious profession, they were made to take off their garments and to undergo the most minute investigation as to their manner of life, observance etc.' However, the upshot of the case was that Judge Caulfield found that no act of parliament could be cited against them (since women were, through some oversight, not included in the penal laws), and that the establishment in King Street was 'only a house of lodgers'. He accordingly allowed the sisters to go free.

Henceforth they were left unmolested but, with a view to attracting as little attention as possible, they decided for the future to dress in lay apparel. And indeed, throughout the eighteenth century the general practice among sisters of all orders was to wear lay attire. I have not seen any evidence that the Poor Clares kept a school in King Street, but they derived some income from keeping lay boarders. In 1729 the reverend mother obtained benefactions to build a chapel, which, we are told, was 'a very good one' and had 'a handsome altar'.[13]

As to the subsequent history of the community, a split occurred in 1752 when the majority of the sisters set up a rival house in the Barley Fields (now Hardwick Street). They remained there until 1804 when they moved to their present convent in Harold's Cross. Although Donnelly states that the two factions were eventually 'fused again under the authority of the Archbishop',[14] that was not in fact what happened. Mrs Concannon tells us that the original King Street convent moved to Dun Laoghaire in 1826 but was dissolved in 1834 due to financial troubles. The sisters were then dispersed to different convents and only one arrived in Harold's Cross.[15]

Dominican convent, Channel Row

The Dominican nuns also originated in Galway, but in 1698 their convent there was suppressed and shortly afterwards they were obliged to quit that city altogether. About 1717 the provincial of the Dominican Order obtained the permission of Archbishop Byrne of Dublin to set up a convent in his diocese.

F

Eight Dominican nuns accordingly arrived in the city and were accommodated in temporary quarters in Fisher's Lane.[16] This lane ran parallel to Bull Lane where Dr Nary had his lodgings. Although there does not appear to be any documentary evidence connecting Cornelius Nary with the arrival of these nuns, they could hardly have been set up in his parish, even temporarily, without his cooperation and consent.

In September 1717 the Dominican nuns moved into the old Benedictine convent in Channel Row, vacated a short time before by the Poor Clares. Before long they were occupying two houses and had at their disposal a large chapel. As well as conducting a boarding school for the daughters of the Catholic gentry and the wealthy merchant and professional classes, the sisters also maintained a home for (mostly) elderly gentlewomen.

Towards the end of the eighteenth century the community moved to Counsellor Plunkett's former home in Clontarf. They made a further move to their present convent in Cabra early in the nineteenth century.

The accounts of their Channel Row convent are available from as early as 1719 and can be examined on microfilm in the National Library.[17] They make absorbing reading. Accounts in respect of the schoolgirls date from 1720, when there were twelve girls on a fee of £4 per quarter. By 1729 the number had risen to thirty. Interestingly enough, Anglo-Norman and English surnames predominate: Butler, Aylward, Grace, Blake, Martin, Plunkett, Cruise, Netterville, Nugent, Dillon, Dalton, Keating, Burke, Taaffe, Power, Holmes, Lyster, Malpas, Esmond, Bodkin, Wolfe, Barnwall, Wyse, Delamor. Some Irish surnames such as Reilly, Daly, Kelly and Egan also occur, but they are decidedly in the minority.

As the school expanded, the sisters found it necessary to employ some extern teachers. Thus we find that in 1727 Miss Molly Reilly's dancing master was paid 9s. 5d., and in 1734 Miss Dolly Egan's music master was paid 15s. There is also mention of a writing master and a tutoress from outside being employed. This boarding school closed in 1777.

The community took over a third, smaller house (known as the Speaker's House) on the opposite side of Channel Row in 1729 or 1730. It was probably intended as additional accommodation for their adult boarders. One such boarder, who went under the name of Mr Egan or Dr Egan, can be identified as Bishop McEgan of Clonmacnoise and later of Meath.

Throughout his entire period as bishop from 1725 to 1756, this house is believed to have been his main residence. As a member of the Dominican Order, he would have had a special claim on the sisters.

Advantage was taken of the community's apparent immunity from interference by the authorities to consecrate three bishops in the convent chapel—Colman O'Shaughnessy as bishop of Ossory in 1736, Laurence Richardson as bishop of Kilmore in 1737, and Peter Kilkelly as bishop of Galway in 1744. However, any ideas they may have had of being immune must have been rudely shattered in 1743, when, during one of those periodic activations of the popery laws, two Dominican priests were arrested at the convent.

As regards the convent's function as a home for gentle-women, or parlour-boarders as they were called, it is of interest that Lady Fingall had quite elaborate apartments there, consisting of a drawing-room, dining-room, parlour and bedchamber. Although her home in Arbour Hill was quite near, the duchess of Tyrconnell is on record as having stayed in the convent for a lengthy period.

The community's accounts contain details of various medicines, purges and potions supplied by the local apothecary, and there are also, here and there, a few eighteenth-century recipes. The inventory of the furniture and effects of the chapel is particularly revealing. Reading through these lists, which relate to the 1720s, it is difficult to credit that all this lavish-ness—everything from several sets of vestments down to eight spitting-boxes and four cushions for Lady Dillon's seat—could be the norm in Channel Row, at a time when the Mass rock was still the reality in parts of the country.[18]

At the more mundane level, we find that Mrs Dillon, the washerwoman, figures a good deal in the accounts. It is also of some interest that in 1738 the community sent a cow to Cabragh 'to be greased' (grazed ?) at a rent of 20*d*. per week.

Dr Nary also comes in for mention in the accounts. In 1727 there is the item: 'Received from Dr Nary for expenses for both Mrs O'Neill's offices £14-5-0'. Around the same time the community received a guinea from Dr Nary for Masses. How this obligation was fulfilled is shown by the further entry: 'Take notice the obligation enjoined by Dr Nary for ye guinea he gave for Masses is complied with by Mr Egan, Mr Scanlon and Mr Nowlan'. Nary is further on record as owing the convent £10 in 1729 but, as against this, he made the convent a donation of

£7. 6s. in February 1731. Finally, in October 1743 the payment of 3s. 3d. 'for Dr Nary's picture' is recorded.

The convent chapel in Channel Row was apparently used on occasion as a venue for musical performances, which some Protestants were known to attend. Stephen Radcliffe, vicar of Naas, in 1727, in reply to a letter believed to be the result of a collaboration between Nary and a Catholic lawyer, refers to 'a famous convent of the latter [nuns] in Channel Row, Dublin, where the most celebrated Italian musicians help to make the voices of the holy sisters more melodious, and many Protestant fine gentlemen have been invited to take their places in a convenient gallery, and hear the performance'.[19]

The Carmelite convent, Arran Quay

In March 1730 the provincial of the Discalced Carmelites wrote to the General Definitory for permission to re-establish a community of Carmelite nuns in Dublin. He stated that the archbishop of Dublin (Fagan) was favourably disposed to the proposal and that the Poor Clares, Dominican and Augustinian nuns had already been permitted to set up in Dublin. It was to be a very weak start, however, for in 1730 a professed nun of only nineteen years of age and a novice arrived in Dublin from the convent in Loughrea to launch the Dublin community. As in the case of the Dominican nuns, they were lodged initially in Fisher's Lane. This must have been quite a pleasant little street, for the houses were nearly all on one side, while on the other side the Bradoge river flowed towards the Liffey.

Again, the setting up of this little community could only have been accomplished with the cooperation of Cornelius Nary, who was vicar-general at this time, and his curates. Two more novices arrived in Fisher's Lane in 1731, and the fortunes of the community were to make a definite change for the better in 1732, when the first of the Bellew sisters, Agnes, was received as a novice. Her sister Lucy joined her shortly afterwards, and when their mother died in 1734 the two sisters inherited some houses which she owned on Arran Quay.[20]

The community moved c. 1734 to a house in Pudding Lane, off Arran Quay, and just behind the Bellew houses. Eventually they were to take over the four Bellew houses together with a further house in Pudding Lane. It is not clear when they acquired a chapel, but it was certainly before 1749, for a Protestant writer, already mentioned, has left a description of it in that year. Like the Dominican nuns, the Carmelites opened, probably in the 1750s, a school for girls, and they also kept some adult lady boarders. Towards the end of the eighteenth century they moved to Ranelagh Gardens and Hotel, where they remained until about 1975, when they made a further move to Seapark, Malahide.

As compared with the other orders of nuns, the Carmelites were rather slow to develop in the city. In 1750, when the Carmelites still numbered only five, the Dominicans numbered thirty, the Poor Clares 25 to 26 and the Augustinians ten to twelve.[21] The Augustinian nuns had their convent in Mullinahack on the south side of the Liffey.

Notes

1. Helena (Mrs Thomas) Concannon, *Irish nuns in the penal days* (London, 1931), 97.
2. The Annals are in the possession of the Poor Clares community in Harold's Cross, Dublin.
3. Mrs Thomas Concannon, *op. cit.*, 9.
4. Nicholas Donnelly (ed.), *State and condition of R.C. chapels in Dublin . . . 1749* (Egerton MS 1772) (Dublin, 1904), 19.
5. Nicholas Donnelly, *Short histories of Dublin parishes* (Dublin, various dates), part XI, 41.
6. Mrs Thomas Concannon, *The Poor Clares in Ireland* (Dublin, 1929), 81.
7. G. E. Cokayne, *The complete peerage,* vol. 7 (London, 1896), 446, however, states that she died at Paradise Row or Arbour Hill, Dublin, while Laurence Whyte, who wrote an elegy on her death, states that she died at her lodgings in Arran Quay—see Laurence Whyte, *Original poems on various subjects* (Dublin, 1740), 201.
8. Reproduced in *Conquest and colonisation* by M. E. Collins (Dublin, 1969), 183.
9. W. P. Burke, *Irish priests in penal times* (Waterford, 1914), 327.
10. List of Catholics permitted to carry arms published in *Archivium Hibernicum* 4 (1915), 59 ff.
11. W. P. Burke, *op. cit.,* 328.
12. Donnelly, *op. cit.,* in note 5, part XI, 52.
13. Donnelly, *op. cit.,* in note 4, 19.
14. *Ibid.,* 39.
15. Mrs Thomas Concannon, *op. cit.,* in note 6, 104–6.
16. Mrs Thomas Concannon, *op. cit.,* in note 1, 74–5.
17. National Library of Ireland, microfilm Pos. 3787.

18. Mass rocks have come down to us as symbols of active persecution. In fact, in the eighteenth century they were often the result of sheer poverty or of an unwillingness on the part of the local landlord to provide a site for a chapel or Mass-house.

19. Stephen Radcliffe, *A serious and humble enquiry* . . . (Dublin, 1727), 69.

20. For further information on these Carmelite nuns see John Kingston, 'The Carmelite nuns in Dublin', *Reportorium Novum* 3, no. 2 (1964), 339 ff.

21. Hugh Fenning, *The undoing of the friars of Ireland* (Louvain, 1972), 199.

Chapter 6

NARY'S NEW TESTAMENT
AND OTHER WORKS

IF, in a moment of retrospection, Cornelius Nary had in his later years looked back over his long life, he would probably have singled out his translation of the New Testament as his most important, albeit his most disappointing, single achievement. Donnelly tells us that the venture 'cost him ten years' hard labour'. Unlikely as it may appear, Nary is said to have done most of the necessary research work in Marsh's Library, in the shadow of St Patrick's Cathedral.[1]

On the face of it, a translation of the New Testament was a rather ambitious undertaking for one man, hampered it must be supposed, given the position of Catholics in the Ireland of the time, by a lack of proper reference books and documents and back-up services generally. Indeed, in his preface to his translation Nary acknowledges the size of the task, the great difficulties facing the translator, and his own insufficiency for so great an undertaking. 'However', he goes on,

> considering that many other private divines have gone before me and succeeded so well as to get the public applause, the approbation of universities and learned men, having attained to a competent knowledge of the oriental languages, and making these my chief study these many years past, I thought I might venture at least by way of essay upon this work, especially considering, on the one hand, the great need my countrymen have thereof, and on the other, that no fault or imperfection in any vulgar translation of the Scripture ought in reason to prejudice the faith or manners of men of sense; because the Latin Vulgate are the standard of our Faith and not any vulgar translation of the Scripture, which is but of private authority.[2]

He took, then, the Latin Vulgate version as the primary source from which to make his translation, because it had been declared authentic by the Council of Trent and had been corrected and amended by that council of the faults and imperfections which had crept into it in the process of time. It was, therefore, the authorised version as used in Gospels and Epistles in what was then a Latin Mass, and 'it was fit the people should understand the Scripture, as it is read in the Catholic Church and as they hear it in the public service and at their private devotions'.[3]

He gives his reasons why a new translation is necessary:

> We have no Catholic translation of the Scripture in the English tongue but the Doway Bible and the Rhemish Testament, which have been done now more than a hundred years since; the language whereof is so old, the words in many places obsolete, the orthography so bad and the translation so very literal that in a number of places it is unintelligible; and all over so grating to the ears of such as are accustomed to speak, in a manner, another tongue, that most people will not be at the pains of reading them. Besides, they are so bulky that they cannot be conveniently carried about for public devotion, and so scarce and dear that the generality of the people neither have, nor can procure them, for their private use.[4]

The Rhemish Testament was first published by the English College of Douai, then temporarily at Rheims in France, in 1582. It is strange that Nary should find the English of this version so foreign to his own time, when it is remembered that it was written only 130 or so years earlier. The fact that we today, 250 years after Nary's death, can find his English so readable, intelligible and, indeed, so modern is an indication that the seventeenth century must be seen as some kind of watershed in the English language, dividing the modern from the archaic.

To overcome the defects in the Rhemish Testament, Nary has endeavoured, he tells us,

> to make this New Testament speak the English tongue now used, as near as the many Hebraisms wherewith it abounds, and which (in my opinion) ought never to be altered, where they can be rendered so as to be intelligible, would allow. I have taken all the care imaginable to keep as close to the Letter as the English will permit, and where the Latin phrase would prove unintelligible in the English, and that a word or two or more must be added to make the sense clear, I took this precaution: If the word or words to be added are evidently implied, though not expressed in the Latin according to the grammatical construction, which every good translator ought always to have before his eyes, I put the same in the text in Italic characters. . . There are certain words in the Scripture, which use and custom have in a manner consecrated, as Sabbath, Rabbi, baptize, scandalize, synagogue, etc. These I have everywhere retained, though

they are neither Latin nor English, but Hebrew and Greek; because they are as well understood, even by men of the meanest capacity, as if they had been English.[5]

He is of the opinion that it is impossible to translate from the Latin Vulgate without a knowledge of the Greek, because in interpreting a Latin word or phrase which may have several meanings it is desirable to be able to fall back on the original Greek version as a sort of sounding-board for determining the exact shade of meaning intended. With regard to Greek, he maintains that it is not enough for the translator 'to understand the Greek of profane authors, but that one must withal be thoroughly acquainted with the Helenist, or the Greek of the Synagogue'. And since the mother tongue of the writers of the original Greek versions of the Gospels and Epistles was Hebrew, they naturally wrote in a Greek in which 'the turn and genius' of Hebrew phrases and particles were reflected. Hence, Nary maintains, in addition to a knowledge of Greek, a knowledge of Hebrew is also necessary for the would-be translator.[6] He goes on to give examples of errors in the various French translations of the New Testament (with which he would, of course, have been familiar from his lengthy residence in France), and even in the Rhemish Testament, which would have been avoided if the translator had consulted the original Greek version and had not depended entirely on the Latin Vulgate.

Nary, later in his preface, goes on to state that his design in bringing out his translation is

> to make this work of as little bulk as possibly I can, so that it may be easily carried about in the pocket for public or private devotion. . . In a word, my chief aim is to encourage my countrymen to read and meditate upon the Will and Testament of their Heavenly Lord and Master by giving it to them in a style and dress less obscure and somewhat more engaging than it has been these many years past. And that it may be the more useful to them, I have annexed a table to the end of the work by looking into which, they shall find in what Chapter and Verse of the Scripture, the beginning and end of every Gospel and Epistle that is read in the Mass every Sunday and great Holyday, all the year over, are to be found, that they may read the same to themselves while the priest reads them at Mass.[7]

So that the reader may get a flavour of Nary's translation, here is his version of the well-known Chapter 13 of St Paul's First Epistle to the Corinthians:

> 1. Though I should speak with the tongues of men and of angels, yet if I have not charity, I am become as sounding brass or a tinkling cymbal.

2. And though I should have the gift of prophecy and should know all mysteries and sciences; though I should have all faith so as to remove mountains, yet if I have not charity, I am nothing.

3. Although I should distribute all my substance to feed the poor, and though I should give up my body to be burned, yet if I have not charity, it profiteth me nothing.

4. Charity is patient, is kind: Charity envieth not, it doeth nothing amiss, is not puffed up.

5. Is not ambitious, it seeketh not its own, it is not easily provoked, it thinketh no evil.

6. It rejoiceth not in iniquity, but it rejoiceth with the truth.

7. It beareth all things, believeth all things, hopeth all things, endureth all things.

8. Charity never faileth, whether prophecies shall fade, whether tongues shall cease, whether knowledge shall be destroyed.

9. For we know only in part and we prophesy only in part.

10. But when that which is perfect is come, that which is in part shall cease.

11. When I was a child, I spoke as a child, I judged as a child, I thought as a child: But when I became a man I put away childish things.

12. Now we see obscurely as through a glass: But then face to face. Now I know in part, but then shall I know even as I am known.

13. Now these three things remain, faith, hope and charity: But the greatest of the three is charity.

Long before his translation was sent to the printers, Nary had had encouraging reactions from Fathers Francis Walsh, Dublin, John Farely, doctor of theology of Paris University and provisor of the Irish College in Paris, and Michael Fogarty, doctor of theology of Paris University. In a letter to Nary dated 19 November 1715, Father Francis Walsh, on behalf of the archbishop of Dublin, wrote: 'It was with a great deal of satisfaction that I read your manuscript version of the New Testament from the Latin Vulgate. You have now by your indefatiguable labour furnished us with what we so long wished for, and so much wanted. Your happy genius has furnished you with the means of reconciling a literal translation with the purity of the English tongue. And your Annotations . . . show manifestly the profoundness of your erudition and the brightness of your wit'.[8]

Such encomiums could not have prepared Nary for the quite hostile reception with which his translation was to meet in certain quarters in Dublin, in Rome and elsewhere. The climate in the Vatican was not conducive to dissent even in the mildest and least intended form. The spectres of Jansenism and

Gallicanism still haunted the Church. The Propositions of Pasquier Quesnel, set out in his *Nouveau Testament avec des réflexions morales* (1695), were all the more dangerous because they encompassed the more acceptable aspects of Jansenism. Quesnel's organising ability had turned Jansenism into a force to be reckoned with, operating through a secret network in the great cities of Europe. The Propositions had been condemned by Pope Clement XI in the bull *Unigenitus* in 1713, but Clement, being of an easy-going nature, was not the type of man to force a showdown with those churchmen (including such powerful fellow-travellers as Noailles, the cardinal archbishop of Paris) who were not prepared to accept *Unigenitus*. Clement, however, died in 1721, and his successors, Innocent XIII (1721–4) and Benedict XIII (1724–30), were forceful men who met the Jansenists with firmness and insisted on submission to *Unigenitus*.[9]

In such a climate it is understandable that the Vatican was in no mood to entertain any tinkering with such a basic document of the Christian religion as the New Testament, even where changes were made, as in Nary's case, with nothing but the best intentions. The establishment in Rome was only too ready to give ear to complaints of unorthodoxy, and there were detractors in Ireland, notably in the ranks of the regular clergy, who were all too eager to have a swipe at Nary and who took an unholy delight in being able to discover something in his translation to complain about.

The sequence of events can best be gathered from the intervention which five members of the Irish hierarchy made to Rome on Nary's behalf in August 1722.[10] The five concerned were Archbishop Byrne of Dublin, Archbishop Butler of Cashel and the bishops of Clonfert, Ossory and Elphin. They pointed out that shortly after the publication of Nary's translation in 1718, some false brother (*'falsus frater'*) made a complaint about it to Rome with such damning effect that the archbishop of Dublin was ordered in 1720 by Santini (internuncio in Brussels) to suppress the translation. This the archbishop immediately did, Dr Nary humbly submitting, notwithstanding all the time and expense the translation had cost him. (This withdrawal of the translation did not, however, mean that Rome was going to forget about it. It still apparently continued under examination by the relevant body; the complaints made about its orthodoxy were found to be proved and it was finally condemned by the Church in 1722.)

The intervention by five members of the hierarchy on Nary's behalf probably saved his translation from the ultimate disgrace of being included in the Index Librorum Prohibitorum. With regard to the justification for a new translation of the New Testament into English, the bishops (in the intervention mentioned), in addition to mentioning the increasing incomprehensibility and unavailability of the Rhemish translation, dwelt at some length on the position in the case of mixed marriages. They maintained that the Catholic partner invariably found him/herself at a disadvantage *vis-à-vis* the Protestant partner because of the latter's much greater familiarity with the Old and New Testaments, the end result quite often being the conversion of the Catholic partner to the Protestant faith. A similar situation arose, the bishops maintained, where Catholics in other circumstances had necessarily to mix on intimate terms with Protestants. An obvious example of this latter would be where Catholic servants were employed in Protestant households. A new Catholic translation was apparently seen as essential to counteract such proselytising influences.

The bishops went on to point out that when Nary's translation was first published in 1718, they and other doctors of sacred theology, English as well as Irish, found it to be in agreement with the Latin Vulgate version. They had delayed making representations on behalf of Dr Nary until the suppression of Quesnel's translation (which both the bishops and Dr Nary 'detested from their hearts') had been effected and the controversy surrounding it had waned. Now that the Quesnellian madness had abated, they beseeched his holiness not to deny any longer to Irish Catholics the favour of being permitted to read this (Nary's) new English version of the New Testament. They claimed it adhered to the tenets of the Council of Trent; if it was otherwise, they would not wish it to be read by anyone.

It was, of course, too much to expect that Rome should make a *volte-face* and grant the bishops' request. Certainly, the reaction of the internuncio (Spinelli) in Brussels could only be described as negative. He recorded in his diary for 19 January 1723 that the Irish bishops had written asking him to allow the publication of an English version of the Bible which had been done by an Irish doctor; that in accordance with the doctrines of propaganda he had replied that he could not approve of the version in question, but that he would be only too willing to accept notes explaining such words in the old version as are no longer in use, these notes to be examined by four religious and forwarded to Rome.

Despite the intervention of the hierarchy on his behalf, Nary's detractors in Ireland continued to lodge complaints about his translation with Rome. We find the father provincial of the Irish Dominicans complaining to the internuncio in Brussels in June 1723.[11] He pointed out that 300 copies of Nary's New Testament had been printed, and that he considered that it should not be let into circulation until some changes had been made. The father provincial pointed out also that Cardinal Allen's (i.e. the Rhemish) translation 'was very easily understood', meaning presumably that there was no need for Nary's.

In 1724 the Irish regular clergy forwarded to Rome lists of books, and quotations from them, which they considered to be Jansenist or Gallican in tone. Among the books complained of were Nary's New Testament, his *Chief points in controversy between Roman Catholics and Protestants,* and his *New history of the world.*[12]

There is evidence too that some of Nary's secular colleagues in the Dublin metropolitan chapter were far from enamoured of his translation. It will be seen in Chapter 9 that the reason given for Nary's omission from the Terno in 1724 (from which the pope would choose a new archbishop) was that his New Testament had incurred the censure of the Vatican authorities.

But the most comprehensive denunciation of Nary's New Testament was yet to come. There is extant a pamphlet[13] published at Douai in 1727 under initials in the form of a monogram, which might be variously deciphered as 'R.N.' or 'R.V.' or 'R.W.' It is evident, however, that the initials were intended to be 'R.W.' and that the author was Robert Witham, president of the English College at Douai, for the same monogram appears on Witham's translation of the New Testament, published in 1730. Witham's pamphlet examines Nary's translation with quite devastating effect.

While there can be no doubt of Witham's qualifications to analyse and criticise Nary's translation, he may not have been without some vested interest in damning it, for at the end of the pamphlet there is an advertisement giving advance notice of Witham's own translation of the New Testament.

Witham prefaces his criticism of Nary's work with some remarks on the need for a new translation and some rules to be observed by any would-be translator. He states that 'a new

THE
NEW TESTAMENT

OF OUR

Lord *and* Saviour
Jesus Christ,

Newly Tranflated out of the Latin Vulgat.

AND

With the Original *Greek*, and divers Tran-
flations in vulgar Languages diligently
compared and revifed.

TOGETHER

With Annotations upon the moft remarkable Paffages
in the Gofpels, and Marginal Notes upon other
difficult Texts of the fame, and upon the reft of
the Books of the New Teftament, for the better
underftanding of the literal Senfe.

By C. N.   C. F. P. D.

[Dublin]

Printed in the Year. 1718.

The title page of Nary's translation of the New Testament, published in 1718. (Courtesy
of the National Library of Ireland.)

translation of the Holy Scriptures from the approved Vulgar Latin . . . has been long and impatiently wished for'. He is in agreement with Nary that the Rhemish translation 'in many places has become scarcely intelligible, so many obsolete words frequently occurring both in the text and in the annotations'. He goes on:

> I must at the same time in this regard do justice to the memory of my predecessors, that in this their version from the Latin, they took great care always to compare it with the original text, I mean the Latin of the New Testament with the original Greek editions, which the late translator [i.e. Nary] has neglected to a strange degree, and by this neglect has fallen into an incredible number of unpardonable mistakes.[14]

Witham then sets out a number of rules which he considers should be observed by a translator. Firstly, whoever undertakes a translation from the Latin Vulgate 'must not give himself the liberty to follow sometimes the Latin, and at other times the Greek, but must always prefer the Latin'. He says that Nary has transgressed against this rule in that he has gone from the Latin text in a great number of places, 'and this, as I conjecture, by so frequently copying the Protestant translation made from the Greek'.

Secondly, the true sense and even the construction of the Latin must be enquired into by examining the Greek, and by comparing them together. He maintains that, while Nary promised to do this in his preface, 'he has been so far from making good this promise that his false translations of this kind, which are very numerous, are visible and altogether inexcusable'.

Thirdly, when the literal sense itself is ambiguous in the text, and when such a sentence is differently understood and expounded by the interpreters of the first and best rank, it is then the business of the translator to make his version as comformable as he can to the text he has undertaken to translate, without using or inserting words which may determine to one exposition more than to another. And if the translator adds any note to explain the text in the margins, he should take care not to make that pass for certain which is only doubtful. He states that he will 'have divers occasions for examining whether Mr Nary has not also transgressed against this rule'.

A fourth rule 'is applicable to such cases only, when the sense being doubtful, the translator, to be understood, cannot avoid using words, which must needs lead the reader to such a particular sense, in which all interpreters do not agree. It is then his duty after a due and careful examin, to make his version agreeable to the expositions of the interpreters of the greatest weight and authority'.

Fifthly, 'an exact translator must avoid as much as possible the addition of any, even the least word, but what is in his text: And when there is an indispensable necessity of adding any word for construction sake, or to represent the very literal sense, such a word must be always printed in a different character' (i.e. in italics). He says that Nary has offended against this rule also.[15]

Witham concludes his prefatory remarks with the following:

> I must needs say I never yet saw any New Testament come from the Press with so many faults, with all of which I do not pretend to charge the translator himself, for whom I have had a great value and esteem ever since I read his little book of controversy against Dr T...n [Tillotson] . . . I am willing to believe that Mr Nary's employments have not allowed him sufficient time to examine thoroughly all the difficulties in the New Testament, all the commentaries of the Ancient Fathers upon it, the interpreters of best note and the writings of the later critics, both Catholic and Protestant; nor even to compare exactly the Greek and Latin texts in such a laborious manner as is necessary for such a performance. This ought to have been done. I rather suppose he employed and trusted others, who have been guilty of such oversights as can never be excused.[16]

Witham then goes on to find fault with Nary's translation on seventy specific counts, of which the following are examples of the kinds of faults involved.

1. *False translations against both the Latin and the Greek texts, relating to matters of faith*

Witham says he first of all turned to some places where Catholic writers have found fault with the common Protestant translation 'from its first publishing, even to this very time'.[17] In four cases, which Witham says cannot be excused, he accuses Nary of sticking word for word to the Protestant translation, even though in one case he admits that there is nothing wrong with the Protestant version. Since the faults mentioned under this heading are, according to Witham, major ones 'which cannot be excused', I have extracted the relevant passages as an appendix to this chapter, so that the reader may see for himself what exactly were the points in Nary's translation to which Witham took such grave exception. Witham's criticism would, I feel, be dismissed today by the vast majority of theologians as so much nit-picking, and one wonders what Witham would make of, say, Ronald Knox's rather free, latter-day translation of the New Testament, which comes to us with the imprimatur of the archbishop of Westminster.

2. *False translations of the Latin text by not comparing it with the Greek*

Witham instances 22 of these cases. He concludes: 'These are faults one would almost blush to take notice of, only that in a version of the Holy Text, no faults are to be looked upon as little. I shall still have occasion to mention some mistakes of this kind: And from these 'tis evident no one should pretend to a translation of the New Testament without both understanding and comparing the Latin with the Greek'.[18]

3. *Other false translations, if the late version be compared with the Latin Vulgate, which the author undertook to translate*

Witham points to seventeen such cases. In seven of these he says that Nary followed the original Protestant translation, even though this had been corrected by a later Protestant divine, Dr Wells. Speaking generally of these faults Witham says: 'Of these [faults] there is the greatest number, and by their number we may without rashness conclude, this happened by the translator's negligence, whilst he followed the Protestant translators, as they, according to their design, followed the Greek. . . I have wondered to find Mr Nary so condescending to the Protestant translators, as to follow them even in words that now sound but oddly'.[19]

Witham's complaints that Nary erred in some instances by not comparing the Latin of the Vulgate with the original Greek version of the New Testament seem to imply that Nary had an inadequate knowledge of Greek. In this connection it is interesting that in his controversy with Clayton (see Chapter 3) Mr Davis, Clayton's friend, also questioned Nary's knowledge of the Greek versions of the Scriptures. It seems probable then that Nary's knowledge of Greek was less than adequate to the job in hand, although criticism of Nary's Greek comes oddly from Witham whose own knowledge of that language was, on his own admission, not perfect. In the preface to his translation of the New Testament Witham states: 'I am far from being so perfect in the Greek as I could wish, and of Hebrew I know nothing'.[20]

Witham's pamphlet comes to us complete with approbations from some of his colleagues in Douai—Richard Challoner, Bernard Clifton, Anthony Codrington and Pacificus Baker. Challoner was then professor of theology at the English College; he was later to be the great pioneering bishop of the English Mission. Bernard Clifton included in his approbation the gratuitous comment that Nary's New Testament contained some errors manifestly smacking of and fostering the Calvinist, Jansenist and Quesnellian heresies.[21]

Robert Witham was president of the English College in Douai from 1715 until his death in 1738. The Douai College was the principal source of priests for the English Mission throughout the eighteenth century. Witham's translation of the New Testament, published in two volumes under the title *Annotations on the New Testament of Jesus Christ,* was drawn on by Richard Challoner in his 1749 translation. In the very extensive annotations—they account for about twice as many pages as the actual text of the New Testament—Witham makes some half-dozen references to Nary's translation (see vol. 1, p. 113, and vol. 2, pp 92, 245, 252, 335 and 348), all of them disparaging.

Another contemporary commentator on Nary's New Testament was John Lewis, who published his *English translations of the Bible* in London in 1739. Although he devotes nine pages of his book to Nary's translation, his comments amount to little more than a précis of Nary's preface. He adds very few comments of his own. He did not appear to know who Nary was, but from the approbations of the doctors which follow Nary's preface he judged that Nary was an Irishman. His only criticism of any account was his objection to Nary's maintaining that the Latin Vulgate was the only authoritative version of the New Testament, and that an English translation could not be authoritative.[22]

In view of all the disparaging criticism, it is hardly surprising that Nary's translation did not achieve its aim of making the New Testament more readily available to the man in the street, more particularly as other English translations were shortly to come on the market. Chief among these was Richard Challoner's translation (1749), which was to serve as a guide and benchmark for future translators. Nary's translation was never reprinted.[23]

Modern scholars, however, have been a good deal kinder to Nary than his contemporaries. The *New Catholic Encyclopaedia*

(1967) concedes that 'his [Nary's] Preface is remarkable for evolving, perhaps for the first time, a reasoned theory of Biblical translation into English—literal, but in current idiom'.[24]

In an article in the *Irish Ecclesiastical Record* (1939) Father Hugh Pope O.P. states that 'the principles of translation which he [Nary] laid down cannot be disregarded by anyone aiming at a correct rendering from the Latin today. . . This retired and comparatively unknown scholar has anticipated the work of Deissman, who seemed to have revolutionised New Testament criticism when he insisted on the necessity of studying the Koine, or common Epistolatory Greek of the New Testament, if one would rightly appreciate the Greek of the Evangelists'.[25] Father Pope later claims that Nary's English has a real sense of rhythm. As to whether Nary intended his translation to be used in public worship, Father Pope states that, although Nary's design was that his translation could be carried about in the pocket for public and private devotion, he doubted if by 'public devotion' Nary meant official use in church.[26]

A new history of the world

A new history of the world is undoubtedly Nary's *magnum opus*. It is a book of 496 folio pages (equivalent to about 1,000 pages of a normal-sized book). Published in Dublin in 1720, it was printed by Edward Waters for Luke Dowling, a Catholic bookseller in High Street, and it is a fine example of eighteenth-century Dublin printing. It is limited in scope since it deals only with the period from the Creation to the time of Christ.

Nary tells us in the preface that his design in publishing this work was 'chiefly to obviate the objections of the Atheists, Deists, Pre-Adamites and Libertins of this age, who ground the whole system of their non-religion (if I may be allowed this term) or rather impiety, upon the vast difference that is between the present Hebrew Text and profane historians in the computation of time'. These 'cunning sophistors' argued that, according to the Hebrew Bible, the period from the Deluge to the Babylonian Captivity was 1,707 years, while according to the 'profane historians' the same period, as measured from the reign of Belus to that of Nebuchadnezzar, was 1,728 years; this would mean that Belus reigned 21 years before the Deluge—a manifest impossibility.[27]

Nary goes on:

> Our modern historians, being sensible of the force of these arguments, and finding no tolerable solution for them, do, as

Alexander did to the Gordian Knot, cut them in sunder, by denying the matter of fact and treating them as fabulous; which is indeed (in my opinion) to subvert all antiquity, and deny what the Holy Fathers and the ancient Ecclesiastical Historians have asserted and maintained from the beginning of Christianity to the last two centuries.[28]

When he speaks of the 'present Hebrew Text' Nary means the version of the Bible prepared by the Jews in the first century A.D., which, he maintains, the Jews 'altered to suit their own ends'. Now, the version of the Bible known to the early Christian Church and the one which would have been familiar to Christ himself was what is known as the Septuagint, a Greek version of the Old Testament said to have been made about 270 B.C. by seventy translators (hence the name 'Septuagint'.)

On the basis of the Septuagint computation of time, Nary maintains that the events recorded in the Old Testament from the Deluge to the time of Christ can be almost exactly correlated chronologically with known historical events and the lives and reigns of known historical characters (such as the kings of Babylon and Assyria, the kings of the Medes and Persians, Alexander the Great, Julius and Augustus Caesar) in the same period. Nary states that he has

annexed to the end of the work a chronological table of the whole from which it appears that the sacred and profane chronology differ only in eleven months; which surely is a convincing argument that the Septuagint computation is the same with that which the Holy Pen-Man Moses left upon record in the Hebrew Text, whence the Septuagint translation was taken, and which continued in its purity in the days of Our Saviour.

He complains that 'they have robbed the World of at least 1500 years by their adherence to the present Hebrew Text, or rather computation of the Jews, who have industriously and on set purpose, abridged the age of the World . . . to serve their own wicked ends'.[29]

With regard to the style and content of his work, Nary states:

As to the embellishments of history, namely, the descriptions of Kingdoms and countries, their situation and bounds, the laws, customs and manners of their peoples, a polite, elegant style, rhetorical flights, choice epithets, true characters and the like; I am sensible enough how much they are wanting through the whole piece. The first [embellishment], indeed, I have industriously omitted, partly because I feared the piece would swell to too great a bulk; and partly, I did not judge such description so necessary in this our age, in which Geography and Topography are brought to that perfection, and charts and maps are in so great plenty, that a man may better learn the limits, extent and situation of any country by looking upon it in a map than by reading it in a book. As to the other embellishment [i.e. the laws, customs and manners of the people] I can only say that, as I have not omitted to touch upon some of them, where I judged it necessary for the reader's information, so I confess I passed by a great many more to avoid prolixity. I was ever content to couch thoughts in the plainest and easiest of terms I could think of, without affecting either lofty or magnificent words or phrases; which in my opinion are proper rather to declamation than to history, whose chief business is to relate matters of fact and that in an easy, even, intelligent style.[30]

So much for the preface. The work proper is divided into nine books, which in turn are broken down into chapters. A recital of the titles of the different books will give the reader some idea of the actual content of the work as a whole:

Book 1: From the Creation to the Deluge
,, 2: The Departure of the Children of Israel from Egypt to the Building of Solomon's Temple
,, 3: Building of Solomon's Temple to its Destruction
,, 4: The Babylonian Captivity to the Birth of Christ
,, 5: Astiages and Cyrus, Kings of Persia
,, 6: The Greeks—origin, rise and progress
,, 7: Alexander the Great
,, 8: The Romans, up to the time of Julius Caesar
,, 9: Chapter 1—the Kings of Asia and Egypt
Chapters 2 and 3—Roman affairs under Caesar

The first four books take us to page 261, and thus it can be said that the work as a whole is divided almost equally between what is known as Bible history and 'profane' history. The title—*A new history of the world*—is a misnomer, since the work does not deal at all with the great civilisations of China and India, nor with the great religions of Buddhism and Confucianism, both of which date from about 500 B.C.

Despite Nary's claim to couch his thoughts 'in the plainest and easiest of terms', his style in practice often borders on the turgid—long, rambling sentences being a feature of the work. However, he disarms criticism when he modestly confesses:

I am very sensible how unequal my capacity is to so great and so difficult an undertaking; and how far short I am of the Judgement and Learning of these great men, which yet have not given the learned world the satisfaction that was expected: However, I hope I may be allowed the privilege of a Dwarf upon Giant's shoulders. I have had the opportunity of perusing the works of most of our modern historians, and of observing their perfections and defects: And if my discoveries be suitable to the advantage of my situation, I aim at no more.[31]

93

He further pleads for his inadequacies at the end of the preface:

> To conclude, as there never was, nor never will be a piece of human invention truly perfect in all points; so I flatter myself the candid reader will make the proper allowances for the mistakes and oversights, proceeding from human infirmity, which may occur in this; since he cannot be ignorant that he himself is surrounded with a like infirmity.[32]

The following description of the death of Julius Caesar will give the reader some idea of the style of the work:[33]

> The fatal day being come, Caesar was no sooner seated upon his throne in the Senate House, when the boldest of the conspirators earnestly entreated him to recall from banishment the brother of Metellus Cimber, one of the conspirators; and upon Caesar's refusal, this Metellus took hold of his robes, and Casca, another of them, wounded him in the back; whereupon Caesar turned about, seized upon Casca's sword, and cried out: 'Traitor, what art thou doing?'. And began to defend himself; but having received many wounds, and seeing Brutus coming with a naked sword to pierce his breast, he looked upon him and said: 'Et tu, Brute!'. Then he drew his robe over his face, fell down on his knees and abandoned himself to the rage of his murderers, who gave him three and twenty wounds; and even designed to drag his body through the streets and to cast it into the Tiber; but being apprehensive, Marc Antony and Lepidus, the General of the Horse, who it seems were the only two friends Caesar had among the Senators on that accursed day, and who by the artifices of Brutus came too late, would be avenged on them, they fled to the Capitol and secured themselves, leaving Caesar's corpse in the Senate House, which was carried by his servants to his Palace, and in two days after interred with great pomp in the Campus Martius.
>
> Thus ended his days the great Julius Caesar, the terror and wonder of the World; the next in every degree to Alexander, if in anything inferior to him: For he had scarce any of Alexander's bad qualities, and possessed all his good ones: As fortunate and bold as Alexander; as great, nay, a greater conqueror than Alexander; as patient of labour and toil as Alexander; as vigilant in danger and as prodigal of his life as Alexander. But as to Alexander's immoderate passion, which put him often upon destroying his best friends, his unmeasurable ambition, his drunkenness, his rage and fury upon the least contradiction, and his insatiable revenge, Caesar was a perfect stranger to all these vices. In a word, were it not that Caesar seemed to want upon some desperate occasions that presence of mind, which Alexander was always master of, and which is an ingredient of no small value in the character of a General, I should not be afraid to pronounce Caesar the greater man of the two.

Other works

Harris, in his mid-eighteenth-century updating of Ware's *The writers of Ireland*, listed the following additional works by

Nary.[34] (While it is not possible to be certain as to the completeness or accuracy of this list, it has to be allowed that Harris was sufficiently contemporaneous with Nary to be *au fait* with his works, or to acquire information from people who had known Nary and were acquainted with his writings.)

1. *Prayers and meditations* (Dublin, 1705; duodecimo).
2. *Rules and godly instructions composed for the spiritual advancement of a devout widow, who hath vowed chastity, and recommended to virgins who have consecrated themselves to God's service* (Dublin, 1716; sextogesimo). (This was probably written for the communities of nuns that were established in Dublin in Nary's neighbourhood. The size sextogesimo denotes that it was a very tiny book indeed.)
3. *A brief history of Saint Patrick's Purgatory and its pilgrimages,* written in favour of those who are curious to know particulars of that famous place and pilgrimage so much celebrated in antiquity (Dublin, 1718).
4. *A catechism for the use of his parish* (Dublin, 1718; duodecimo).
5. An argument showing the differences in Sacred Writ, as well in the Old as in the New Testament (MS).

He is said to have translated the following:

6. *The bishop of Angers' pastoral letter to the clergy of his diocese together with the answers made to him by Mons. Dublineau, and the letters which he wrote to him on the subject of the Constitution Unigenitus*; as also the bishop's mandate (Dublin, 1721; octavo).
7. Cardinal Noailles' *Mandate on the subject of a miracle wrought at the Procession of Corpus Christi, Anno 1725* (Dublin, 1726; octavo).
8. Mons. Rapin's *Polemical tracts* (Dublin, 1732).

Of the foregoing works I have been able to trace only *The bishop of Angers' pastoral letter* and Cardinal Noailles' *Mandate on the subject of a miracle.*

The bishop of Angers' pastoral letter, a pamphlet of 48 pages, is available in the Royal Irish Academy[35] but it does not contain Mons. Dublineau's correspondence with the bishop. Dublineau was a doctor of divinity of the Sorbonne. The pamphlet is stated to have been 'faithfully translated into English from the French original', but the name of the translator is not given.

The pamphlet begins with a letter from Bishop Michael of Angers to his clergy, stating that he has received a letter inviting him to join with those who have appealed to a future General Council of the Church against *Unigenitus*. (*Unigenitus* was Pope Clement XI's bull, issued in 1713, condemning Jansenism.) The bishop feels obliged to make public the reply he has given, because it may contribute to make his clergy more steady in faith and 'divert them from the snares that are laid, in order to make them forget what they owe to the Church, to the Holy Father the Pope, and to the Ordinances of their Bishops'.[36]

There then follows the bishop's answer to Mons. Dublineau, who had written to him claiming that there had been 'a general insurrection of the Faithful against *Unigenitus*'. The bishop refutes this claim and states that of about 120 bishops in France, 100 supported *Unigenitus,* and that only in Paris was there any great opposition to the bull. He goes on to question Dublineau: 'Has the insurrection [in Paris] been general even in your own Faculty, Sir? Have not many Doctors of the House of Sorbonne . . . formally protested against your last deliberations?'[37] It is clear that the bishop of Angers comes down very much in favour of *Unigenitus.*

The translation of Cardinal Noailles' *Mandate on the subject of a miracle* is available in the Early Printed Books section of Trinity College Library. A pamphlet of 38 pages, it is stated to have been 'faithfully translated into English from the original French', and to have been printed in the year 1726. The name of the translator is not stated. A note on the title-page states that 'this is the miracle mentioned in our [presumably Dublin] News Papers of last June'. The pamphlet relates how a Paris lady, Dame De La Fosse, wife of a cabinet-maker, was cured of an issue of blood at a procession of the Blessed Sacrament in the parish of St Margaret, Paris, on the Feast of Corpus Christi, 31 May 1725. Noailles, having examined the report of a team of physicians on the cure, pronounced it to be 'extraordinary, supernatural and miraculous'.[38]

As regards Nary's translation of Mons. Rapin's *Polemical tracts,* I have failed to discover anything, published in Dublin, answering to this description. René Rapin (1621–87) was a Jesuit theologian and literary critic. Like the other members of his order, Rapin was active in repelling Jansenism in France. He wrote a history of Jansenism which, though strongly biased, is held to be a valuable record of the movement. His polemical and theological works include *L'esprit du christianisme, La perfection du christianisme* and *La foi des dernier siècles,* and it was no doubt some of these works which Nary is believed to have translated into English.[39]

The bishop of Angers' pastoral letter and Rapin's *Polemical tracts* were decidedly anti-Jansenist, and, if Nary was indeed the translator of these works, this would be a positive indication that he had no sympathy with Jansenism, although he was accused of Jansenist leanings in some of his writings. Indeed, Nary's translations of these works may have been a conscious effort on his part to rid himself of the Jansenist label which his detractors so sedulously endeavoured to burden him with.

Appendix

Extract from Robert Witham's pamphlet on Nary's New Testament

False translations against both the Latin and the Greek text, relating to matters of Faith

As soon as this Translation came to my hands, having first with a pen corrected all the Errata, I turned to some places, where our Catholic writers have found fault with in the common Protestant Translation from its first publishing, even to this very time.

Matt. c.19 v.11 Latin: 'Non omnes capiunt Verbum istud'. The Greek agrees exactly with the Latin [Greek version] which is truly translated 'All men take not, or receive not this word'. The Protestant Translation: 'All men cannot receive this saying'. I was much surprised to see the very same, as fully expressed by Mr N——: 'Everyone cannot receive this saying'. This gentleman [Nary] surely cannot be ignorant of what has been writ both against the Protestant and against the Mons translation on this subject; nor what connection such expressions have with the errors and heresies condemned by the Catholic Church.

I. Corinthians, c.7 v.9: 'Quod si non se continent, nubant'. The Greek is in like manner [Greek version].

The true Translation from both texts—'But if they do not contain themselves'. The Protestant: 'But if they cannot etc'. Mr N—— hath exactly the same words with the Protestant.

Gal. c.5 v.17: 'Caro . . . concuspiscit adversus Spiritum . . . ut non quaecumque vultis, illa faciatis'. The Greek agrees exactly [Greek version]. The Protestant against both texts: 'The flesh lusteth against the Spirit . . . so that you cannot do the things that you would'. Mr N—— has again copied word for word the Protestant in this place, which is even worse than either of the former. The true Translation: 'So that you do not whatsoever you would'.

Mr N—— is here much more to be blamed, after that the learned Protestant, Dr Wells, had been so just ten years before, an. 1709, in his new edition, as here to correct the Protestant, and to put: 'So that you do not, whatsoever you would'.

Romans c.9 v.19: 'Voluntati, eius quis resistit?' There's nothing here amiss in the Protestant: 'for who hath resisteth his will?'. 'Tis very strange Mr N—— should translate again: 'for who can resist his will?'. 'Tis true 'tis only an objection in Saint Paul, but what need of clapping in 'can' contrary to both the Latin and Greek? Mr N—— might remember the words of St Stephen, Acts 7.5, to the obstinate Jews 'You always resist the Holy Ghost'. He might have remembered the 2nd Proposition of Jansenius, condemned by the Church as heretical, and other Propositions condemned in Quesnelle.

Notes

1. Nicholas Donnelly, *Short histories of Dublin parishes* (Dublin, issued in parts, various dates), part XI, 51–2.
2. C. N. [Cornelius Nary], *The New Testament of Our Lord and Saviour Jesus Christ* (1719), 2. (Place of publication not given.)
3. *Ibid.*, 1.
4. *Ibid.*, 2. It will be recalled in this connection that one of the arguments put forward by Nary against the use of the vernacular in the Mass (see Chapter 2) was that vernacular languages change' markedly with the passage of time, requiring regular updating.
5. *Ibid.*, 2–3.
6. *Ibid.*, 3–4.
7. *Ibid.*, 9.
8. Hugh Pope, 'A Dublin priest translates the Latin New Testament into English', *Irish Ecclesiastical Record* 54 (July–Dec. 1939), 236.
9. *New Catholic Encyclopaedia* (Washington D.C., 1967), vol. 12, 21.
10. National Library of Ireland, microfilm Pos. 5370, p. 142 (in Latin).
11. Cathaldus Giblin, 'Catalogue of material of Irish interest in the collection Nunziatura di Fiandra, Vatican archives', *Collectanea Hibernica,* no. 15 (1972), 31.
12. *Ibid.,* 32.

13. R. W. [Robert Witham], *The English translation of the New Testament by C. N. examined and compared with the Latin Vulgate and the Greek* (Douai, 1727).

14. *Ibid.*, 3.

15. *Ibid.*, 4–5.

16. *Ibid.*, 5.

17. *Ibid.*, 6–7.

18. *Ibid.*, 10.

19. *Ibid.*, 11.

20. Quoted in Henry Cotton, *Rhemes and Doway* (Oxford, 1854), 305.

21. R. W., *op. cit.* in note 13, 24.

22. John Lewis, *English translations of the Bible* (London, 1739), 365.

23. As to the place of printing of Nary's New Testament, it does not appear to have been Dublin for the Corrector of Press (initials J. S.) apologised for the numerous printers' errors and wholly exculpated 'the learned translator [Nary] who was at a great distance when the same was printed'. Henry Cotton in *Rhemes and Doway* (p. 38) tells us that some rare copies have a title-page endorsed 'London printed for J. Moore in Cornhill 1718', but this is by no means conclusive evidence that it was printed in London, since a London attribution such as this was sometimes made where it was desired to sell a section of a print-run of a book in London through the agency of a particular bookseller or publisher.

24. *New Catholic Encyclopaedia* (Washington D.C., 1967), vol. 2, 465.

25. Hugh Pope, *op. cit.*, 238.

26. Hugh Pope, 'Should we continue to use Challoner's version in church?', *Irish Ecclesiastical Record* 59 (Jan.–June 1942), 122.

27. Cornelius Nary, *A new history of the world* (Dublin, 1720), 1. Deists believed in the existence of a personal God, based solely on the testimony of reason, and rejected any supernatural revelation. Pre-Adamites believed that there were men on earth before Adam. Libertins was another name for Quakers.

28. *Ibid.*, 2.

29. *Ibid.*, 3.

30. *Ibid.*, 4.

31. *Ibid.*, 6.

32. *Ibid.*, 4.

33. *Ibid.*, 482–3.

34. Walter Harris, *The writers of Ireland* (Dublin, 1746), book 2, 299.

35. Anon., *The bishop of Angers' pastoral letter to the clergy of his diocese* (Dublin, 1721). Royal Irish Academy Haliday tract, box 167, no. 2.

36. *Ibid.*, 6.

37. *Ibid.*, 8.

38. Anon., *Cardinal Noailles' mandate on the subject of a miracle* (Dublin, 1726), 38.

39. *New Catholic Encyclopaedia* (Washington D.C., 1967), vol. 12, 84.

Chapter 7

THE TROUBLE WITH THE REGULARS

BAD relations between the regular and secular clergy had already become entrenched in the seventeenth century. In 1678, in their report to the pope on the state of the Catholic religion in various countries, the Sacred Congregation of Propaganda had this to say with regard to Ireland:

> They [bishops] are frequently crossed and disturbed by the monks, especially the Franciscans, who have many convents there, but do not live according to their Institution, but continually make an ill use of their privileges, celebrating more Masses than is necessary, granting dispensations [for marriages] to the Second Degree, taking money for the Sacraments, and administering them at Easter against the will of the Parish Priests, or making them [secular clergy] stay at the altar until they have done begging and wholly exempting themselves from the jurisdiction of the Ordinaries'.[1]

John Brenan, then bishop of Waterford, in his report to Rome in 1675 complained that the regulars 'intruded on the pastoral functions of Baptism, Matrimony and Extreme Unction in the districts which had their own Parish Priests'. He further complained that the regulars, and especially the Franciscans,

> induce several of the Faithful to take the habit of the Order when they are stricken with severe sickness. Such persons, after death, are laid out on a table, dressed in a habit and uncovered, with lighted torches around them in the houses of the laity. . . The Bishops have repeatedly applied to Rome for a decision in this matter, but up to the present there has been no reply'.[2]

The animosity between the two groups became increasingly virulent as the eighteenth century advanced. Although the regulars had been banished from the country under the Banishment Act of 1698, several went into hiding, and of those who left many returned later. They increased in numbers until by 1742 it was estimated that they were about equal in numbers with the seculars at around 700 members. Some 90% of the regulars belonged to the four main orders of friars—the Franciscans, the Dominicans, the Augustinians and the Calced Carmelites. Other orders, such as the Discalced Carmelites, the Capuchins and the Jesuits, totalled only about 75 members at that time.

The primary cause then of dissension between the regulars and the seculars was that, with a total of around 1,400 clergy, there were far too many competing for support from the laity, the majority of whom were very poor. The seculars had lost all their church property and tithes at the time of the Reformation and were forced to adopt the methods of the regulars, i.e. to collect money at church doors and to go about the country looking for donations in money or kind, a practice known among the regulars as 'questing'.

Secondly, there was a difference in theological outlook between the two groups, which had its origin in the fact that the seculars tended to be trained in French colleges (Paris, Nantes, Lille, Bordeaux, Rouen, Charleville, Douai, Toulouse), while very few regulars were trained in France but had their colleges chiefly in Rome, Lisbon, Spain and Belgium. There was a consequent juxtaposition of a secular clergy that had been exposed to, and influenced to a greater or lesser degree by, anti-papal French principles, and a regular clergy conditioned by their training to an ultramontane outlook of extreme loyalty to the pope. Indeed, the seculars were known to refer to them derisively as 'the Pope's Dragoons'. The regulars were accordingly much more likely to push the pope's arrogated powers to depose monarchs and to dispense subjects from their oaths of allegiance, powers which many seculars, such as Cornelius Nary, openly opposed.

Thirdly, the regulars' loyalty to the pope, as well as to the Pretender (who by papal indult had it in his gift to nominate bishops to Irish sees), was rewarded with an unduly high proportion of episcopal appointments, a development that was greatly resented by the seculars. The result was an Irish hierarchy composed of regular and secular appointees, and *ipso facto* a divided hierarchy.

Lastly, the regulars were inclined to insist on exemption from episcopal authority. Their convents were often makeshift affairs, a few thatched houses perhaps, and the idea of their

101

living a normal community life was difficult of achievement. Numbers of them roamed aimlessly around the country and were very difficult to bring under any kind of discipline, although after 1750 the bishops had been given the whip hand by Rome and could no longer complain that they were powerless in the face of the regulars.[3]

Such were the general causes of friction between the secular and regular clergy in the first half of the eighteenth century. Turning now to the particular situation in the archdiocese of Dublin, we find that, if anything, the animosity between the two groups was more bitter there than anywhere else in the country, and that there were some factors in the situation which were peculiar to Dublin. In 1728 the Irish regular clergy drew up a formal list of grievances which they forwarded to the nuncio in Brussels. A commission, consisting of Archbishop Murphy of Dublin and Stephen McEgan, a Dominican, then bishop of Clonmacnoise, was appointed by the nuncio to enquire into and report to him on the grievances. The Leinster regulars had complained that 'by the wiles of certain innovators new and pernicious doctrines are creeping into Ireland, by which the Catholic Faith is much shaken, and the minds of the Faithful perplexed with doubt, especially as regards the infallible authority of the Supreme Pontiff'.

In proof of the foregoing grievances, the regulars adduced a number of pamphlets and pastoral letters that had recently been published. One of the publications complained about was an anonymous pamphlet entitled *Letter to the Reverend Stephen Radcliffe, Vicar of Naas,* five passages from which were quoted verbatim. It was stated that this letter had been published 'with the approbation of a Catholic Parish Priest'. As will be seen in Chapter 10, this letter was evidently a collaboration between Cornelius Nary and a Catholic lawyer.

In the Dublin archdiocese the regulars complained that their right to support by the alms of the faithful was being invaded by the parish priests, who, in addition to their parochial rights and stipends, likewise quested for alms, both by collections at church doors and by house-to-house collections several times yearly. Further, three new parish churches had been erected, in each of which there were no fewer than six priests, and there was no necessity for this since the regulars also had public churches in those areas. The regulars requested that this abuse should be reported to the proper ecclesiastical authorities as a very serious grievance, on the grounds that the citizens of

Dublin were so burdened by the continual collections of the pastors that they were unable to contribute sufficient for the support of the regulars. They complained that this abuse had been introduced in late years and was contrary to the ancient practice which obtained in the city.

The regulars further complained that certain Dublin parish priests publicly preached to their parishioners that they were bound 'under sin' to hear the parochial Mass [i.e. the Mass in a parish church as distinct from a Mass in a church belonging to a religious order] on Sundays and holydays, at least once a month, and that confessions made to regulars were invalid.

There was a reply by the seculars to these complaints and a rejoinder by the regulars. The seculars replied that the three new parish churches in Dublin were necessary because of the increase in the Catholic population in the previous thirty years. The regulars denied the statement of the seculars that if all the churches in the city were open from 6 a.m. to 1 p.m. they could hardly accommodate all the worshippers; in fact, the churches of the regulars were almost empty until 10 a.m., at which hour the sermon was preached. In particular, the Carmelites thought it was useless to open their church before 8 a.m.

With regard to collections at church doors, the regulars outlined as follows the origin of this practice. In the case of the seculars, collections were not held at church doors prior to the Banishment Act, 1698. On the passing of that act some regulars remained in this country and were allowed by the seculars to say Mass in their churches and to make a collection at the church door, a deduction from the amount collected being made in respect of expenses. When, however, a degree of toleration returned and the regulars were able to open their own churches again, the seculars continued the practice of collecting at church doors, although, considering its origin, they should have discontinued it.

Another complaint of the seculars was that the regulars made their 'quest' throughout the whole city and suburbs. The regulars replied that they did this only once a year and that the money so collected went to meet the chapel rent; their only means of subsistence (i.e. food, clothing, etc.) was the money collected at church doors. The seculars pointed out that the regulars did themselves harm by complaining that the support they received from the people was barely sufficient for their needs, for this only embittered the people. To this the regulars retorted that, in order to cause mischief, the seculars had leaked the regulars' original complaint on this matter to the laity.[4]

Cornelius Nary had been the target of complaints by the regulars from early in the century. A letter in the Vatican Archives, dated 22 May 1707, from a Dublin person 'worthy of credence', paints a very revealing picture of the situation in Dublin and Nary's part in it.[5] According to this writer the state of the regular clergy in Dublin at that time was pitiable. The secular clergy, who enjoyed some tolerance from the government, spoke ill of them, with the exception of Dr Russell, and these anti-regulars would not tolerate a member of a religious order in the city if they could help it. They (seculars) maintained that the regulars were coming back into the country as '*vagabundi*', in order to avoid giving obedience to their superiors in the friaries overseas and to seek in Ireland a life free from restrictions. In confirmation of this, the writer referred to 'a certain Dr Nary', who had preached publicly in this vein to the scandal of the Catholics. It was well known that since the Reformation in Ireland missionaries of all kinds, who had no churches or chapels, were in the habit of celebrating Mass in the private houses of Catholics and of giving instruction there secretly. Since the decree for the banishment of the regulars was promulgated in 1698, the missionaries of the mendicant orders followed this custom without scruple and with profit, as 'they were strictly forbidden by Parliament to frequent churches or indeed to live in Ireland'. In fact, the writer goes on, they could not stay in hiding, instruct the people, or receive any means of sustenance except by living in private houses and by exercising their ecclesiastical functions in such places. The seculars, however, maintained that if a regular priest did more than was permitted him by the law, he should not reside in Ireland and should leave the country. Accordingly, the seculars had stated in private and in public that it is not lawful to celebrate Mass in private houses.

Our writer goes on to point out that Dr Nary, who had written a book in English which had been the occasion of much controversy, and who was striving with all his might to obtain possession of a parish which had been granted to another priest 'by the Pope', had stated publicly from the pulpit that it was less blameworthy to omit one's religious duties than to attend them in a private house. This doctrine had not been voiced before and had as its sole purpose the extinction of the regular clergy in Ireland.

The question had to be asked, the writer went on, whether such statements were in accordance with charity. The writer had not written these things without due consideration; they were definite facts and had been heard by many. In writing them he was not moved by spite or hatred nor by 'the Expulsion Order of 1697'; it upset him that their enemies had made it impossible for the regular clergy 'to tend the vineyard of the Lord', which they (seculars) neglected, or to which they could not attend properly because of paucity of numbers. However, tribulations and troubles would come and patience was the only remedy in the face of them. Finally, the writer wished it to be noted that Dr Nary himself had no objection to saying his Mass in private houses, especially if he were sure he would receive a generous donation for doing so.

Nary's book, mentioned above as giving rise to controversy, was no doubt his *Chief points in controversy between Roman Catholics and Protestants*. We can only speculate as to which parish Nary was alleged to be trying to get possession of. It may well have been St Nicholas Without, which fell vacant about this time following the appointment of its parish priest as archbishop, and which was acknowledged to be the best parish, as regards income, in the diocese.[6]

A measure of Nary's antipathy to the regulars is his outburst in his pamphlet *The case of the Roman Catholics of Ireland*, published in 1724, which is dealt with at some length in Chapter 8. It will be seen that in this pamphlet he made a distinction between the registered priests and unregistered ones (mainly regulars), which must have raised the hackles of the regulars. Granted, the great influx into the country of mostly regular clergy had queered the pitch for the secular priests and given the authorities an excuse for proposing further penal legislation against all kinds of priests. It is, nevertheless, difficult to excuse Nary's remarks, and not to look upon them as other than partisan and selfish. It may have been as a result of these remarks by Nary that some regular clergy forwarded to Rome about this time a list of books, including some by Nary, which they considered to be Jansenist or Gallican in tone.[7]

But despite the bad feeling between himself and the regulars, Nary had no problem about cooperating with the Franciscan Order to bring the Poor Clare nuns to Dublin in 1712. The establishment at a later date of Dominican and Carmelite convents must also have been done with his coopera- tion (see Chapter 6). Nary no doubt saw the establishment of

105

these convents as providing for definite needs—education of the daughters of the Catholic upper and middle classes in the case of the Dominican and Carmelite nuns, and charitable works among the poor in the case of the Poor Clares.

As was seen in Chapter 3, the Jesuits were active in St Michan's parish throughout Nary's period as parish priest. They appear, however, to have been involved to a large extent in education, and Nary would probably have seen such a non-pastoral role as a proper and useful one for regular clergy. There is the further point that if, as seems probable, Nary was prepared for the priesthood at a Jesuit school, this would be an added reason for his viewing that order with special favour.

Nary's particular difficulties with Father Francis Lehy, a member of the Calced Carmelite Order (White Friars), should also be noted here. Lehy first came to prominence around 1726 as the founder of the Carmelite Chapel in Ash Street, off the Coombe. Lehy and his supporters liked to portray his brush with the ecclesiastical authorities in Dublin as just another manifestation of the harsh treatment meted out to the regulars by the secular clergy, but it seems likely that this was not the whole story and that Lehy was guilty of misdemeanours, the precise nature of which has not come down to us.

A sermon supposed to have been given by S. J., 'a Popish priest', and printed in 1728[8] sets out Lehy's side of the story. Launching straight away into an attack on the seculars, the sermon begins: 'This is, Dear Christians, to let you plainly understand the case of Mr Francis Lahey, and several other Romish clergymen in Ireland, who are cruelly prosecuted by their Brethren (I mean the Popish clergy) without the least show of justice or reason; but out of pure malice, envy, jealousy and especially interest'. S. J. goes on to accuse the 'Romish Clergy' of condemning Lehy without giving him a chance to defend himself, as required under canon law. We gather further on in the sermon that the Catholic authorities in Dublin had sometime in 1727 proclaimed in their chapels 'that no one should hear another priest's Mass but their own'; in other words, that they should attend Mass only in their parish churches and that they should not attend Mass in the chapels of the regulars. The seculars, S. J. affirms, compared such a Mass by a regular priest to 'a dog barking'.

S. J. claims that the archbishop (at this time Murphy)

> had been very careful in his visitation of his diocese to forbid his diocesan gentlemen not to entertain or give any aid or assistance,

106

directly or indirectly, to any poor clergyman [i.e. a regular] without his positive order. . . I am surprised to hear his Lordship so careful of their purses about extending their charity, and neglect at the same time their idle and unnecessary expenses in Gaming and Drinking, a Thirteen Pence [i.e. an English shilling] or a Sixpence would not be missed given for God's sake, even to a Turk or Jew, when many pounds are spent in Gaming and Drinking. . . I am sure his Lordship would not like to be served so himself. No, no, he will have the best of meat and drink.

S. J. has some interesting remarks to make about Lloyd's translation of the Montpellier Catechism:

As to Mr Lloyd's translation of Montpellier's Catechism, this city and Kingdom are sensible how they recommended it to be read by all Christians, as both excellent, pious and edifying; and soon after forbid it again as pestiferous and heretical. A fine proof of their infallibility. I expect they may have the same turn to cry-up Mr Lehy, as they cried him down.

The chapel which Lehy had opened in Ash Street is referred to throughout the sermon as 'the new chapel'. S. J. accuses the head curate (presumably of St Nicholas Without, Francis Street) of 'thundering out of house and home' anyone who frequented the new chapel, and goes on:

If his penitents confess they have been guilty of enormous crimes, as Swearing, Cursing, Sabbath-breaking, Murder, Theft, Adultery, Whoredom, Lies and the like Transeat [*sic*]; but if they went to the New Chapel, 'tis the greatest crime, the Absolution is to be denied and severe Penances inflicted upon them, poor souls, though innocent, for going to the House of God.

S. J. claims that there were very few Good Shepherds to be found among the Roman clergy of Ireland. He says that he could name many large parishes in country districts where the parish priests

are so covetous that for fear of lessening their purse, they will not employ a curate even if they could get him for £5 a year; as to their flocks' fine instruction, they never take pains to teach 'em their Catechism, nor give one half-penny to any schoolmaster to do that duty . . . so that scarce one in twenty know that there is a God at all, and a great many, even old men and women, cannot repeat the Lord's Prayer or the Creed, so that, as to their belief, they know not what it is; they think it a great matter if they see a priest vested at the altar, but to what purpose? They are as wise coming home as going to it, they do not know their Christ nor their Shepherd, nor their Shepherd does not know them, (he only says his Mass.) As for explaining the Gospel and putting them in mind of their duty to God and their neighbour, there is no such thing; yet if they have a good Bit, or a good firkin of ale, he [parish priest] will be sure to have a good share; he is every day feasting abroad, seldom at home, in the meantime the people die in this large district without the rites of the Church, for they live like beasts and for the most part so they die.

S. J. concedes that the cities are 'more regular' and that 'they teach them their Catechism after a manner'. He goes on:

> I know not any Parish Priest in Dublin, except one or two, that take pains to exhort their congregation, in expounding of the Gospel every Sunday and Holy Day in all the chapels established in Dublin. There are about eighty priests, among all of which there are not but six that preach, the rest for the most part thinking that function to be too troublesome or not worth their while. They respect and honour the Holy Scripture so much that I believe not one in twenty has read it through in all his life-time; 'tis out of date with them . . . although I don't at all deny there are famous, learned men among them, but I am sorry to see they endeavour by Malice, Envy and Jealousy to destroy a great many souls by their Cursing, Damning and Calumniating, rather than after the example of Our Lord and Saviour, Jesus Christ.

S. J. complains that the secular clergy will not allow poor priests (the regulars)

> one half-penny or one morsel of bread; trade they have not, Work they cannot,—must they rob and steal to be hanged? We do not care, says our infallible Romish Clergy of Ireland,—let 'em quit the Kingdom! But I assure and can prove a great many of themselves deserve better a hundred times to be banished, for many faults in their pastoral Government, negligence in the care of souls, and bad life and bad examples. . . If the Kings of Spain, France, the Pope and others who give a deal of money towards the Mission in these countries, knew the bad uses made of it, they would doubtless be more careful, when they would consider that our present Holy Missioners in Ireland, as they pretend—instead of preaching and expounding the Gospel to the people Sundays and Holy Days, instead of instructing them in the principles of the Christian Religion, instead of visiting each family in their several districts, to see and know their life and behaviour, that both old and young may know their duty to God and Man, to shine to their flock by their good life and example, to be, as Our Saviour says, 'the Light of the World'—they strive to excel who shall be greatest with Ladies and Gentlemen, drink bravely full bumpers, gather most money, calumniate and curse their Brethren.

It might appear from the foregoing that Lehy was unfairly treated. It is significant, however, that he appears to have got little support from his colleagues in the regular clergy. The formal complaint made by the regulars to the nuncio in Brussels (already noted above) does not mention Lehy's case, although it instances several similar cases of harsh treatment of regulars in Dublin and elsewhere. One Dublin newspaper reported that he had been suspended by his own superior[9] and this would point to misdemeanours on Lehy's part which his colleagues were unwilling to excuse or condone.

Lehy's troubles attracted a great deal of publicity in the Dublin newspapers of the time. We find the *Dublin Intelligence* of 11 March 1729 reporting:

> Most of the Papists of this city seem at present under great concern at the proceedings which were carried on, on Sunday last, against their new favourite, Father Lehy . . . who was openly declared in all the Romish chapels, especially that great one in Saint Francis Street of which Father Austin is the head, to be a vile and disorderly person, incapable and unqualified by some of his misdemeanours of the function he professes himself a worthy practitioner in, and that all those poor deluded people, who had already confessed or received Absolution or bore part in holy ceremonial conjunctions, Penance etc. with him, must forthwith on the first opportunity, apply themselves to some other priest of the Catholic Faith for Absolution etc. On the other side we hear Father Lehey is not behindhand with them in his accusation for their unwarrantable dealings against him, who has as much authority for keeping, attending and curing his flock as any of them have, and so will maintain it . . . in some memorials he is like to make against them.

Lehy was denounced with special vehemence in Francis Street chapel no doubt because his chapel in Ash Street came within the parish of St Nicholas Without. Nary's part in the affair becomes clear when the *Dublin Intelligence* of 29 March 1729 expresses the hope that 'the laws should be invoked against them [Catholic clergy] for daring to assume jurisdiction in these Kingdoms from any authority derived from a foreign power, as Dr Nary seems to have done, in his putting those people to their oaths, at the trial held of the test of Mr Lehy's good or bad actions since he came to these Kingdoms'.

It appears that, in his dealings with Lehy, Nary was acting in his capacity as a vicar-general. The diocese was without an archbishop at this time, Archbishop Murphy having died the previous December, and the vacancy remained unfilled until near the end of 1729. It will be seen from Chapter 9 that, because of dissension in the diocesan chapter, apparently no vicar capitular was appointed to administer the affairs of the diocese *pro tem.,* but that instead two vicars-general, Cornelius Nary and Joseph Walsh, were appointed.

That Lehy was prepared to stoop to some decidedly low strategems is apparent from what turned out to be a quite spurious 'vindication' of him by Nary, published in the *Weekly Post* of 8 March 1729. The piece is headed: *Dr Nary's Vindication in the behalf of Father Francis L—y by reason of*

*his many good sermons, having an authority from the Pope, for
his so doing.*

The 'Vindication' reads:

> Having rightly considered the many scandalous reports that have
> been spread abroad upon one of our Fathers, I thought it the part of a
> Christian to clear him, as far as lies in my power; having examined
> his Prerogative and Authority for so doing, I find that the many
> irregular proceedings that have been transacted against him, are
> entirely false and scandalous, he being a gentleman of extraordinary
> parts, being one of the greatest orators and excellent preachers of our
> Function in the Kingdom, being both admired and beloved by all
> who have heard him, and I think it a duty incumbent on me to let the
> World know how far he is wronged. This I can certify that he has a
> power from the Pope, and has read his Orders to the King of France
> and several other Powers; he has been grossly abused by several
> persons, and particularly last Sunday he was excommunicated, both
> he and all those that would go to hear him preach or pray; notwith-
> standing all this, he preached the same afternoon and read a long
> Memorial, which he sent by three gentlemen, some of which were
> men of above £4,000 per An. He continued above an hour reading of
> his Memorial, which was so full of feeling and tender expressions to
> clear his innocence, that the whole congregation wept bitterly. I wish
> the peace of the Church and of its members with all my soul, which
> God of His infinite mercy grant us all, Amen.

The printer of the *Weekly Post,* Nicholas Hussey, in the
issue of 15 March felt it necessary to publish a disclaimer of the
foregoing, when he stated that 'there is nothing of truth or
sincerity in that scandalous paper, being only sent to me by an
unknown hand, believing it to be true, but now am convinced of
the falsehood thereof, and desire the Public may not give any
credit to any papers that shall appear in print from the said
Father F———s L—y'.

Matters had gone from bad to worse for Lehy when the
Dublin Intelligence mentioned the case again in its issue of 22
July 1729:

> We hear that the Romish clergy have made a declaration against
> Father Lehy, and that on Sunday last he was read out of all their
> chapels, for high crimes and misdemeanours against the reverend
> body of their divines. On the above account we are informed from a
> public paper, that Mr Lehy went to Dr Nary's chapel, as divine
> service was began, and then bred a great disturbance; loudly
> demanding what Mr Nary had to allege against him; but received
> from that gentleman no satisfactory answer.

Some weeks following this confrontation, however, Lehy
was reported to have made 'an ample recantation in several
chapels'.[10]

When we next get a glimpse of Francis Lehy, he is conducting a series of non-denominational conferences at the house of one James Tomson, a turner in Indian Alley, in St Catherine's parish. In reporting the matter to the lords' committees, the local Church of Ireland rector stated that the conferences

> first began about the month of September 1730 and continued till the March following; and further that to gain admittance. . . all comers were obliged to pay two pence for the said Lahy's use and also to pay two pence more for ale for ye benefit of Tomson's alehouse and I do further certify that I am well assured that said Lahy was under severe censure from his own side and was interdicted in ye several parish mass-houses in the city and suburbs some years since, and so continues.[11]

He was not, of course, the only priest in the city conducting such conferences. It will be seen from Chapter 12 that Cornelius Nary held several such interdenominational conferences in his parish around the same time.

The last mention I have seen of Lehy is in the Fottrell papers. These were documents discovered by the authorities on Father John Fottrell, provincial of the Dominicans, when he was arrested on 6 June 1739. A list of 'demi-Protestant converts from the Roman Church', found on Fottrell, refers to Lehy as 'the famous impostor' and 'a notorious reprobate Carmelite'.[12] It might appear from this that Lehy eventually conformed to the Established Church. His name does not, however, appear in the Convert Rolls, a list of people who conformed in the eighteenth and early nineteenth centuries by legal process.

Notes

1. National Library of Ireland, microfilm Pos. 3142.
2. Quoted in Emmanuel Curtis, *Blessed Oliver Plunket* (Dublin, 1963), 212.
3. Hugh Fenning, *The undoing of the friars of Ireland* (Louvain, 1972), *passim*.
4. For information on friction between the regular and secular clergy in Dublin I am indebted to 'Father Fintan's Records' (N.L.I., microfilm Pos. 3142, 367–75). The actual complaints of the regulars (in Latin) can be found in the Dublin diocesan archives, item 79.
5. Cathaldus Giblin, 'Catalogue of material of Irish interest in the collection Nunziatura di Fiandra, Vatican archives', *Collectanea Hibernica*, no. 4 (1961), 114–15.
6. W. P. Burke, *Irish priests of the penal times* (Waterford, 1914), 307.
7. Cathaldus Giblin, *op. cit.*, no. 8 (1965), 65.

8. S. J., Popish priest, *Sermon in vindication of Mr Francis Lehey, against the Romish clergy of the city of Dublin; which sets forth their cruelty to their poor brethren, particularly to the said Mr Lehey* (Dublin, 1728), Ref. P. gg. 9. no. 33 in Early Printed Books section, library of Trinity College, Dublin.

9. *Dublin Intelligence,* 15 March 1729. Quoted in John Brady, *Catholics and catholicism in the eighteenth century press* (Maynooth, 1965), 48.

10. Peter O'Dwyer, *The Irish Carmelites of the ancient observance* (Dublin, 1988), 130.

11. 'Report on the state of Popery in Ireland, 1731', *Archivium Hibernicum* 4, no. 10 (1915), 144. In the same year (1731) Lehy was 'particularly under suspicion' by the Irish authorities in regard to proposals for sending Catholic missionaries from Ireland to Jamaica. (See Public Record Office, Northern Ireland, Deputy Keeper's report for 1934, p. 25.)

12. L. P. Murray (ed.), 'The Fottrell papers', *County Louth Archaeological Journal* 7 (1930), 151.

Chapter 8

THE PUBLIC MAN (1720–30)

WHEN a Catholic, James Cotter, was executed in Cork in 1720 for the rape of a Quaker woman there was a great deal of unrest and agitation throughout the country because, rightly or wrongly, it was generally believed that he was innocent. Protest in Dublin took the form of an attack on the Quaker meeting-house in Meath Street. The authorities believed, no doubt wrongly, that the Catholic clergy had instigated this attack and a number of them were arrested. Probably as a precaution against possible attacks by Protestants, the chapels the following Sunday were closed—all, that is, except Nary's chapel in Mary's Lane, where, as *Whalley's Newsletter* recalls, 'it's said the chapple was hung in mourning and prayers offered up for the soul of Mr Cotter'.[1]

This was typical of the independent, calculated stance adopted by Nary throughout his entire period as parish priest of St Michan's. The same stance is apparent in the different controversies he engaged in with Protestant divines. That he was not afraid to adopt such a stance, and, what is more, was allowed to get away with it, probably derives in large measure from the fact that he was a doctor of civil law as well as a doctor of canon law. Protestants had no difficulty, then, in allowing him his title of doctor, i.e. doctor of law, and it is evident that he was on the same account treated by them with a great deal of deference and respect, almost of admiration. Indeed, in the eyes of many Protestants he must have been the 'acceptable face' of popery.

In a situation where the Catholic archbishop was not in law deemed to exist, it seems clear that Nary evolved as a sort of unofficial representative of the Catholics of Dublin. The acquittal of Archbishop Byrne by the courts in 1718 on a charge of taking on himself the title of archbishop was almost certainly the result of outside pressure, and may have given that dignitary a false idea of the extent of the 'connivance' to be afforded him, for by the early 1720s he was, to quote a contemporary source, 'going constantly and publicly his visitations with his chaise and retinue without any question or interruption'.[2]

That the authorities in Dublin had no intention of relaxing the Penal Laws is evidenced by the fact that in 1719 the Irish privy council forwarded to London heads of a bill which included provisions for the castration of unregistered Catholic priests, a truly monstrous proposal which was turned down by the British authorities. Since the archbishop could have no role as a public man, Nary, whether unconsciously or by his own design, found himself cast in the role of spokesman on both religious and political matters.

When the lord lieutenant, the duke of Grafton, prorogued the Irish parliament in 1722, he enjoined the members to keep a watchful eye on the papists, since he had reason to believe that 'the number of popish priests is daily increasing in this kingdom, and already far exceeds what by the indulgence of the law is allowed'.[3] Accordingly, when parliament reassembled in 1723 it was in a mood to pass a number of resolutions directed against Catholics. On the basis of these resolutions a bill was prepared under which, *inter alia,* no registered Catholic priest, under the penalty of high treason, could say Mass in the kingdom except those who had taken the Oath of Abjuration. It was also provided that all unregistered priests, as well as bishops and regular clergy, should depart the country by 25 March 1725 on pain of high treason.[4] The significance of the date, 25 March, was that this was New Year's Day under the old Julian calendar then operating in Britain and Ireland.

The Catholic clergy in the autumn of 1723 brought the new bill to the attention of the internuncio in Brussels, who had responsibility for Irish affairs.[5] Cornelius Nary must at the same time have decided that action against the bill at home was also called for. This action took the form of a twenty-one-page pamphlet entitled *The case of the Roman Catholics of Ireland,* published anonymously in 1724. Nary does not appear to have been publicly cited as the author of this pamphlet until after his death, when it was included as an appendix to *The impartial history of Ireland* (attributed to Hugh Reily) when the latter was reprinted in 1742 (four years after Nary's death), and in 1744 and 1762. On all these occasions the pamphlet was attributed to Nary. I have not been able to trace any copy of the original pamphlet published in 1724. (Incidentally, Reily's history, which is also known as *The genuine history of Ireland,* and Nary's *The case of the Roman Catholics of Ireland* were translated into Irish by Uilliam Ó Murchadha in 1772 but did not appear in print in Irish until 1941.) Since it is the only substantial pamphlet published in the first four decades of the eighteenth century which makes the Catholic case, it is a highly important document from the purely historical point of view.

In the early pages of the pamphlet Nary cites the main clauses of the Articles of Limerick. He then goes on to show how these Articles were contravened by the various Penal Laws against Catholics. 'All and every Roman Catholic of the Kingdom', he tells us, 'bating [except] a few Lords and three or four Colonels of the troops that were actually in Limerick and Galway at the time they surrendered, are disabled under severe penalties to carry arms, offensive or defensive, for their own, or defence of their houses and goods, other than pitch-forks and other such instruments as the peasants till the earth with; nay, many gentlemen who formerly made a considerable figure in the Kingdom, are nowadays, when they walk with canes or sticks only in their hands, insulted by men armed with swords and pistols, who of late rose from the very dregs of the people'.[6]

He records that Catholic lawyers have been disabled from practising, 'so that of about an hundred Roman Catholic lawyers and attornies, that attended the courts of Dublin and in the country, not one of them is allowed to get a morsel of bread by those studies upon which they spent their youth and their time'.[7]

He points out that Catholics may only take leases of land for terms not exceeding thirty-one years, and that at not less than two-thirds of the improved rent.[8] He castigates the law under which heirs apparent, on becoming Protestants, can make their parents tenants for life, 'so that the fathers cannot, may not, provide for their other dutiful children or other extraordinary exigencies of life'.[9]

Nary refers to the law requiring registered Catholic priests to take the Oath of Abjuration on penalty of being punished as regular clergy. The same Oath of Abjuration is required also from the laity, the penalty for refusing to take it being ultimately the forfeiture and confiscation of all their real and personal estates, 'notwithstanding that they had stipulated by

115

the Articles of Limerick, and had the public faith given them, that no other oath but that of allegiance should be required of them, which oath they were always ready to take'.[10]

He points out that all civil offices but that of petty constable are barred to Catholics, and that Catholic tradesmen and shopkeepers are not allowed to work at their respective trades 'except they pay exorbitant taxes, which they call Quarterages, to the respective masters of their corporations'.[11] 'Add to this', he continues,

> as often as England or Ireland have been alarmed by the attempts made by the French or Spaniards or by the Pretender upon England or Scotland, the Roman Catholics of this Kingdom were sure to be taken up, to have the arms, which the few of them had, taken from them . . . to have their saddle and even their draught or plough-horses taken from them, and kept while the alarm continued. And had these foreigners or the Pretender succeeded in their attempt, the Lord of Heaven knows what should have been our fate![12]

Nary highlights the Oath of Abjuration as the main bone of contention between Catholics and the administration. He devotes four pages to explaining why it is not possible for him to take this oath, while at the same time he would have no problem at all about taking an oath of allegiance. Under the Oath of Abjuration a Catholic was required to swear that the late King James or his son, the Pretender, had no right or title whatsoever to the crown of England, a proposition so manifestly untenable that many Protestant divines and persons of note and learning had been unable to accept it.[13] With regard to the clause in the oath requiring men to swear that they will maintain the succession to the crown in the Protestant line, Nary adverts to the difficulty that, if the existing sovereign were converted to Catholicism, a Catholic on that ground alone would be bound to withdraw allegiance from him. He maintains that this is not as far-fetched as it sounds, since there had been several cases in Europe where a monarch had turned Catholic, including Charles II, James II and Henry IV of France. Furthermore, the oath contained the assertion that it was taken 'heartily freely and willingly', which in the case of a sincere Catholic would certainly be untrue.

Reverting to the Articles of Limerick, Nary recalls that King William,

> of happy memory, did not suffer the least attempt to be made upon the Articles which his generals made with the Roman Catholic army at Limerick, of which we have a pregnant instance. For in the third year of his reign, when an Act of Parliament passed in England

116

entitled an Act for abrogating the Oath Of Supremacy and appointing other oaths, requiring all Officers, Magistrates, Lawyers etc. in Ireland to take the same, there was a saving for such Roman Catholics as were entitled to the benefit of the Articles of Limerick; and it was expressly provided by the said Act that they should be obliged to take the Oath of Allegiance and no other.[14]

He goes on to pay a characteristic tribute to liberal-minded Protestants:

But alas! this great monarch was no sooner laid up with his fathers, but the Roman Catholics began to feel the dire effects of some men's spleen. I say some men: for God Almighty be thanked, we have always had many worthy gentlemen of great honour and integrity in the House of Commons and many also in the House of Lords, without whose help we would have been long since consumed.[15]

The trouble was, as he notes, that such liberal-minded people were in the minority and, accordingly,

There was scarce a session of Parliament in this Kingdom in the reign of Queen Anne, in which one point or other has not been invaded of the Articles and Conditions upon which we submitted to King William, and which are in themselves no more than what was natural for subjects and Free-born Men to expect. Nay, much less than our neighbouring nation, the Scots, obtained upon their submitting to the Crown of England. . . And we challenge all the World to show us one instance in which we have not demeaned ourselves, as dutiful and as loyal subjects as the Scots, if not more. . . But I would beg of them [the administration] to consider that there is a God in Heaven, an avenger of wrongs, a God of vengeance to those who violate Public Faith; a crime which never fails to bring visible judgments from Heaven, especially when it is public and national, as may be manifestly seen both in sacred and profane history.[16]

He proceeds to give instances from ancient and more recent history of the Nemesis which pursues rulers who violate treaties and solemn agreements. He mentions in particular Louis XIV's abrogation of the Edict of Nantes and the subsequent flight of 'at least 100,000' Protestant Huguenots from France,[17] and how this proud prince, once the terror of Europe with a seemingly invincible army, was finally brought to heel and had to accept peace on terms prescribed by his enemies.

And yet the vengeance of Heaven did not cease to pursue him . . . till his son, his two grandsons and his two great grandsons were swept away almost in one year, so that his family (though in appearance the best stocked with a numerous issue of any Prince in Europe) was reduced in his own sight to a single infant of five years old, and his Kingdom to so much misery and desolation, both of pestilence and famine, as is hardly to be expressed. And will not the vengeance of Heaven (think you) pursue those who so flagrantly broke the Public Faith, solemnly given to the Catholics of Ireland, now indeed honest, innocent and loyal subjects to King George? . . . And who can tell but the Bill now under consideration, should it pass into law, is the filling up the measure of the sins of those gentlemen, who so often before have violated the Public Faith? It seems indeed, as far as human reason can penetrate into God's secrets, to be so. For it is calculated for the utter ruin and destruction of all the Roman Catholics in the Kingdom, notwithstanding the Public Faith given them at Limerick, of enjoying all the liberties, privileges, immunities and freedom, as well in civil as religious matters, which they enjoyed in the reign of King Charles the Second.[18]

With regard to the requirement in the Bill for priests to take the Oath of Abjuration, he notes that 1,100 priests were registered under the Act of 1704 and of these not above 33 took the Oath of Abjuration required under the Act of 1709.[19] He calculates that more than two-thirds of the 1,100 originally registered were by then (1724) dead. He asks: 'What shall so many thousands of Roman Catholics in every province of the Kingdom do then to serve God in their own way? . . . What shall they do when sick or dying? To send for a priest . . . it's to themselves certain death, considering the greatness of the reward offered to the informer, who doubtless will be one of their own domestics'.[20]

Nary gives four reasons why it is impolitic, and against the interest of the government, that the bill should pass into law. First, it is impolitic to prosecute the Roman Catholics of Ireland at a time when the king is labouring to get toleration for Protestants from Catholic powers.[21] Secondly, the passage of the bill would have the effect of draining the country of the greatest part of the people. 'For if this Bill passes into law, all the estated Roman Catholics, all the merchants, dealers, shopkeepers, all the tradesmen and farmers, with their respective clans, will dispose of their effects and quit the Kingdom, as will also the little people [i.e. poor people] who are able to purchase their passage; and such as are not will become thieves and robbers, having no clergymen to teach or instruct, or to keep them within bounds'.[22] Thirdly, Catholics thus forced from the country may indeed be replaced by Protestant Huguenots: 'These indeed we may have: But then they are and will be still Huguenots or Calvinists, will wear swords and carry arms; and though they will readily take all the Oaths, which our laws require, yet still will be of a different religion from that which is by law established, and will endeavour to propagate it'.[23] Fourthly, the passage of such a bill would be against the interest of the government, 'for it is well known that the Roman Catholic merchants and dealers carry on more than half the trade of the Kingdom, and pay more Custom and Duty for imported goods, than all the Protestants in it. Now if this Bill should pass, all these merchants and dealers would be necessitated to leave the Kingdom, to the great diminution of the Revenue, and God knows in how many years this could be retrieved, if ever'.[24]

He again bemoans the breach of public faith and points to the peaceable manner in which Catholics have nevertheless conducted themselves: 'Their behaviour being so even, their Demeanour being so peaceable, and their loyalty so untainted, that they challenge the worst of their enemies to find the least flaw or blemish in their conduct. Nay, the only thing I could ever hear them charged with is that their hearts and affections are not for the Government, and there are a great many priests come of late from foreign countries into this Kingdom'. To overcome the first charge, Nary says, what is required is for the government to treat the Catholics fairly: 'Be pleased, most excellent Lords and noble Senators, to give us the same liberty and freedom as our fellow subjects have to use our industry and enjoy the fruits thereof; let no distinction be made but of good and bad, and I will engage the Government will have our Hearts, our Affections and our Hands'.[25] In reply to the second charge above—that too many priests have been coming into the country—Nary makes a surprising, some would say an unworthy, answer:

> In answer to the Second, I shall only ask the same question that Abraham asked of God Almighty: 'Wilt thou also destroy the righteous with the wicked'. Must the civil and quiet priests, who have lived these many years in the country, be destroyed for the indiscretion of other priests whose coming they knew nothing of; nor, if they had, was it in their power to prevent. No, they hope better things from the mildness and lenity of the present Government; and flatter themselves that, as they have been overlooked [i.e. tolerated] since the accession of His Sacred Majesty King George to the throne . . . and enjoyed, without any trouble or molestation, the free exercise of their religion, which they gratefully accept with all thankfulness, and for which they continually pray for the blessings of Heaven upon His Majesty and his Magistrates.[26]

Such is Nary's pamphlet, *The case of the Roman Catholics of Ireland*. All in all, it is an expertly argued, economically worded piece of polemical writing, which compares favourably with anything written in the polemical vein by Nary's contemporary, Swift. As one might expect in this kind of writing, there is the occasional exaggeration, as when he claims that the number of Catholics allowed to carry arms amounted to no more than a few lords and three or four colonels. In fact, an official list published in 1704 shows 115 Catholics entitled to carry arms; nineteen of these could keep a sword only, while nearly all the others were licensed to keep a sword, a case of pistols and a gun.[27] When he refers to the position of lawyers he neglects to mention that Catholic solicitors were still practising at the date in question, to such an extent, indeed, that the government saw fit in an act passed in 1734 to require all solicitors, except those covered by the Articles of Limerick, to take the Oath of Abjuration.

Although Nary strives to paint the plight of the Catholics in the blackest colours possible, he nevertheless makes, unconsciously, a few surprising disclosures as to the real, and quite favourable, situation of certain Catholic sectors. Firstly, in complaining about the exorbitant quarterage payments required from Catholic tradesmen, he discloses that they were allowed to continue as members of their guilds, although admittedly on discriminatory terms. Secondly, he discloses that Catholic merchants and dealers carried on more than half the trade of the country, and this, it should be noted, as early as 1724. As to how this strong Catholic merchant and tradesman sector came about, the most likely answer is that they were, for the most part, there all the time, at least as far as Dublin was concerned. We have to remember that the original Norman and English settlers in Dublin were all Catholics and a high proportion of these must have continued to adhere to the old faith following the Reformation. It is no accident, then, that so many of the Catholic merchants and tradesmen in Dublin had non-Irish surnames such as Lincoln, Usher, Hall, Ambrose, Linegar, Sweetman, Atkinson, Hay. A further proportion of Catholic merchants consisted of Catholics who lost landed property and turned to trade as an alternative means of livelihood.

Whether 'this very powerful memorial', as the historian Lecky termed Nary's pamphlet, had any effect at all in changing the minds of the members of the Irish parliament with regard to the bill before them is a moot point. One possible indication of a change of heart on the part of that body is that when Edward Synge, prebendary of St Patrick's, preached a sermon to the members of the House of Commons in St Andrew's Church on 23 October 1725, advocating a degree of toleration for Catholics, his audience were so pleased with what they heard that they congratulated Synge on an excellent sermon and ordered it to be printed. That the same body of men shortly before could have been proposing in a bill quite penal provisions against Catholics suggests a lack of direction with regard to the treatment of Catholics. There appears to have also been a change of heart on the part of the Irish House of Lords on this issue, since the latter on 3 December 1725 resolved that 'the most probable way of restraining popish priests and regulars coming into this Kingdom, will be to allow a competent number of secular priests to exercise their functions under such rules and limitations as may be for the security of the civil state'.[28]

In the event, it appears that the bill was killed largely by the not inconsiderable weight of Vatican diplomacy which was brought to bear against it. In the latter months of 1723 the inter-nuncio in Brussels, on being informed of the provisions of the bill, requested the papal representatives in Catholic countries to implore their respective governments to use their good offices in favour of the Irish Catholics. The pope, following the receipt of the report sent to him by the internuncio, wrote with all speed to the rulers of the Catholic states and instructed the various nuncios to do everything they could to persuade the Catholic rulers to come to the defence of the Irish as resolutely and as speedily as possible.[29] For a time it was feared that the execution of a number of Protestants at Thorn in the Catholic kingdom of Poland might engender a backlash against the Catholics of Ireland. However, on 2 March 1726 we find Cardinal Secretary of State Spinola informing the internuncio in Brussels that the news sent by the latter, that the Irish parlia-ment had been prorogued without taking measures against the Catholics, had brought great relief to the Holy See. Spinola went on to say that the authorities at Rome gave much of the credit for what happened to the intervention of de Fleury (effective prime minister of France and later cardinal) with Walpole, the English minister at the court of France.[30] But it will be clear from the foregoing paragraph that the decision to drop the bill had been taken long before the prorogation of parliament in January 1726.

It will be gathered from the foregoing, then, that the way to prevent penal legislation against Catholics in Ireland was to persuade the government in London that such legislation was impolitic having regard to the implications for Protestants in Catholic countries. Under Poynings' Law and the Sixth of

George I (which could be termed blessings in disguise as far as Catholics were concerned), the Irish parliament was the mere creature of the British government and privy council. In effect the Irish parliament could not enact any legislation without approval from London. The 1723 bill was not the only one to be negatived by the British authorities.

The question of an oath and the Address to the King

In a letter dated 27 June 1722[31] to the archbishop of Canterbury, Archbishop Synge of Tuam put forward proposals for a form of oath to the king which might be acceptable to Catholics who were genuinely loyal. These proposals are indeed further evidence of the muddled and quite contradictory thinking emanating at this time from the establishment in Dublin. To give an adequate indication of Synge's proposals, it is necessary to quote from his letter at some length:

> Some Papists, with whom I have discoursed, affirm that they are ready in the strongest terms to swear allegiance to King George and to renounce the Pretender, which (say they) is as great a security as can be given to the civil power. But, (say they) to renounce the Pope's authority or jurisdiction in *matters purely spiritual,* is against a known principle of our religion. And to swear that the Pretender has *not any right* to the Crown, is to swear to the truth of doctrine, which ought not to be made the matter of an Oath. Or to swear that *we believe he has no right,* is to take an Oath concerning a thing of which we are not capable of forming a judgment. The distinction between a King *de jure* and *de facto* having not only been received by men of learning, but also into some of the English Acts of Parliament.

Synge goes on to express the belief that there were as many Catholic bishops and priests in the country as at any time for the previous sixty years, and continues:

> And some there are who think it hard to require an Oath from them, which even an honest Papist, who desires to be faithful to the present Government, cannot in conscience take. . . To obviate all these pretences, and for the relief of all Papists that are sincere and honest, and the detection of those that are not so, I have often thought that an Oath might be framed against which they can have no manner of pretence, except they will openly profess themselves not to be subjects to King George, but to the Pretender and the Pope. . . A Papist, whose interest as well as duty obliges him to be faithful to the King, positively told me that, if I could draw up the form of an Oath of Fidelity, that should be free from those objections which he made, and I have above mentioned, he would propose it to as many of his persuasion as he could; and was content that all who refused it should be treated as rebels.

122

James Francis Edward Stuart (1688–1766), the 'Old Pretender'. (Courtesy of the National Library of Ireland.)

Synge enclosed with his letter a draft of the oath he proposed and asked for the opinion of the archbishop of Canterbury upon it and on whether he should 'communicate it, or anything of that sort to the person who desired me to draw it up, in the hope that the Papists may at the next sitting of our Parliament, make some proposal to the Government that may be a means to distinguish such as are honest from those who are not so'.

The form of oath proposed by Synge is included as Appendix 1 to this chapter. As to the identity of the Catholics with whom Synge says he had 'discoursed', there are good grounds for believing that one of them was Nary. The criticism of the Oath of Abjuration conveyed by 'some Papists' to Synge is broadly in line with Nary's criticism of the oath in *The case of the Roman Catholics of Ireland*.

We do not know the reaction of the archbishop of Canterbury to Synge's proposed oath; if he put his views in writing, they do not appear to have survived. In any event the proposal appears to have remained dormant for a few years. In the light of the further disabilities on Catholics proposed in the 1723 bill, already discussed, Synge may have considered that the time was not ripe to proceed with such a liberal measure as a special oath for Catholics. However, following the abandonment of that bill and when saner counsels appeared to prevail in the Irish parliament, we find Synge's oath surfacing again in 1726 in the course of the controversy between Synge's son, also named Edward, and the vicar of Naas (see Chapter 10).

The previous October, as already mentioned, Synge *fils* had preached, before members of the Irish House of Commons, a sermon in St Andrew's Church, Dublin, in which he argued that a toleration might be granted to Catholics under certain conditions.[32] This was a sermon given annually to commemorate the alleged massacre of Protestants during the 1641 rebellion, and was preached by Synge in his capacity as chaplain to the lord lieutenant. In view of his position as chaplain and of the audience he was preaching to, Synge no doubt put forward his proposals in the knowledge that there would be considerable support for them at establishment level. They were also in line with the resolution of the Irish House of Lords of 3 December 1725, already mentioned in this chapter.

In the course of his sermon Synge argued that neither the governors of the Christian Church nor the civil magistrates had a right to use force 'to restrict or punish any opinions or practices in religion'. He drew 'the very important conclusion that all persons in a society, whose principles of religion have no tendency to hurt the public, have a right to a toleration'. By toleration he meant 'a liberty to worship God according to their consciences, without any encouragement from the civil government on the one hand, or fear of infliction of punishment on the other hand'.[33] With regard to pretended papal powers to depose princes and to absolve subjects from their allegiance, he stated:

Though the church of Rome does, as I have shown, maintain or countenance these wicked doctrines, yet all the members of it do not. The church of France has, as I have already said, declared fully against the deposing powers; a late noted professor at Louvain, a native of this kingdom [Francis Martin], has not long since written freely against it, and the design of his book is to prove it to be the duty of the Romanists of both kingdoms to renounce this doctrine, and not only so, but to swear and to pay all dutiful allegiance to his Majesty and to abjure the pretender. And all this, if I am rightly informed, many of them declare they are ready to do. They do indeed make one objection to the Oath of Abjuration, as it now stands, which possibly may be obviated, without lessening the binding force of the Oath itself, but as to the other doctrines mentioned, they say they do not own them and are ready in the most solemn manner to renounce and disclaim them.

Synge goes on to argue that such people 'ought at least to be allowed some benefit of a toleration'.[34] As regards people who were not prepared to swear allegiance to King George, he claimed that ''tis evident they could not justly complain though they were at once banished out of the society'.[35]

Following an attack on these proposals by Stephen Radcliffe, vicar of Naas, Synge *fils* published a vindication of the proposals, in the course of which he put forward a form of oath which he thought might be acceptable to Catholics. It differed in a few minor points from Synge *père*'s original draft oath. It was part of the package that the country would be served by 500 secular priests, but no regulars. He had no plans for revoking any of the other Penal Laws against Catholics, but he pointed out that the consequence of their not being able to purchase land was that they turned mostly to trade and 'have their wealth chiefly in money, which is not so sure a pledge for their quiet and peaceable behaviour as an estate of land, and may much more quickly and effectively be applied to carry on an enterprise against the government'.[36]

The Synges, father and son, were not alone at this time in putting forward proposals for toleration for Catholics. Bolton, bishop of Elphin and later to be archbishop of Cashel, who as well as being a member of the Irish House of Lords was also a privy counsellor, put forward in the House of Lords proposals for an establishment of 600 Catholic priests and, in order to preserve a succession of priests, one popish bishop who should be allowed to reside constantly in Ireland. He also proposed that arrangements should be made for the education of Catholic priests in Trinity College, Dublin.[37]

125

In the early months of 1726 there were rumours of an approaching war, a possibility which spurred the government in the direction of conciliatory overtures to Catholics, with a view, no doubt, to countering latent Jacobite sympathies. The Franciscan Sylvester Lloyd, a committed Jacobite and bitter opponent of the projected oath, reported on 1 June to the court of the Pretender:

> As to affairs of religion, the catholics are treated of late with extraordinary mildness. The judges in their circuits everywhere recommended moderation to the magistrates, as they did in the most earnest manner good behaviour and fidelity to the catholics. . . The Oath of Allegiance is no longer talked of. . . I hope we shall be able to disabuse some deluded people with regard to their notions on that head, or any other that may be to the prejudice of his Majesty's [i.e. the Pretender's] undoubted right to our allegiance.[38]

But it appears that even as Lloyd wrote these words the situation, always volatile, was rapidly changing. The Catholic mob in Dublin, far from being conciliated by the government's show of lenity, took advantage of this lenity so far as to demonstrate openly on the streets of Dublin, and indeed the summer of 1726 turned out to be a particularly violent one in the capital. The authorities at one stage feared that what the papists had in mind was not simply rioting but open rebellion and the murder of Protestants. There were ugly rumours going the rounds that, in order to facilitate the murder of Protestants, Catholic houses were being marked with a special sign. *Dublin Intelligence* reported:

> This ten or twelve days past almost in every part of this city, there has not been any discourse of moment but of a sermon which ('tis reported) was lately preached in some papist chapels here on a text taken from the ninth chapter of Ezekiel: 'Go through the midst of the city and set a mark upon the forehead of the men that sigh and that cry for all the abominations that be done in the midst thereof. . . Slay utterly both old and young, both maids and little children and women, but come not near any man upon whom is the mark; and begin at my sanctuary'—on purpose to stir up in the minds of their people an itching for some dangerous attempt. We further hear, but of it have no confirmation, that information being made of the abovesaid passage, an Eminent Doctor did preach a sermon of quite a different intention to appearance in one of the mass-houses, on which a Protestant who out of curiosity stood by, remarked it were well if the good man, as he looked one way, did not row th'other.[39]

There can be little doubt but that the ambivalent Catholic priest referred to here was Cornelius Nary. Nary was the best-known Catholic priest in the city and arguably the only one to whom the Protestants would accord the title 'eminent doctor'. He cannot have condoned the action proposed, but neither can it have escaped his notice that protest by the mob had a significant deterrent value where active prosecution of the Penal Laws was concerned.

The government, alarmed by these rumours, decided on a show of strength, and we are told that 'an armed force was marched in hostile array through the streets of the metropolis, and an unresisting multitude of either sex and of every age were fired upon and put to flight'.[40] The Pretender's birthday, 10 June, had been celebrated by the Catholics for several years by meetings in St Stephen's Green. Despite the show of strength by the authorities, the celebrations on 10 June 1726 went ahead as usual, for we read that 'in the evening a great mob gathered in Stephen's Green . . . expecting something extraordinary, which not happening as they expected . . . they fell to toss dead dogs and cats about'. Lord Abercorn, who lived nearby, spoke to them from a window of his house, asking them to disperse. Their reply was to shower his lordship's house with stones, brickbats and dead creatures. The mob then got completely out of hand and the Main Guard had to be called to deal with them. The rioting did not cease until 'a great number were desperately wounded and taken prisoners'.[41]

But to revert to the question of the oath, the reaction of the Pretender to the idea of Irish Catholics swearing an oath of allegiance to King George was predictable. His secretary of state, John Hay, wrote on 29 May 1726:

> The only answer which can be made to Mr Lloyd's [i.e. Sylvester Lloyd's] long letter . . . is that the King [i.e. the Pretender] never can give his consent to his subjects of Ireland taking any oaths which can hinder them from coming to his assistance and taking a forward part in his service when we shall have occasion to call upon them.[42]

Pace Lloyd's assertion of 1 June 1726 (above) that the Oath of Allegiance was then no longer talked of, it is clear that Archbishop Synge had at least the intention of reactivating his proposal for an oath in 1726, for we find Bishop Nicolson of Derry writing to Archbishop Wake of Canterbury in that year:

> The archbishop of Tuam said he had met with a great many Popish priests, who profess their readiness to abjure all manner of power in the Pope to absolve them from their allegiance; which they were ready to swear in the most binding and solemn manner to King George. But they pointed to an expression or two in the Oath Of Abjuration which they thought might be omitted without hazard to the Government. And his Grace [of Tuam] seemed to intimate his own intention shortly to give the House [of Lords] his reasons for agreeing in the same opinion.[43]

Again, the 'Popish priests' whom Synge is said to have met must have included Nary, for it will be apparent from Chapter 11 that these two men were well acquainted with one another.

At what point Nary decided to draw up his own form of oath we do not know. That he did draw up a form of oath is certain, for it was reproduced years afterwards by Charles O'Conor of Belnagare in a pamphlet entitled *Vindication of Lord Taaffe's civil principles,* published in 1768.[44] In the course of a letter dated 9 December 1767 to Dr John Curry, O'Conor commented on Nary's oath:

> King William required of our people no more than a simple Oath of Allegiance; and did the wisest men now in the Kingdom club hands to frame a Test against perjury, duplicity etc., they could not produce one more full to every point than Doctor Nary's, which is annexed to the *Vindication* etc. Appendix no. 2.[45]

Nary's form of oath is included as Appendix 2 to this chapter. The very clear declaration in that oath that 'it is no article of my faith that any person whatsoever has power to absolve me from my obligation to this oath, or that the Pope hath power to depose princes' is in line with the following views expressed in the anonymous *Letter to the vicar of Naas* (see Chapter 10), believed to be the joint work of Nary and a Catholic lawyer.

> He [the vicar's informant] tells you also of the famous decree of Sorbonne, which, had you read, you might see that no person whatsoever can take a degree in that famous Faculty, who doth not first swear and declare that he will (among other things) maintain that the Pope hath neither directly nor indirectly any authority or power over the temporals of kings, nor can dispense with the subjects of any crown or state to break their Oath of Allegiance, and thousands of others might have told you that this is the doctrine of all the universities of the French Dominions. . . So that the doctrine of the deposing power and of dispensing with subjects' allegiance is only the opinion of a few divines and canonists, and the doctrine contrary to it, that of all the rest of the Catholic Church.[46]

In accepting a degree of doctor of laws from the University of Paris, Nary had as early as 1694 accepted that the pope had no dispensing or deposing powers. The decree of the Sorbonne mentioned above was of course an indication that these alleged powers of the pope were just as obnoxious to Catholic monarchs as to Protestant ones.

Nary does not appear to have finalised his form of oath until mid 1727 at the earliest, for it mentions George II, who succeeded his father as king in June of that year. The question of an oath appears at that stage to have become bound up with the Catholic Address to the new king, which, as we shall see, was to split the Catholic community.

George II had already, before coming to the throne, acquired a reputation for liberality and toleration. Some Catholics therefore thought that an Address of loyalty to him might have the effect of securing in time some easement of the Penal Laws. Towards this end about thirty of 'the chief citizens' of Dublin met in 'The Lion' in Werburgh Street, under the chairmanship of Lord Delvin. According to a report sent to the nuncio in Brussels it was Lord Delvin who drew up the Address and falsely informed the meeting that it had the support and approval of Cardinal de Fleury, prime minister of France. When they were well filled with wine and had glasses in their hands, the report goes on, Delvin arranged that those present put their signatures to the Address. Many of them came back the following morning, however, and insisted that their names be erased from the document. The report to the nuncio went on to state that 'the whole thing may be said to be the work of eighteen or twenty people, at most'.[47]

The Address was brief and to the point:

To the King's Most Excellent Majesty,
The most humble Address of the Roman Catholics of the Kingdom of Ireland.

Most Gracious Sovereign,

We Your Majesty's most loyal and dutiful subjects, the Roman Catholics of your Kingdom of Ireland, are truly grieved for the unspeakable loss that this nation, as well as Your Majesty's other Dominions, has sustained by the decease of our late most Gracious Sovereign, Your Royal Father; the goodness and lenity of whose Government we are deeply sensible of, which emboldens us thus in a most humble manner to approach Your Majesty's Most Sacred Person, to congratulate Your Majesty's happy accession to the Throne, and to crave leave to assure Your Majesty of our steady allegiance and most humble duty to Your Majesty's Person and Government. And we most humbly beseech Your Majesty to give us leave to affirm that our resolution of an inviolable duty and allegiance to Your Majesty proceeds not only from our inclination and the sincerity of our hearts, but also from a firm belief of its being a religious duty, which no power on earth can dispense with.[48]

Lord Delvin was an absentee who came over from London to Dublin specially to draw up the Address and to organise support for it. He then returned to London and presented the Address to the king. Father Sylvester Lloyd, in a letter dated 15 July 1727 to the court of the Pretender, tells us that the Address was signed by the earls of Carlingford, Westmeath and Fingall,

Lord Trimleston, another lord whose name is illegible, and about twenty of 'the chief of the commons' in and about Dublin.[49] However, Bishop Stephen McEgan, likewise in a letter to the court of the Pretender, states that the Address was signed by 'not above sixty or a few more'.[50]

According to Lloyd 'no clergyman' was consulted in regard to the Address, and we can conclude from this that the Address was not signed by any of the Catholic clergy. It soon emerged that the regular clergy in particular were vehemently opposed to the Address, and at the instigation of Lloyd[51] they drew up the following Queries upon it.

A few queries seriously offered for the consideration of the Lords and gentlemen who lately signed an Address intended to be (and since presented to King George the Second) in behalf of the Roman Catholics of the Kingdom of Ireland.

Q.I. Whether about twenty or thirty lords and gentlemen, without election or deputation from the Roman Catholics of Ireland, can in any sense be understood to be the Roman Catholics of Ireland?

Q.II. Whether at their meeting at the Lyon in Warburgh Street on the 8th day of July 1727, the proper parties concerned were all present, and time for full deliberation, or a full freedom of debate allowed to those that were?

Q.III. Whether the peremptory signing of an Address of this high nature at first reading, was not precipitate, passionate and presumptuous?

Q.IV. Whether any arguments were made use of to terrify the weak, or catch the unwary, which were anarchical, contrary to the fundamental laws of these realms, injurious to the sentiments of our Holy Mother, the Church, and dishonourable to the much-renowned Fidelity of an Irishman?

Q.V. Whether these words 'the goodness and lenity of whose Government we are deeply sensible of, which emboldens us thus in a most humble manner to approach etc.', do not wipe away our tears without removing the cause? And, whether they do not wipe away some men's scores? While they disarm our Mediators on all occasions and future times, when a sharp execution of the Laws still in force may make it as necessary as it is natural for us to complain?

Q.VI. Whether these words 'and we most humbly beseech Your Majesty to give us leave to affirm that our resolution of an inviolable duty and allegiance to Your Majesty proceeds not only from our inclination and the sincerity of our hearts', may not be understood to be vile and nauseous flattery?

Q.VII. Whether the continuation 'but also from a firm belief of its being a religious duty, which no power on earth can dispense', be not making a new Creed for the Roman Catholics of Ireland, and arrogantly deciding of a question of right, which no conscience can affirm, because no understanding can reach?

Q.VIII. If duty and allegiance to King George II be a religious duty, his right and power which are their necessary correlatives, must be of course divine. Why then did not the Junto go generously and take the Oath of Abjuration for all the Roman Catholics of Ireland, and so save Lord Delvin the trouble of going for England?

Q.IX. Though allegiance to the Lord's anointed may be perhaps a religious duty, with which no power on earth can dispense, yet since it is evident from our history that there may be Kings de facto and since Coke and other of our great lawyers say that allegiance is due to Kings de jure in their natural capacities; and since allegiance does in our language and laws signify something more than mere fidelity, which is reciprocal to mere protection, (We mean as the Flemings swear to their successive Governments, Spaniards, Germans, French, Dutch or English). Whether then, and in every such case, allegiance be a religious duty equally due to all Kings de facto, as well as de jure, and finally, in all cases, whether the Parliament be not a power on earth actually existing, that often has, and still can dispense with such duty?

Q.X. Whether such of the subscribers as were hurried into this affair, without seeing into the private views of the scheme, ought not to think it as just, as it will be undoubtedly honourable in them, to withdraw their names and acknowledge they were imposed upon?

Q.XI. Whether the Junto were not obliged to answer these and innumerable other queries to all Irishmen, before they presume to present their famous Address in the name of the whole Kingdom?

Q.XII. Whether if the Address must absolutely go, it ought not to be entitled *The humble address of us the Subscribers?*

Q.XIII. And last to be forthwith answered, whether an humble petition to the King, and a Remonstrance of our Grievances, notwithstanding the public faith given at Limerick, and our peaceable behaviour ever since that time, would not be much more proper on this critical occasion, and contribute more to our relief at a future Congress?[52]

In a further letter dated 20 July 1727 to the court of the Pretender,[53] Lloyd recites substantially the foregoing Queries, with the exception of Queries X and XIII. The absence of Query XIII from Lloyd's letter may be significant: it is likely that Lloyd himself, as an ardent supporter of the Pretender, did not agree with it. Lloyd in this letter claimed that the Queries had the effect of persuading one lord and some commoners to withdraw their signatures from the Address. Bishop Stephen McEgan, in the letter already mentioned, states that the Address was opposed by a vast many as soon as they heard of it, 'judging a Remonstrance of grievances with assurances of fidelity [to King George] to be more proper'.[54]

Meanwhile representations had evidently been made to Nuncio Spinelli in Brussels, presumably by one or more members of the Irish hierarchy, for we find Spinelli writing to Cardinal Secretary of State Lercari on the matter on 29 August 1727.[55] Spinelli maintained that this was the first time since the reign of Henry VIII that the Catholics of England, Ireland and Scotland had given recognition in a formal manner to a non-Catholic king; and even though many Catholics thought they should swear an Oath of Loyalty to the monarch who preceded the present ruler, provided they were granted freedom of conscience, none of them considered that it was permitted to them to swear at the same time, as the court desired, that they were of opinion that the pope had no authority over the temporal jurisdiction of princes, an opinion which was to be found in the present Address in a somewhat mitigated form.

Having described Lord Delvin's part in summoning the meeting in Werburgh Street and in finalising the Address, Nuncio Spinelli goes on to maintain that such an Address may be of advantage to the person responsible for it, but that it would certainly do great harm to Catholics generally; that a declaration of this kind could create scandal and schism among them; that, in so far as the government was concerned, the joy it would experience in seeing that only twenty Catholics signed this new oath of fidelity will not be nearly so great as its sorrow on considering that the other Catholics refused to put their signatures to it; and that, finally, the references made in the Address to the moderation of the last government will provide the heretics with a satisfactory answer, should they wish to reply to the Catholic powers whenever the latter speak in favour of the British or Irish Catholics, or try, by some other means, to keep the non-Catholics of Germany and France from abusing their power.

It will be seen that the Address was blown up out of all proportion by describing it as an oath of fidelity. This was the aspect which the Vatican concentrated on in a dispatch to Nuncio Spinelli on 11 October 1727, intimating that the secretary of state was not yet in a position to give a precise answer concerning 'the oath taken by the Irish catholics to the present king of England'; that the pope had referred the matter to the Holy Office for detailed examination; and that he (the pope) would then decide what should be done.[56]

Sylvester Lloyd makes a further progress report on the results of the Address in the course of a letter to the Pretender's court dated 9 March 1728:

Our Addressors, at least a great many of them who were brought into that scandalous affair without being let into the secret views of the first promoters of it, begin to be confounded and ashamed of the deed. Whether this proceeds from principle or considerations of guilt or rather from disappointment, I can't say. They promised themselves mountains from the present parliament in reward of their great loyalty, but the thing was quite otherwise understood than they expected. For the majority of members in the late election proved to be Tories, who were in their hearts offended at them. And the old true blue party took it to have been a scheme set afoot by some of the ministry and entered into by these few catholics in order to procure an English act for the repealing of the Penal Laws made in this kingdom against them. And so establish a Popish party here to make a kind of balance against the Protestant spirit which in the last parliament made so obstinate a stand in assertion of their independence of the English parliament and against the patent granted to one Mr Wood. . .

These reasons, or perhaps others which I can't penetrate, have hindered the parliament having hitherto done anything for the Addressors, for, though they made a petition to the House of Commons for leave to take long leases, mortgages, and perhaps lands etc., their petition at last reading was not only rejected but to their great confusion hissed with indignation out of the house.[57]

In the early summer of 1728 Lloyd spent some weeks in London on his way to the Continent, when he had an opportunity of keeping a watchful eye on Lord Delvin. In a letter from Douai dated 1 June 1728 he reported as follows to the court of the Pretender:

The Lord Delvin is very obsequious to the English court. He was about a fortnight ago introduced to the Elector [i.e. George II] and his lady by the Duke of Richmond and was received, as the newspapers call it, very graciously. I watched him as narrowly as possible and could only find that he intended to give in a petition in the name of the Irish Catholics, begging that they may have leave to purchase lands and to take long leases, inasmuch as their behaviour to the Government has always been peaceable, and that besides their late loyal Address they are ready to give the Government all such further security for their future fidelity and allegiance as shall be thought necessary. I did not see the petition but have it from very good hands that this is the substance of it, which is I think as injurious as it possibly can be, because it not only confirms the late Address but tacitly surrenders the Articles of Limerick which are our sheet anchor, and leaves us absolutely at the discretion of the Government for such oaths and tests as they shall think proper.[58]

It appears then that, having been rebuffed by the Irish parliament as indicated by Lloyd, some Irish Catholics were during 1728 concentrating their efforts on a direct approach to the king, and it is clear that at that stage something more than a mere Address of loyalty was involved.

As to what part Cornelius Nary played in the Address and its sequel, he was apparently not a signatory of the original Address, and it seems unlikely that he played even a behind-the-scenes part in it. Indeed, he was probably one of those, mentioned by Bishop McEgan, who were opposed to the Address on the grounds that a remonstrance of grievances, with assurances of fidelity to the king, would be more proper. McEgan and Nary were near neighbours and it will be seen in Chapter 9 that Nary actively supported McEgan's bid to be appointed archbishop of Dublin in 1729. But whatever about his attitude to the Address, it appears very likely that in regard to the petition to the king in the spring of 1728 'involving further security for their future fidelity and allegiance' Nary played a significant role since, as we have already noted, it must have been around this time that he finalised the form of the Oath of Allegiance reproduced by Charles O'Conor of Belnagare.

Rome was no doubt kept fully informed as to these further developments for there is a reference to the question of an oath in a dispatch of 24 July 1728, wherein the cardinal secretary of state warned Spinelli that if the latter should learn that the Irish Catholic clergy intended to take some kind of oath to the 'Duke of Hanover' (George II) he was to see to it that no decision was taken until the matter had been examined at Rome and precise directions issued by the Holy See.[59] This must have had the effect of stopping Nary and others of a like mind in their tracks as far as further progress with an Oath of Allegiance was concerned.

But while Rome prevaricated, the climate at home with regard to toleration of Catholics again worsened. In December 1729 the Irish House of Lords noted that 'several pretended popish archbishops, bishops and their officiates had of late exercised ecclesiastical jurisdiction within the realm in defiance of the laws, and that the behaviour of papists within the kingdom had of late years been very insolent in building many public mass-houses and erecting convents of friars and nuns, and on many occasions insulting the protestants'. Their lordships went on to resolve that the judges be directed to give in charge to the justices of the peace and all other magistrates more effectually to put the laws against popery in execution, particularly those against regulars and all persons exercising ecclesiastical jurisdiction. The lord lieutenant undertook to have their lordships' wishes carried out.[60]

This hardening in attitudes towards Catholics took the form in 1731 of the promotion in the Irish parliament of five bills injurious to Catholic interests, viz. (a) a bill closing loopholes in the law on the holding of arms by Catholics, (b) an amendment of the law in relation to popish solicitors, (c) a bill for registering the popish clergy, (d) a bill for better putting in execution the laws for banishing popish regulars, etc., and (e) a bill to annul and make void all marriages celebrated by popish priests and friars.[61]

The first two of the foregoing bills were duly approved in London,[62] but approval was withheld for the other three for the reason that they were 'of an extraordinary nature and very different from the laws of England against papists'.[63] But this may not have been the only reason for rejection for there is strong evidence in the Stuart Papers that the Austrian emperor intervened with the British government to have the bills rejected.[64] One of the bills—no doubt that for registering the Catholic clergy—evidently included an oath to be taken by Catholic priests, and on this subject Bishop Bernard Dunne of Kildare had this to say in a letter to the Pretender:

> Had matters succeeded with them [the Irish Lords and Commons] there was an oath to be tendered to those of my cloth which none but men void of both honour and conscience could swallow. 'Twas the second part of the same tune with the A—— [the Catholic Address to the king] and could not miss to meet with the same fate among men of untainted principles.[65]

It has not been possible to trace a copy of the proposed bill, and the form of the oath to be prescribed must be a matter for conjecture. It may well have been on the lines of Archbishop Synge's oath, in which case its principal shortcomings in the eyes of committed Jacobites such as Bishop Dunne would have been that it involved swearing allegiance to King George II to the exclusion of the Pretender.

A Catholic oath again became a live issue in 1756 in the penal bill of that year for a register of popish priests. The Catholic side on that occasion resurrected Cornelius Nary's form of oath with a view to its inclusion in the bill instead of the oath proposed.[66] In the event the bill was not proceeded with, largely because of opposition to it in the Irish House of Lords by the majority of Protestant bishops, led by Primate Stone who was quite favourably disposed to Catholics.[67]

It was not until 1774 that the question of an oath for Catholics was finally settled with the act of that year 'to permit his Majesty's subjects of whatever persuasion to testify their allegiance to him'. The oath then prescribed was subscribed to by the vast majority of Catholics with a stake in the country, both lay and clerical, either under the 1774 act itself or under the relief acts of 1778, 1782 and 1793.[68] The point must be made that the oath subscribed under these acts was no improvement, as far as Catholics were concerned, on the oath proposed by Archbishop Synge and his son in the 1720s, to which such grave exception was taken.[69] The conclusion is inescapable that opposition to an oath for Catholics in the 1720s and 1730s derived from political, rather than religious, considerations, centring around papal recognition of the Pretender as king of Great Britain and Ireland, and the large measure of support in Ireland for the Pretender.

The questions of an oath and the Address to the king thus showed that the Catholic clergy and, to a lesser extent, the Catholic laity were deeply divided on two separate issues. At one level they were divided into those who supported the claims of the Pretender to the British throne and refused to acknowledge King George as king, and those who, like Nary, were prepared to accept the reality of the Hanoverian succession and to swear an oath of allegiance to King George, while at the same time acknowledging that the Pretender had a *de jure* right to the British crown. At another level they were divided into those who supported the pope's deposing and dispensing claims and those who, like Nary, rejected such papal claims. Generally, those who supported the Pretender also supported the papal claims.

These divisions must be viewed in tandem with the machinations of the Pretender (and later his son), over a period of forty years, for the restoration of the Stuarts to the British throne. While there were actual attempts by the Jacobites at invasion or insurrection in Scotland or England in the years 1708, 1715, 1719 and 1745, there was hardly a year during this period when the Pretender was not plotting with some great European power or other with invasion of Scotland or England as the desired end. It was always on the cards that if England was brought to heel in any of the many European wars she engaged in over this period the restoration of the Stuart dynasty in Britain would have been one of the conditions of the peace. In these circumstances the British and Irish authorities cannot be greatly faulted if in times of tension they took measures to intern suspected Jacobites (in Ireland mainly Catholics) or to disarm them and take away their horses.

While the main support for the Pretender was in Scotland and England and came mostly from Protestants, he had his adherents also in Ireland, particularly among the Catholic clergy. The regular clergy were particularly vocal in his cause, but he also enjoyed some support among the secular clergy. This support was not devoid of self-interest since as long as Irish bishops were appointed to their sees on the nomination of the Pretender, it behoved every Catholic priest with episcopal ambitions to demonstrate his loyalty to the Pretender. Certainly, any priest who campaigned actively for an oath of loyalty to King George would stand a poor chance indeed of a nomination to a bishopric from the Pretender. And the Stuart Papers at Windsor Castle show that this power of nominating bishops to Irish and the few British sees was one which the Pretender took very seriously, for the very good reason that it was about the only real power he possessed.

Succeeding popes proved to be the Pretender's most enduring supporters and eventually he was to find that, in the see-saw of alliances between the different states in Europe, the only permanent refuge he could count on was Rome, and it was there he made his headquarters from 1718 onwards. The pope's continued recognition of the Pretender as king of Great Britain and Ireland meant that he was not prepared to countenance his Irish clergy taking an oath of allegiance to King George.

While, then, throughout the first half of the eighteenth century the Vatican was untiring in its efforts to protect the interests of Irish Catholics by enlisting on their behalf the good offices of the Catholic powers in Europe, the imposition of the Pretender as well as the outmoded papal deposing and dispensing powers as a sort of albatross around the necks of the Irish Catholics did much to offset the quite considerable achievements of Vatican diplomacy. If Catholics had been allowed to make their peace with the Irish authorities by accepting the reality of the Hanoverian succession and by renouncing papal pretensions as advocated by some Catholics, including Cornelius Nary, the path towards toleration and eventual emancipation might have been considerably shortened.

Archbishop Synge's form of Oath of Fidelity

I, A.B., do promise, testify and declare before God, that I am and will continue a true and faithful subject unto our Sovereign Lord King George; and that I will bear faith and allegiance to him as a good subject ought to do.

I do also profess, testify and declare before God that I hold myself bound in conscience to pay all that duty and allegiance unto our Sovereign Lord King George, which according to the Laws of God, and the present Constitutions of this realm now in force, is due to the King of Great Britain and Ireland in all matters and things which concern the lives, liberties and properties of the subjects of this land.

I do also promise and swear, that I will not at any time, directly or indirectly, by word or deed, encourage or assist any person or persons whatsoever in any design to deprive our Sovereign Lord King George of the crown or Supreme Authority which he now enjoys within the Kingdoms of Great Britain and Ireland, or either of them, or to set up a right or title to the same in any other person whatsoever; and that I will immediately discover every such design that is, or shall hereafter come to my knowledge; so as that the same may, to the best of my power, be prevented, and the promoters thereof brought to punishment according to the laws now in force within this realm.

I do also profess and swear, that I do not believe the Pope, or Bishop of Rome, or any Council or Assembly of Bishops, or Ecclesiastical Persons, has or have any lawful power, in any case whatsoever, to depose Kings or Princes, or to deprive them of their authority, or any part of it; or to absolve their subjects from their allegiance; Neither do I believe that either he or they or any of them, have power to absolve me from that allegiance which I have now sworn to Our Sovereign Lord King George, or to dispense with any part of the Oath which I now take: Neither have I already taken, nor ever will accept of any such Dispensation.

I do also promise and swear, that I will not either directly or indirectly, by word or deed, attempt or endeavour to hinder or alter the Succession of the Crown of Great Britain or Ireland, as the same stands now limited to the heirs of the late Illustrious Sophia, Electress and Duchess Dowager of Hanover; But will to my power maintain and defend the same against all persons whatsoever, and particularly against the person pretending in the life of the late King James to be Prince of Wales, and since his death pretends to be King of England and Ireland, or of Great Britain by the name of James the Third, or of Scotland by the name of James the Eighth. And if I shall at any time know of any attempt or endeavour to defeat or alter the said Succession, I will with all speed make such discovery of the same, as that to the best of my power such attempt or endeavour may be rendered ineffectual, and the authors and promoters thereof punished according to the laws now in force.

And all this I do sincerely and faithfully profess, promise and swear, according to the ordinary sense of the words now read unto me, in the true faith of a Christian, without any secret collusion, equivocation, or mental reservation; and will in like manner honestly and sincerely to the best of my power perform what I have now sworn, and every part thereof; so help me God.

Appendix 2

Cornelius Nary's proposed form of oath

I, A.B., do promise and swear to bear true faith and allegiance to his Majesty King George the Second, his heirs and successors, and that I will make known all treasons, traitorous conspiracies and plots, against his Person, Crown or Dignity, if any such shall come to my knowledge. I also profess that I detest and abhor from my heart as impious, scandalous and abominable to believe that it is lawful to murder or destroy, any Person or Persons whatsoever, for, or under pretence of being heretics; and also that base, unchristian principle that no faith is to be kept with heretics. I further declare that it is no Article of my Faith, that any person whatsoever has power to absolve me from my obligation to this Oath, or that the Pope hath power to depose Princes: And therefore I do promise and swear that I will not teach, preach, hold, maintain or abet any such doctrines or tenets, and that I will not accept of any Absolutions or Dispensations whatsoever with regard to this Oath, or any Part thereof. And all this I promise and swear upon the Faith of a Christian freely, readily and willingly, in the plain and ordinary sense of the words now read unto me, without any secret Collusion, Equivocation, Evasion or Mental Reservation whatsoever. So help me God.

Notes

1. *Whalley's Newsletter,* 19 May 1720.
2. Gilbert Library, Dublin, Newenham Collection, vol. 50, pamphlet entitled *Considerations upon considerations for promoting agriculture and providing for the poor* (Dublin, 1723), 58.
3. Quoted in Thomas Wright, *History of Ireland from the earliest period to the present time* (London, 1854), vol. 3, 309.

4. Cornelius Nary, *The case of the Roman Catholics of Ireland,* in Hugh Reily, *Genuine history of Ireland* (1762 edition), 127. This history is also known as *The impartial history of Ireland.* Although it is generally attributed to Hugh Reily, it in fact consists of Reily's pamphlet *The case of Ireland stated,* with additional material included after Reily's death.

5. Cathaldus Giblin, 'Catalogue of material of Irish interest in the collection Nunziatura di Fiandra, Vatican archives', *Collectanea Hibernica,* no. 14 (1971), 38. The papal representative in Brussels, who had *inter alia* responsibility for Irish affairs, held the rank of internuncio until September 1725, after which date he held the rank of nuncio.

6. Cornelius Nary, *op. cit.,* 116.

7. *Ibid.,* 116.

8. *Ibid.,* 116.

9. *Ibid.,* 117.

10. *Ibid.,* 117.

11. *Ibid.,* 117.

12. *Ibid.,* 118.

13. *Ibid.,* 119–22. The most notable non-juror, as they were called, was the archbishop of Canterbury, Sancroft, who was superseded by Tillotson in July 1691.

14. *Ibid.,* 123.

15. *Ibid.,* 123.

16. *Ibid.,* 124.

17. *Ibid.,* 125. Some historians put the figure at more than 400,000.

18. *Ibid.,* 126.

19. *Ibid.,* 127.

20. *Ibid.,* 127–8.

21. *Ibid.,* 128.

22. *Ibid.,* 128–9.

23. *Ibid.,* 129.

24. *Ibid.,* 130–1.

25. *Ibid.,* 131.

26. *Ibid.,* 132.

27. *Archivium Hibernicum* 4 (1915), 59 ff.

28. *Journals of the Irish House of Lords,* vol. 2, 830.

29. Cathaldus Giblin, *op. cit.* in note 5, 39.

30. *Ibid.,* 40.

31. Gilbert Library, Dublin, MS 28, 174 ff.

32. Edward Synge, *Sermon preached in Saint Andrew's Church, Dublin, before the Honourable House of Commons, 23 October 1725* (Dublin, 1725), *passim.*

33. *Ibid.,* 30.

34. *Ibid.,* 49.

35. *Ibid.,* 30.

36. Edward Synge, *A vindication of a sermon preached before the Honourable House of Commons of Ireland on Saturday 23 October 1725* (Dublin, 1726), 78.

37. Gilbert Library, Dublin, MS 27, 380. This letter from Bishop Nicolson of Derry to the archbishop of Canterbury is undated but evidently relates to some time in 1726.

38. Stuart Papers, RA SP(M) vol. 94/54, British Library MFR 762.

39. *Dublin Intelligence,* 7 June 1726.

40. Matthew O'Conor, *History of the Irish Catholics* (Dublin, 1813), 196.

41. *Dublin Intelligence,* 11 June 1726.

42. Stuart Papers, RA SP(M) vol. 94/48, British Library MFR 762. I can find no trace of Lloyd's long letter in the Stuart Papers.

43. Gilbert Library, Dublin, MS 28, 380.

44. Charles O'Conor, *Vindication of Lord Taaffe's civil principles* (Dublin, 1768), appendix ii.

45. Royal Commission on Historical Manuscripts, *Appendix to Commission Report No. 8* (London, 1881), 487.

46. Anon., *A letter to Revd. Stephen Radcliffe. . .* (Dublin, 1727), 34.

47. Cathaldus Giblin, *op. cit.,* no. 5 (1962), 121. The earl of Westmeath (at the time in question Thomas Nugent) appears to have been generally known throughout the eighteenth century as Lord Delvin, although this is a courtesy title which properly belongs to the eldest son of the earl of Westmeath. Thomas Nugent was a colonel in the Jacobite army at the siege of Limerick and was one of the hostages handed over to the Williamites as an earnest of the good faith of the Jacobite side. In accordance with the Articles of Limerick Thomas Nugent retained all his extensive estates in Westmeath, Cavan and Meath. He died in 1752 at the age of ninety-six, outliving his son by a few months. He was succeeded briefly by a brother, and then by a nephew, who conformed to the Established Church.

48. This version of the Address is taken from the *Dublin Journal* of 25–7 July 1727. It should be accepted as the official version since it was sent to that newspaper with a covering letter from the authors of the Address. It differs in some minor respects from other published versions.

49. Stuart Papers, RA SP(M) vol. 108/80, British Library MFR 768.

50. *Ibid.,* RA SP(M) vol. 112/36, British Library MFR 770.

51. It is clear from a letter dated 19 March 1728 from Francis Stuart, provincial of the Irish Franciscans, to the Pretender that Sylvester Lloyd was the prime mover in organising opposition to the Address. Stuart states: 'His [Lloyd's] behaviour in this affair having made him many powerful enemies, and having reason to believe that they have stirred up some even of the most eminent of the clergy against him, who, perhaps conscious of their omission of duty, may be ready to misrepresent him abroad for their private ends' (Stuart Papers, RA SP(M) vol. 114/138, British Library MFR 771).

52. Edward Synge, *Sermon preached in Christ Church Cathedral, Dublin on Saturday 23 October 1731 . . . by Edward, Lord Bishop of Clonfert* (Dublin, 1732), appendix. The Queries were not, apparently, printed independently as a pamphlet, since Synge states that they had 'never, that [he] could hear, been made public' (see appendix to his sermon, p. 20). The congress referred to in Query XIII was the Congress of Soissons in France in 1728.

53. Stuart Papers, RA SP(M) vol. 108/99, British Library MFR 769.

54. *Ibid.,* RA SP(M) vol. 112/36, British Library MFR 770.

55. Cathaldus Giblin, *op. cit.,* no. 5 (1962), 121–2.

56. *Ibid.,* no. 14 (1971), 40.

57. Stuart Papers, RA SP(M) vol. 114/136, British Library MFR 771.

58. *Ibid.,* RA SP(M) vol. 116/152, British Library MFR 772.

59. Cathaldus Giblin, *op. cit.,* no. 14 (1971), 41.

60. Trinity College, Dublin, Early Printed Books, Press A 75, no. 157. *Resolutions of the Lords Spiritual and Temporal* (Dublin, 1729).

61. National Library of Ireland, microfilm pos. 3651, 11.

62. *Ibid.,* 7.

63. *Ibid.,* 74.

64. Stuart Papers, RA SP(M) vols 147/24 and 152, British Library MFR 786.

65. *Ibid.,* RA SP(M) vol. 153/28, British Library MFR 788.

66. Charles O'Conor, *op. cit.,* appendix no. ii.

67. R. R. Madden, *Historical notices of penal laws against Catholics* (London, 1865), 8–12.

68. Some 1,531 persons took this oath under the 1774 act itself—see Commons Journal, Ireland, 6 February 1792. For the names of those who took the oath under the 1778 and 1782 acts see the Catholic Qualification Rolls index in the National Archives, Dublin.

69. While the Synge oath would require subscribers to maintain and defend the Hanoverian succession against all persons whatsoever, and particularly against the Pretender, the oath under the 1774 act went much further in requiring subscribers to utterly renounce and abjure any obedience or allegiance to Charles Edward, the Young Pretender. Under both oaths subscribers were required to reject the papal deposing and dispensing claims.

Chapter 9

A MATTER OF A MITRE

CANON Patrick Boyle, in his book *The Irish College in Paris from 1578 to 1901,* tells us that in 1693 Cornelius Nary was appointed bishop of Kildare but never took possession of his see.[1] I have not come across any evidence for this, and unfortunately Canon Boyle does not cite his authority. Nary, at least in his earlier years, can scarcely have had much ambition to be raised to the episcopal bench as either an archbishop or a bishop. Indeed, he must have known that if he was appointed archbishop of Dublin, for example, he would necessarily have had to forgo his roles as a public man, as a voice of Catholic public opinion, and as a writer and apologist on Catholic rights and beliefs. Furthermore, as is discussed in Chapter 8, he was quite vocal in his opposition to the pope's presumed powers to depose princes and to release subjects from their oaths of allegiance, and this in itself would have been enough to make him unacceptable to Rome. It was the view of Spinelli, the nuncio in Brussels with responsibility for Irish affairs from 1721 to 1731, that the country should be ruled by bishops 'notoriously attached to the Holy See',[2] and this, it seems, was by and large the policy which Rome adopted. In addition, in advocating an oath of allegiance to King George, Nary virtually ruled himself out of a nomination to a see by the Pretender.[3] It is difficult to see, then, how Nary could have had any real expectation of becoming archbishop of Dublin, although it appears that in his later years he coveted that post.

Following the sudden death of Archbishop Edmond Byrne in February 1724, there was a period of about ten years during which the priests of the archdiocese of Dublin indulged in an unseemly wrangle on three separate occasions in regard to the appointment of a new archbishop. Despite the many restraints under which the archbishop operated, and the very real dangers to his person in the event of the Penal Laws being activated, there was no shortage of takers for the post left vacant by Edmond Byrne's death. Chief among those interested was Sylvester Lloyd, who at that time was commissary provincial and actual definitor of the Irish Franciscans. As will be apparent from the previous chapter, he was also a Jacobite activist and a sort of secret agent for the court of the Pretender. He had some time previously translated the French *Montpellier Catechism* into English, and when the original *Montpellier Catechism* was banned by the Holy Office in 1721, the orthodoxy of Lloyd's translation was also called in question.

The catechism was in fact being widely used in the archdiocese. When its orthodoxy was initially questioned, it was examined by a group of Dublin theologians, including Cornelius Nary, who declared in August 1723 that they had found nothing in Lloyd's translation which was contrary to faith and morals, and, indeed, that Lloyd's skill was especially noticeable in the way he ingeniously omitted whatever was superfluous or dubious in the original French, or amended such passages to bring them into line with Catholic teaching. Consequently the theologians considered this translation, which took so much study and hard work, 'suitable to provide knowledge of salvation to those who sit in darkness and the shadow of death'.[4] At about the same time theologians from the Irish Augustinians and the Irish Dominicans also examined the catechism and found nothing in it opposed to faith or morals.[5] But while the catechism had ardent defenders its critics were no less powerful, and the discord which was shortly to manifest itself among the members of the Dublin diocesan chapter is said to have derived at least in part from their differences over Lloyd's catechism.[6]

His translation of the *Montpellier Catechism* was not the only matter which rendered Lloyd unsuitable to be archbishop. The Vatican Archives disclose that two gentlemen, 'noted for their learning, standing and holiness', gave it as their opinion to Nuncio Spinelli in Brussels that Lloyd was completely unsuitable for promotion to the Dublin post, even though there were many who would back him for the position. These two gentlemen further asserted that Lloyd was born of a Protestant father 'who was not ashamed to have two wives at the same time'; that since he came to Ireland he had made many friends by his charm of speech and his pleasant manner, but that he did not show signs of holiness and gravity which would merit his promotion to archbishop. When forwarding this information to Rome, the nuncio stated that he would let the cardinals know about the qualities of the other candidates as soon as he got definite information concerning them.[7]

Another man with an eye on the vacant see was Bernard Dunne, who was originally from the diocese of Dublin but had been a curé in Paris for some time. He was said to have the support of the archbishops of Armagh, Cashel and Tuam, had the honour of being known to the Pretender, and was 'universally esteemed by everybody'. However, the Pretender, despite his high opinion of Dunne, did not find it possible to give him his nomination because 'it was in the present circumstances found by no means desirable to send into the capital of that country [Dublin] any person from France, however qualified he was for the highest dignities', and in the end Dunne had to be content with the bishopric of Kildare.[8]

In the meantime it was necessary for the Dublin chapter to elect a vicar capitular to manage the affairs of the diocese pending the appointment of a new archbishop. But when the votes of the members present at the meeting for that purpose were duly counted, it was found that the candidate highest on the list had not obtained the necessary two-thirds of the votes required by canon law. The chancellor (i.e. the legal officer) of the archdiocese, Joseph Walsh, then proposed as a compromise that they should have a second vote, and that whoever obtained an absolute majority should be acknowledged as vicar capitular. This would obviate having to convene a second meeting of the chapter at a later date, a circumstance it was thought highly desirable to avoid, given the possibility of such a meeting coming to the attention of the authorities. Following a further vote on the basis mentioned, Russell, the dean of the chapter, was elected vicar capitular.[9]

According to the submission made to Rome by Archbishop Murphy a few years later,[10] seeking decisions on certain points arising from the election of the vicar capitular, all the members of the chapter, without exception, accepted Russell as the legitimately appointed vicar capitular. It is clear, therefore, that at this point Nary made no objection to Russell's appointment.

The chapter (Murphy's submission tells us) then proceeded to the selection, for submission to Rome, of three names (the Terno) from which the pope might choose the new archbishop.

145

The three names which emerged, in order of preference, were: Edward Murphy, bishop of Kildare; Dean Russell; and Joseph Walsh, the chancellor. Walsh, in his capacity as chancellor, drew attention to the fact that neither he nor Russell held the degree of doctor, prescribed as a necessary qualification by the Council of Trent for aspirants to the episcopacy; he no doubt assumed that the chapter was in a mood to gloss over this requirement, as it had apparently glossed it over in the selection of Russell as vicar capitular. In any event, he must have been taken aback by the attitude adopted by the prebendary for Maynooth, Cornelius Nary, who, we are told, became very annoyed at colleagues who were not doctors being included in the Terno, while he, apparently the only doctor among the members of the chapter, was excluded. The members, however, refused to consider the inclusion of Nary for the reason that his translation of the New Testament had recently been condemned by Rome.

Nary apparently recognised that there was little he could do about his non-inclusion in the Terno, the selection of a future archbishop being eventually a matter for the pope and the Pretender. He could, however, make a fuss about Russell's selection as vicar capitular, since a doctorate was a requisite for that position also and Russell was not a doctor. The upshot was that Nary wrote a long letter[11] to the senior suffragan bishop of the Dublin province (Verdon of Ferns) drawing attention to Russell's lack of qualification, and apparently persuading Verdon that he, as senior suffragan, had a role to play in the selection of the vicar capitular. At all events, about two months later Verdon suddenly appeared in Dublin and, 'led solely by an itch to dominate', declared that not only the election of the vicar capitular but also the selection of the Terno for submission to Rome was null, ineffective and invalid. However, he confirmed Russell as vicar capitular but made it clear that Russell owed his appointment to him as senior suffragan, and not to his election by his colleagues in the chapter.

The members of the chapter were understandably annoyed at this high-handed meddling with the affairs of their diocese, and it was arranged that three canons of the chapter should meet Verdon. At this meeting the deputation, in the name of the chapter, rejected Verdon's decree in regard to their selection of a vicar capitular and a Terno, and emphasised the rights and prerogatives of the chapter. 'Then the Suffragan', Archbishop Murphy's submission to Rome goes on, 'more audacious and wonderfully inflamed because the three Canons in the name of seventeen members of the Chapter were unwilling to submit to his judgment or decree, imposed the sentence of excommunication on the said three Canons, and he threatened to deprive the Vicar Capitular of office, unless he subscribed to the judgment against the Canons.'

Nary, it can be assumed, had not reckoned with such a serious turn of events, and no doubt he regretted having drawn down such a temperamental character as Verdon upon the chapter. Whether his colleagues ever discovered his part in drawing Verdon upon them is not clear. There is nothing in Murphy's submission to Rome about Nary's letter to Verdon. However, it was a situation, serious as it was, which by its nature could not last very long. Once a new archbishop was appointed, Verdon would cease to have any claim to a role in the Dublin archdiocese and would have to confine his activities to his own diocese of Ferns.

The pope duly accepted the first choice of the members of the chapter and appointed Edward Murphy archbishop of Dublin. He was no stranger to the Dublin scene, for he had been parish priest of St Audoen's for several years prior to his appointment as bishop of Kildare. According to his will[12] he lived in St Audoen's parish most of his life—he died at an address in Cook Street—and it is indeed probable that he continued to live in that parish after his appointment to Kildare. His appointment as archbishop cannot have been seen as other than a stop-gap arrangement, since he was already 73 years of age.

In July 1725 we find Cardinal Secretary of State Spinola informing Nuncio Spinelli in Brussels that the pope had granted Archbishop Murphy the usual indult to exercise pontificals and to describe himself in documents as archbishop. The secretary of state remarks that an indult is normally granted to Irish archbishops instead of the pallium for the reason that acceptance of the latter required a public profession of their status in consistory, which would expose them as Catholic archbishops to the authorities in Dublin.[13]

During his term as archbishop, Murphy put to Rome the whole sorry business outlined above and obtained the following decisions: (1) the selection of Russell as vicar capitular by the chapter was legal and valid; (2) the presentation of the Terno by the chapter was legal and valid; (3) persons without the degree of doctor, who in the opinion of the chapter are considered more suitable for the administration of the church, are to be preferred to those with the degree of doctor but who are not at all suitable; (4) the actions of the suffragan bishop were neither lawful nor valid; (5) the excommunication of the three canons by the suffragan did not stand.[14]

The Nary faction continued to be active and in August 1728 succeeded in scoring a minor victory. The position of dean, who as head of the chapter was the first dignitary among the priests of the diocese, became vacant earlier that year. The majority of the chapter postulated Archdeacon Doyle as dean, but in the event—and by what method it was effected we do not know—Denis Byrne, one of Nary's curates and his protégé, was appointed dean by the Holy See.[15]

In the meantime Murphy's health had deteriorated rapidly to the point where he felt it necessary to ask the pope to appoint a coadjutor with the right of succession. His choice for the post was the chancellor, Joseph Walsh, who was as old and nearly as feeble as Murphy himself. It will be remembered that Nary had previously found himself in opposition to Walsh over the appointment of a vicar capitular in 1724. Nary, along with five other members of the Dublin chapter, now took the quite unusual step of protesting to Rome, through the nuncio in Brussels, against the appointment of Walsh as coadjutor.

In their submission dated 23 November 1728,[16] Nary and his fellow signatories stated that Archbishop Murphy had been seriously ill for some months and, because of his great age, there was little hope of his recovery. They complained that Murphy, at the instance of some members of the chapter who had not the interests of the diocese at heart, was seeking as coadjutor a man who was in bad health, feeble and almost eighty years of age, and who in their opinion was entirely incapable of bearing the burdens of the office of archbishop. They represented themselves as forming the 'saner part of the chapter', in proof of which they pointed out that when the pope had recently appointed a new dean of the chapter they had humbly obeyed, while all those who had signed the postulation in favour of Walsh were reluctant to accept the new dean. (This claim sounds very laudable until it is remembered that the new dean was one of Nary's curates.) The petition was signed by the aforesaid Dean Byrne; Simon Murphy, P.P. St Audoen's and treasurer of St Patrick's; John Clinch, P.P. St Michael the Archangel and prebendary of St Patrick's; Cornelius Nary, 'Consult(issimae) Facult(atis) Parisiensis Doctor' (i.e. doctor of laws), P.P. of St Michan's, canon of the cathedral of Dublin and prebendary of Maynooth; Daniel and George Byrne, both P.P.s and canons of St Patrick's Cathedral.

Archbishop Murphy died only a month later, in December 1728, and with his death the appointment of a coadjutor was no longer an issue. However, the appointment of an archbishop to succeed Murphy led to a further wrangle and great dissension among the members of the chapter.

A letter from Nuncio Spinelli to Cardinal Secretary of State Lercari in January 1729 shows that the nuncio was only too well aware of the parlous situation in Dublin.[17] Spinelli pointed out that the state of affairs in Dublin could lead to sadder consequences than heretofore unless a man of experience and authority was chosen without delay to govern the see. He referred to the rift between the members of the chapter over the appointment of a coadjutor, and went on to point out that the chapter was for all practical purposes without a head, even though a short time before the pope had appointed Denis Byrne as dean. The majority of the canons refused to recognise him for reasons 'which were frivolous and false', and Spinelli was at a loss to know how they were even going to go about selecting a vicar capitular, since the canons refused to come together at the behest of the dean. Furthermore, Spinelli maintained that the bitter disputes between the secular and regular clergy must be given the most careful consideration when the new archbishop was being chosen. He felt that the best solution would be to transfer Christopher Butler, the archbishop of Cashel, to Dublin; his piety, prudence and nobility of birth gave him such standing and authority in Ireland that he alone would be capable of terminating the disputes which existed in Dublin. Spinelli anticipated, however, that Butler would resist transfer to Dublin since he was quite comfortable in the diocese of Cashel, where he lived among his brothers and relatives.

Whether Dean Byrne succeeded in bringing the entire chapter together to select a vicar capitular is not clear. Donnelly in his *Short histories of Dublin parishes* implies that the chapter did meet and that a majority of the members, numbering fourteen—a figure which was something short of the necessary two-thirds majority—and backed by a formidable array of parish priests, elected the chancellor, Joseph Walsh, to be vicar capitular. According to Donnelly a minority of the members of the chapter, including Dean Byrne, were in favour of Nary, but Donnelly does not state who, if anyone, was appointed vicar

149

capitular.[18] Interestingly enough, there is documentary evidence that one from each camp was appointed vicar-general of the diocese at this time, Joseph Walsh from the majority faction and Cornelius Nary from the minority faction. It seems likely, then, that no vicar capitular was appointed.

Donnelly states that the two factions sent forward separate postulations to the Holy See on the appointment of an archbishop, and that 'Father Walsh was the favourite with one side and Dr Nary with the other'. I have not been able to trace either of these original postulations. However, there is extant a postulation[19] in respect of a new archbishop dated 16 September 1729, sent to Rome by the majority of the chapter. It refers back to an earlier postulation by that faction which set out five names, one of whom they hoped would be acceptable to the pope, viz. Christopher Butler, archbishop of Cashel; Bernard Dunne, bishop of Kildare; Joseph Walsh, chancellor and vicar-general *sede vacante*; and two further members of the chapter, Richard Murphy and Matthew Kelly. The postulation mentioned that certain others, particularly from the ranks of the regular clergy, were known to aspire to the archbishopric. They mentioned in particular that Stephen McEgan, a Dominican, then bishop of Clonmacnoise ('*septem ecclesiarum episcopus*'), had such aspirations and had secured the support of some of the laity.[20] The postulation particularly warned against the appointment to the archbishopric of a reluctant person; they did not want a new affliction imposed upon a diocese already sufficiently afflicted in other ways.

This postulation was signed by eleven members of the chapter, including the two archdeacons, by ten parish priests and by twenty curates. Four of the signatories were doctors of theology, although none of these were members of the chapter. If we add the three members of the chapter nominated in the postulation—Walsh, Murphy and Kelly—to the eleven chapter signatories, it will be seen that there were fourteen members of the chapter in favour of the postulation.

Although I have not come across the original postulation by the minority faction mentioned by Donnelly, I have uncovered in the Stuart Papers a highly interesting memorial,[21] dated 28 August 1729, by 'the nobility, clergy, gentry and inhabitants of the city of Dublin', supporting Stephen McEgan's candidature. This memorial was apparently sent to Bishop Michael MacDonagh in Rome with the following letter, dated 28 August 1729, from Cornelius Nary,[22] vicar-general, L.L.D. (Michael

MacDonagh, who in 1728 was appointed bishop of Kilmore, had for some years acted as intermediary between the pope and the Pretender.)

Hond. Sir,

As you are near our Master and can have easy access to him, I beg you will present him with my profound respects, with the assurance of my daily prayers for his prosperity and that of his family. At the same time pray let him know that great numbers of this city and county are extremely astonished and scandalized that Doctor Stephen Egan should be represented as disagreeable and very unacceptable to this clergy and laity. I think that their being acquainted with the extraordinary pains that he took these twenty years past in preaching the word of God and administering the Holy Sacraments to them, should oblige them to have singular respect and esteem for him, especially since his life and conversation never clashed with his profession, or doctrine, as to my own knowledge they did not. 'Tis impossible to have everybody's good word on such an occasion as this; nevertheless I can assure you that he has the heart and wishes of the generality of the people and of a great many of the secular clergy, whatever is suggested for the contrary. I am satisfied that even those who don't sign for him have not the least aversion or dislike for his person or conduct. This is my humble and very sincere opinion; which I beg you will make known to our Master and others whom it may concern. I am with due respects, Hond. Sir, your most humble and obedient servant,

Cornelius Nary:
Vicar General L.L.D.

The memorial was signed by sixty-two persons, including ten clergy. The latter included Denis Byrne, dean of the chapter, and two other members of the chapter but, strangely, Cornelius Nary was not a signatory. Since the memorial discloses the names of some of the more prominent Catholics in Dublin city at that time, it is of considerable interest and has been included as an appendix to this chapter.

Support from the Nary faction was probably the kiss of death as far as McEgan's chances of being appointed archbishop were concerned. He would have stood a much better chance of being appointed if he had put himself forward as a compromise candidate, unsupported by either faction.

When Nary speaks of 'our Master' in the letter quoted above it is reasonably clear from the context that he means the Pretender and not the pope. It seems odd, to say the least, that the man who was guilty of such obsequiousness to the Pretender could have been a short time before actively involved in the formulation of an oath of fidelity to the Pretender's mortal enemy, George II.

151

The fact that the memorial in support of McEgan was signed by Dean Byrne and two other members of the chapter casts doubt on Donnelly's suggestion that the minority faction had previously sent a postulation to Rome in favour of Nary as archbishop, since it seems unlikely that the dean and two canons would sign a memorial in favour of McEgan if they had already postulated in favour of Nary. Nary's support for McEgan is an indication that he had by this time abandoned any ambition to be archbishop of Dublin himself, and is a further argument against Donnelly's suggestion of a minority postulation in his favour.

With regard to the persons nominated by the majority faction, Christopher Butler, as anticipated by Spinelli, had no desire to move to Dublin. Bernard Dunne, bishop of Kildare, had only recently been accused of Gallicanism in the course of a lengthy complaint, already mentioned, by the Irish regular clergy to the nuncio in Brussels,[23] and although there was a strong lobby in his favour from the Catholic gentry,[24] the nuncio and the Holy See could scarcely be enthusiastic about his elevation to Dublin. As regards the remaining three names in the postulation, the Holy See, faced with a rival postulation, no doubt saw the desirability of not allowing either side the victory, and opted for a compromise appointment in the person of Luke Fagan, the bishop of Meath.

Fagan scarcely fulfilled the specification which Spinelli had set of appointing an archbishop of experience and authority, capable of holding the ring between the warring factions in the archdiocese. He was indeed a most reluctant archbishop— probably the reluctant appointee whom the postulation already mentioned had warned against. In a letter of 1 February 1730 to the Pretender he states:[25]

> If your Majesty had no concurrence in my promotion, it was no fault of mine for I knew nothing of the matter till the Bull came to my hands, nor ever directly or indirectly solicited that honour of which I thought myself unworthy; but now being seventy years of age, infirm and daily decaying, I am disabled to undergo the fatigue necessary for the administration of so large a district. The good of the people cannot, without hazard to their salvation, suffer a long vacancy, and therefore I beg your Majesty may be pleased to represent to his Holiness my request of making a thorough renunciation of this heavy burden, altogether improportionable to my present strength.

But his protests were in vain and the diocese found itself saddled with another caretaker archbishop, quite inadequate, on his own admission, to the job in hand. The fact that while bishop of Meath Fagan had allowed himself to be conned into ordaining twelve young men for the Jansenist (and schismatical) Church of Utrecht is a measure of his capacity and judgement.[26] But the authorities in Rome were unaware of this quite unpardonable piece of folly, else he would never have been appointed to Dublin.

There are indications that relations between Fagan and Nary were close during his term as archbishop. Fagan retained Nary as vicar-general, no doubt because of his knowledge of theological questions and his experience generally of the affairs of the diocese. Fagan was quite a wealthy man with a private fortune salted away in France. He made two wills, one dated November 1733 in respect of his Irish estate, which did not amount to very much, and one dated June 1732 in respect of his French estate, valued at 25,000 *livres*. He directed that the interest on this sum should be used to provide burses for four Irish students (two from the diocese of Meath and two from the archdiocese of Dublin) at the Irish College in Paris.[27] It must be of some significance that Nary figures in both wills, in the French will as a witness, along with his curate, Dean Byrne, and in the Irish will as a go-between in the case of a donation by Fagan to the Charitable Infirmary.

Fagan died in November 1733 in Phrapper Lane (now Beresford Street) in Nary's parish, and he may indeed have resided there for most, if not for all, of his period as archbishop. He directed in his will that he be buried in St Michan's (Protestant) Churchyard in Church Street 'in such decent manner as to John Reilly, of ye Citty of Dublin, Esquire, and Thomas Kearnan of ye said Citty, merchant, shall seem meet'.[28] The 'decent manner' of his interment decided on by these two gentlemen, whom he nominated as his sole executors, did not apparently extend to erecting a tombstone over his grave, which remains unmarked and unknown.

Following Fagan's death, the metropolitan chapter met to elect a vicar capitular: Father John Linegar, parish priest of St Mary's, obtained fourteen votes and Doctor Nary eight votes. The supporters of Nary drew attention to the requirement that the vicar capitular should be a doctor, and insisted that Linegar could not be appointed while there was another so qualified (Nary) among the members of the chapter. Since there was clearly a majority in favour of Linegar, not only in the chapter but among the priests of the archdiocese generally, a petition dated 4 December 1733 on behalf of Linegar,[29] signed by a total

St Michan's Church of Ireland church, Church St. (Photo: John Kennedy, The Green Studio.)

of 44 priests, was dispatched to Cardinal Imperiali in Rome. A reply was requested to be sent to Francis Lynch, a Dublin Catholic merchant, since, of course, all such business had to be carried out under a veil of secrecy.

This petition sets out four reasons why Linegar should be appointed vicar capitular:

1. The election of a vicar capitular who was not a doctor was sanctioned by custom in Dublin and other dioceses.
2. If the requirement of a doctor's degree was insisted on, and if there was only one person (Nary) so qualified in the chapter, then an unsuitable person would be preferred to others who were highly suitable. Furthermore, if there was only one person eligible for election, this made a nonsense of the liberty of members of the chapter to vote for the person of their choice.
3. Several members of the chapter had been educated in seminaries abroad conducted by the Jesuits, where Irish students were debarred from progressing to a degree of doctor.[30] Such men, in accordance with the rule, would always be excluded from election to vicar capitular, however conspicuous they might be for learning, good morals and judgement.
4. The death of the archbishop and the sickness and old age of Dr Nary necessitated the urgent appointment of two vicars-general.

This reference to the state of Nary's health was no doubt intended as a further reason in favour of Linegar's appointment and against Nary's. That Nary was in poor health at this time is borne out by the independent evidence of one of his curates (see Chapter 12). Why his supporters should be pushing his election as vicar capitular is in these circumstances difficult to understand; it may be that the duties of a vicar capitular were such as to be within the capability of a man in poor health, and his supporters may have wished to pay Nary one final tribute. According to Donnelly,[31] the nuncio in Brussels, pending a decision from Rome, advised that the Council of Trent rule should be adhered to and that Dr Nary should act as vicar capitular.

With regard to the appointment of a new archbishop, the following were in contention for the Pretender's nomination: Abbé Wogan, a brother of a notable Jacobite, Chevalier Charles Wogan; Stephen McEgan, Dominican, bishop of Meath;

Ambrose O'Callaghan, Franciscan, bishop of Ferns; and John Linegar, parish priest of St Mary's, Dublin.[32] In a letter to the Pretender's secretary of state, O'Callaghan, while shamelessly pressing his own case for appointment to Dublin, pleaded 'at least don't set your farm [code for 'diocese'] to any decrepit old man, who may start at his own shadow',[33] no doubt with the two previous archbishops in mind. The Pretender eventually gave his nomination to Linegar, and he was appointed archbishop by the pope in March 1734. He was to occupy that post until his death in 1757.

W. Maziere Brady in his book *The episcopal succession in England, Scotland and Ireland* claims that the nuncio in Brussels recommended Cornelius Nary for the bishopric of Kildare[34] following the death of Bishop Bernard Dunne in August 1733. Brady does not cite any authority for this claim, and I can find no evidence to support it either in the abstracts from the Nunziatura di Fiandra collection in the National Library of Ireland or in the Stuart Papers. According to the latter there were four priests in the running for the Pretender's nomination to the Kildare vacancy, viz. Abbé Wogan, already mentioned; John Clinch, parish priest of St Michael's, Dublin; a Father Skelton (probably Walter Skelton, a Dublin priest who was vicar-general of Leighlin); and Stephen Dowdall, who had spent some time on the English mission.[35] A month or so before his death Archbishop Fagan, in his capacity as metropolitan, had recommended John Clinch for the vacancy.[36] Abbé Wogan would have been the Pretender's choice had he wanted the appointment. The Pretender in the end came down in favour of Stephen Dowdall, who was duly appointed by the pope.

Linegar's appointment as archbishop brought to an end a ten-year period of dissension and bickering in the Dublin chapter. The Nary faction must have decided to accept the new archbishop with a good grace, for we find Cardinal Secretary of State Firrao informing the nuncio in Brussels in July 1734 that it was very consoling for the Holy See to hear that at times its decisions in regard to appointments met with approval, as happened on the appointment of the archbishop of Dublin, which was reported by the nuncio to have greatly pleased everybody.[37]

One of the conditions of Linegar's appointment was that he should vacate the parish of St Mary's. Linegar objected very strongly to this, pointing out to the Holy See that he had been known to the civil authorities for many years as the registered

John Linegar, archbishop of Dublin 1734–57. (Photo: John Kennedy, The Green Studio. from *Repartorium Novum* vol. 2 (No. 1) (1958), p. 128.)

parish priest of St Mary's, and tolerated by them as such; any change made in the administration of the parish would reveal him as the new archbishop. If this happened, he would, he claimed, be liable to incur the penalties laid down in the laws. As a result he would have to cease functioning and would be able to do very little in the interests of religion. Linegar also protested that he would have no means of support if he were no longer parish priest of St Mary's, and he implored his holiness not to make him destitute in the new dignity he had conferred upon him.[38]

The pope apparently accepted the case made by Linegar and in July 1734 agreed that he should retain the parish of St Mary's.[39] Linegar's experience serves to indicate that bishops at that time did not have a prescriptive right to a mensal parish, as was the case later.

Nary cannot be said to have emerged from these ten years of wrangling with any degree of credibility. One gets the impression of a man only too well aware of his own abilities and of his own importance both in the archdiocese and the country as a whole. While some of the objections put forward by him—for example, against the appointment of Walsh as coadjutor—were entirely justified, there were others of the nit-picking variety, out of all proportion to the harm caused to the peace and good order of the archdiocese. He perhaps had a chip on his shoulder owing to the lack of recognition of the part he had been playing for many years as the foremost champion in the country of Catholic rights and beliefs. It must have been galling for such a man to see men of vastly inferior capabilities raised to a position of authority over him. Nevertheless his actions do smack of a dog-in-the-manger mentality, since he must have known that, because of his outspoken views on the pope's supposed deposing and dispensing powers and the condemnation of his translation of the New Testament, he was necessarily out of favour with Rome and could never be acceptable as an archbishop. But notwithstanding these realities, he appeared to be hell-bent at every opportunity on spoiling the pitch for other aspirants.

It is interesting, too, to take note of what else was taking place while the priests of Dublin were thus engaged in internecine strife. From 1723 to 1726 there was a bill before parliament (see Chapter 8) which, if it had passed, would have left them with very little to fight about, for some of its provisions amounted to a banishment from the country of the Catholic bishops. From 1726 to 1728 the Catholics, laity as well as clergy, were split on the question of an oath of loyalty to the king, and the heat engendered by that issue was mirrored in the wrangles in the metropolitan chapter. There was as well the long-standing feud between the secular and regular clergy which people of Nary's kidney did little to alleviate.

Appendix

Stuart Papers, RA SP(M) vol. 130/100, British Library MFR 777

Memorial by the nobility, clergy, gentry and inhabitants of the city of Dublin, dated 28th August 1729

Whereas the Very Reverend Doctor Stephen Egan, now Ordinary of the diocese of Ferns, hath for these two and twenty years strenuously laboured in this Metropolis of Dublin with singular zeal and extraordinary advantage of our holy religion as well as great satisfaction of the Roman Catholics thereof.

We, the undermentioned nobility, clergy, gentry and inhabitants of the city of Dublin do declare and attest to all whom it may concern that the said Very Revd. Doctor Stephen Egan, now Ordinary of Ferns, far from becoming the cause of any future division or discontent in this diocese in case of further promotion, as hath been suggested, his advancement on the contrary to this see would be highly acceptable to us as witness our hands this 28th day of August 1729

Pat Usher Esq.	Richard Barnewall
John Walsh Esq.	Andrew Aylmer Bart.
John Masterson Esq.	J. Bellew Bart.
Thomas Woulfe	James Dowdall Bart.
Gerald Byrne Gent	Anthony Alen Esq.
Walter Burne Gent	John Mapas Esq.
Standish Martin Gent	Richard Bellew Esq.
Richard Masterson Gent	Maurice Eustace Esq.
Joseph Clinch	John Plunkett Esq.
Thomas Luttrell	Val. Cruise Esq.
Will Eustace Esq.	Michael Bellew Esq.
Richard Aylmer Esq.	An. (?) Byrne Esq.
Edward Eustace Esq.	Edward Walsh Gent
John Taylor Esq.	
Christ. Eustace Gent	
Robert Eustace Esq.	
Domk. Ryan	

(Second page of memorial)

John Fitzpatrick Esq.	Dionysius Byrne Presbiter et
James Dillon Esq.	Ecclesiae Cathedrali Divi Patricii
Edmund Barry Esq.	Dubls. Decanus
Michael Loghlin Esq.	Georgius Byrne Presbiter eiusdem
Jo: Fergus Esq.	Eccles. Canonicus

John Howard Esq.
Edwd. Archer
Oliver Knaresborough
Chas. Reilly
Patt Browne
James Butler
Lawr. Comings
Jon (?) Corbally
Con Matthews
John Haughton
John Andrews
Pat Creagh
James Mason (?)
Cha. Dillon
Thomas Mahon
Aneas McDonnell
Gill McDonnell

Daniel Byrne Eiusdem Eccles.
Canonicus et Pastor
James Byrne Eiusdem Dioecesis Pastor
Valentinus Teeling S.T. Baccalaurens
Formatus in Universitate Lovaniensi
olim Theologiae Professor in absentia (?)
Glardimontensi (?) in Flandria, nuper
Examinator Synodalis Archidioecesis
Dubliniensis
Nicholas Gibbons Paroch. de Kil . . .
eius dioec.: Dubt. et Vicar. Foran. (?)
Henricus Wise Parochus et Presbiter
in Archidioecesi Dubliniensi
Patricius Byrne Presbiter Supra
dictae Dioecesis
Gulielmus Lush Presb. eiusdem
Dioecesis
Fr. Melicius Reily . . . eiusdem Dioec.

Note: Persons described as 'esquire' on the above list (apart from medical men) can be taken to be generally men of property. The names Val. Cruise, John Fitzpatrick, James Dillon, Edmund Barry, Michael Loghlin, John Fergus and John Howard correspond with the names of physicians in Dublin about the time in question. Dominick Ryan was probably a Catholic apothecary and Patt Browne a Catholic lawyer. The names Thomas Woulfe, Thomas Luttrell and Pat Creagh correspond with names on a list of merchants, not free of their guild, who opposed 'Wood's halfpence' in 1724. (See *Dublin Gazette* for 18–22 August 1724.) Oliver Knaresborough was also a merchant—see Sir Arthur Vicars, *Prerogative wills of Ireland* (Dublin, 1897). It will be seen that Egan is described in this memorial as ordinary (i.e. bishop) of Ferns. It appears that plans to appoint him bishop of Ferns fell through, and he was appointed to the diocese of Meath instead. Although he is known to historians as McEgan, it will be seen that he was known as Egan to his contemporaries, and that was how he himself spelled his name.

Notes

1. Patrick Boyle, *The Irish college in Paris from 1578 to 1901* (Dublin, 1901), 47.

2. Hugh Fenning, *The undoing of the friars of Ireland* (Louvain, 1972), 46 ff.

3. The Pretender's right of nomination of bishops to vacant Irish sees has been mentioned in previous chapters. There is evidence in the Stuart Papers of a high degree of consultation between the pope and the Pretender on appointments to vacant sees, and clearly the Pretender's influence on such appointments was very considerable. But when all was said and done the pope held the whip hand, since it was always within his

power to withdraw the right of nomination from the Pretender. There were cases where the pope overruled the Pretender: Hugh McMahon was not the Pretender's choice as archbishop of Armagh in 1715, nor was Michael MacDonagh his choice as bishop of Kilmore in 1728 nor John O'Hart of Achonry in 1735. In the case of important sees, such as Dublin, the Pretender's influence on appointments may not have been all that critical. It is significant that out of six archbishops appointed to Dublin during the Pretender's 'reign' not one was a regular, although the regular clergy, in particular the Dominicans and Franciscans, were very close to the heart of the Pretender. For further information on this subject see Cathaldus Giblin, 'The Stuart nomination of Irish bishops 1687–1765', *Irish Ecclesiastical Record* 105 (1966), 35–47, although I would not fully agree with Father Giblin's conclusions.

4. Cathaldus Giblin, 'Catalogue of material of Irish interest in the collection Nunziatura di Fiandra, Vatican archives', *Collectanea Hibernica,* no. 5 (1962), 107–8.

5. *Ibid.,* 108.

6. *Ibid.,* 107.

7. *Ibid.,* 76. Lloyd, in fact, later became successively bishop of Killaloe and Waterford.

8. Stuart Papers, RA SP(M) vol. 76/72 (British Library MFR 754).

9. Nicholas Donnelly, *Short histories of Dublin parishes* (Dublin, issued in parts, various dates), part XI, p. 52.

10. Dublin diocesan archives, Liber Decanatus No. 1 (in Latin), not paginated.

11. The letter from Nary to Verdon is not mentioned in Murphy's submission to Rome. My source for this information is Donnelly (*op. cit.,* part XI, 52) who gives the impression that he had seen the letter. I understand from Bishop's House, Wexford, that they can find no trace of the letter in the Ferns archives.

12. William Carrigan, 'Catholic episcopal wills', *Archivium Hibernicum* 4 (1915), 68.

13. Cathaldus Giblin, *op. cit.* in note 4, no. 14 (1971), 39.

14. Dublin diocesan archives, Liber Decanatus No. 1 (in Latin), not paginated.

15. Nicholas Donnelly, *op. cit.,* part III, 53. It has to be said, however, that, although a curate, Byrne was fairly senior as a member of the chapter—in fact senior to Nary who was appointed to the chapter only in 1722, while Byrne was appointed to the chapter in 1720 (see *Reportorium Novum* 1 (1956), 377). It is probable that, because of Nary's many other commitments, the task of administering St Michan's parish was largely Byrne's responsibility, and that this was recognised in his admission to the chapter and his later appointment as dean.

16. Cathaldus Giblin, *op. cit.,* no. 9 (1966), 10. In his translation of this document Father Giblin has erroneously rendered Nary's qualifications as 'Consultor of the Theological Faculty of Paris University, Doctor of Theology'. (See microfilm of the original document in National Library of Ireland, Pos. 2814, vol. 123, no. 351.)

17. *Ibid.*, p. 11.

18. Nicholas Donnelly, *op. cit.*, part III, 53–4.

19. P. F. Moran (ed.), *Spicilegium Ossorense* (Dublin, 1893), vol. 3, 134–7 (in Latin).

20. Although the small diocese of Clonmacnoise was also known as 'The Seven Churches', to describe McEgan as bishop of 'The Seven Churches' was no doubt an attempt to cut him down to size.

21. Stuart Papers, RA SP(M) vol. 130/100 (British Library MFR 777).

22. Stuart Papers, RA SP(M) vol. 130/99 (British Library MFR 777).

23. *Father Fintan's Records,* National Library of Ireland, microfilm Pos. 3142.

24. Stuart Papers, RA SP(M) vol. 131/85 (British Library MFR 778).

25. Stuart Papers, RA SP(M) vol. 102/106 (British Library MFR 766). The date in this case could be read as either 1727 or 1729. The Windsor Castle archivist read it as 1727 and filed the document accordingly. The letter evidently refers to Fagan's appointment as archbishop of Dublin in September 1729 and the date should therefore be read as 1 February 1729 (i.e. 1730 New Style).

26. Catholic apologists, such as Cardinal Moran in the last century, have sought to dismiss this story as unlikely, but Ruth Clarke, in *Strangers and sojourners at Port Royal* (Cambridge, 1932), 212–15, puts the matter beyond question.

27. A. Cogan, *History of the diocese of Meath* (Dublin, 1874), vol. 2, 156–7.

28. William Carrigan, *op. cit.,* 68.

29. National Library of Ireland, microfilm Pos. 5371, part 1, 317 (in Latin).

30. This appears to be a reference to priests, such as Linegar, who were educated at colleges in Spain and Portugal which were under the control of the Jesuits. The return made under the 1704 act shows that 23 of the priests registered for the Dublin diocese were ordained in Spain or Portugal, and there may have been others who were ordained in Ireland and who went to colleges in Spain or Portugal to complete their education.

31. Nicholas Donnelly, *op. cit.,* part III, 54.

32. See Stuart Papers, RA SP(M) vol. 166/70 (British Library MFR 794), vol. 166/139 (MFR 795), vol. 168/106 (MFR 796), and vol. 168/186 (MFR 796).

33. Stuart Papers, RA SP(M) vol. 166/81 (British Library MFR 794).

34. W. Maziere Brady, *The episcopal succession in England, Scotland and Ireland 1400 to 1875* (Rome, 1876–7), vol. 1, 357.

35. See Stuart Papers, RA SP(M) vols 165/213, 165/112, 165/138, 166/111 (all in British Library MFR 794), and 166/169 (MFR 795).

36. Stuart Papers, RA SP(M) vol. 164/106 (British Library MFR 793).

37. Cathaldus Giblin, *op. cit.,* no. 14 (1971), 50.

38. *Ibid.,* no. 9 (1966), 39.

39. *Ibid.,* no. 14 (1971), 50.

Chapter 10

A JOUST WITH THE
VICAR OF NAAS

A MONG the works of Cornelius Nary listed by Walter Harris in *Writers of Ireland* is *A letter of controversy to the vicar of Naas*. In the Early Printed Books section of Trinity College Library I came across a pamphlet by an anonymous author entitled *A letter to the Reverend Stephen Radcliffe M.A., vicar of Naas, on the subject of his letter and reply to Mr Synge's sermon and vindication*[1] (referred to below as 'the T.C.D. pamphlet'). Is this the 'letter of controversy' by Nary mentioned by Harris? I believe there is convincing evidence that it is, but whether it is entirely the work of Nary is questionable.

Walter Harris (1686–1761), a lawyer by profession, published his updating of Ware's *Writers of Ireland* in 1746, only eight years after Nary's death. It will be seen that he was to an extent a contemporary of Nary, and would have been familiar with the various works attributed to him. True, he gives the date of publication of *A letter of controversy to the vicar of Naas* as 1722 while the T.C.D. pamphlet is dated 1727. But this discrepancy is of no great significance because Harris can be shown to be generally unreliable as regards dates of publication. He gives the date of Nary's *Chief points in controversy* as 1699 when it should be 1696; Nary's answer to Clayton he dates as 1722 when the correct date was 1703. Dates of publication of Nary's New Testament he gives as 1705 and 1718 instead of 1718 and 1719. Nary's translation of Cardinal Noailles's *Mandate* is dated 1728 instead of 1726.

It is apparent that the author of the T.C.D. pamphlet was living in Dublin, had a detailed local knowledge of the town of Naas, a knowledge of the position of Catholics in the Protestant

163

states of Europe, and a knowledge of the universities of France. Nary satisfies all these particulars.

Tell-tale phrases such as 'in my humble opinion' which occur in the T.C.D. pamphlet will also be found in Nary's *The case of the Roman Catholics of Ireland* and, to an even greater extent, in his replies to Archbishop Synge (see Chapter 11). The caustic, cutting, sardonic tone of Nary's answer to Prebendary Clayton will be found also in the T.C.D. pamphlet. One finds too in that pamphlet echoes, similarities and some repetitions of Nary's *The case of the Roman Catholics of Ireland.* Furthermore, in taxing the author of the pamphlet with 'erecting' a famous convent of nuns in Channel Row,[2] in Nary's neighbourhood, Radcliffe (the vicar of Naas) may have been signalling that he believed the author of the pamphlet to be Nary.

But there is other evidence to suggest that the most which can be safely claimed for the T.C.D. pamphlet is that it is a collaboration between Nary and some prominent Dublin Catholic lawyer of the day. In the first place, when the pamphlet states: 'neither did any living soul, as yet, see or hear of it [i.e. this letter to Radcliffe], but myself, one clergyman of my religion and my amanuensis',[3] is this Nary planting a false clue with a view to preserving his anonymity, or has it to be taken simply at its face value? If the latter, it is clear that at any rate consultation with a Catholic priest was involved.

Secondly, in an obvious reference to the T.C.D. pamphlet the Franciscan priest Sylvester Lloyd, writing to the court of the Pretender in July 1727 at the time of the Catholic Address to King George II, states:

> You must remember that I last summer sent you a sermon that was preached before the House of Commons with an answer and a reply or vindication wherein this scheme [i.e. the question of an oath] was laid open. *And I again last spring gave you an answer of a pamphlet written by a catholic lawyer of this city in defence of the whole scheme*[4] [my emphasis].

When Lloyd speaks of a 'catholic lawyer of this city', could he be referring to Nary? True, Nary liked to project himself as a lawyer as well as a churchman. The fact that it was he and not a practising lawyer who wrote *The case of the Roman Catholics of Ireland,* with its high legal content, and who drafted an oath of fidelity for Catholics (again, primarily a legal document) shows to what extent his legal prowess was recognised. Nevertheless, it is difficult to see how Lloyd could refer to a clerical colleague as 'a catholic lawyer of this city'. It seems

Cornelius Nary in clerical dress, by Andrew Millar. (Courtesy of the National Library of Ireland.)

more likely that Lloyd accepted the pamphlet for what it purported to be, a letter to Radcliffe from a practising Catholic lawyer.

Lastly, there is the evidence of the regular clergy, who, in their list of grievances drawn up in 1728, quoted five passages verbatim from the T.C.D. pamphlet as evidence of the Irish secular clergy's Gallican tendencies, and pointed out that it had been published by Luke Dowling, a Catholic bookseller in High Street, *with the approbation of a Catholic parish priest.*[5] Since the pamphlet was published anonymously the regulars would have felt precluded from naming the 'catholic parish priest', but since the pamphlet emanated from Dublin city, where there were then only eight or nine parish priests, the finger of suspicion, on the basis of other internal evidence, pointed inexorably to Cornelius Nary. And the regulars must have believed that the parish priest in question had made a substantial contribution to the pamphlet since otherwise there would have been no point in citing passages from it as evidence of the secular clergy's Gallicanism. It was not, of course, the first time that they had accused Nary of such tendencies.

It appears, then, that it would be unsafe to regard the T.C.D. pamphlet as other than a collaboration between Nary and some Catholic lawyer. As to whether Nary agreed entirely with the views expressed in the pamphlet, the regular clergy implied that he did.

A letter to the Revd Stephen Radcliffe, vicar of Naas (to revert to the proper title of the T.C.D. pamphlet) is in the nature of an intervention in a controversy which had been going on between Edward Synge *fils,* then prebendary of St Patrick's Cathedral, Dublin, and Stephen Radcliffe, Church of Ireland vicar of Naas. The controversy had its beginning in a sermon preached by Synge in St Andrew's Church, Dublin, on 23 October 1725 before members of the Irish House of Commons. Synge put forward proposals in his sermon for toleration for Catholics under certain conditions. (These proposals have been dealt with at some length in Chapter 8.)

Synge's sermon of 37 pages drew a reply of 45 pages from Radcliffe,[6] in which he vehemently disagreed with the proposals for toleration for Catholics. This was followed by a 93-page vindication of his original sermon by Synge,[7] in the course of which he put forward a very detailed form of oath of allegiance, which he felt might be acceptable to Catholics who were genuinely loyal to the king.

Synge's *Vindication* was followed by a 216-page reply by Radcliffe, in which he again argued vigorously against Synge's toleration proposals and instanced his own position in Naas, where he was being bested by an unregistered Catholic priest. 'This one thing I know', he states, 'and appeal to the whole country for the truth of it, that the Romish priest of this place stands indicted for above these twelve months past, as unregistered and unlawful; upon examinations given that he had presumed to baptise even the children of Protestants inter-married with Papists, against the express will and consent of the Protestant parents. And tho' the Capias be out against him, yet he (with impunity and in defiance of the laws) officiates to this day as publicly as ever; tho' I have used all the prudent and legal methods and applications to remove him; out of no personal prejudice to him, but with a sincere intention to labour more abundantly and effectually for the conversion and edification of those souls committed to my charge.'[8]

Radcliffe goes on:

> How the case would be altered if he, or any other were tolerated by law, I cannot at present say, but believe I should soon see the dismal effects. And I think in the meantime I have reason to complain that I, an established minister in duty bound, should endeavour to put the laws in execution; and yet be hitherto baffled by a Romish priest and his adherents in defiance of the law. . . How a religious assembly of above a thousand persons in the very midst of the Borough of Naas, can in any grammatical construction of the words, be said to be quite removed from the Magistrate's inspection, is a most surprising Paradox. The Magistrate of the place may, if he please, wink hard or shut his eyes from inspecting into that which he does not desire to see or think he cannot redress. But I will venture to say he has certain knowledge of such an assembly upon full information given; and therefore it is not quite nor at all removed from his inspection, unless he is pleased, for fear of such schemes as Mr Synge's, to take no cognisance of it.[9]

Someone appears to have been deliberately misleading Radcliffe with regard to Professor Francis Martin of Louvain for Radcliffe says he had been warned 'that my priest was to be removed and he [Martin] settled here in his place'. He beseeches Mr Synge 'to keep his Professor to himself and leave me as he found me, if I cannot get rid of the nuisance altogether. For I am persuaded it is less hazardous to guard against an open enemy than a treacherous, seeming friend'.[10]

A pamphlet published at this time by one R. M. Weaver gives a very unflattering description of the vicar: 'I suppose by your silence, gentlemen, you have neither heard of the man nor his writings. Lord! he's that great, overgrown, lubberly, indolent, ignorant priest, distinguished from men of sense for his compositions and from all others by his bulk, voraciousness and avarice, and from the rest of his ingenious brethren by the title of Vicar of Naas. I'll be hanged if this be not he who lately run mad for the loss of a long-awaited benefice'.[11]

Radcliffe was born in Belfast in 1677 or 1678 and obtained his early education from a Mr Curran. He entered Trinity College, Dublin, in 1694 and graduated B.A. in 1698. He was later ordained in the Established Church. He died in Naas in 1732. His son Richard, who was born in Naas, followed in his father's footsteps and was later rector of Lisnaskea.[12]

The controversy between Radcliffe and Synge attracted the attention of the ballad-makers. There is extant *An excellent new song to a good old tune* which begins:

> I Synge of a sermon, a sermon of worth,
> which newly was printed, and newly came forth;
> a sermon of late,
> which raised a debate,
> and many opinions, of Church and of State:
> It was made by a priest of six foot and more,
> but the like of it scarce has been heard of before.

The author of the ballad repeats R. M Weaver's allegation that Radcliffe had been disappointed by not obtaining an expected promotion in the Church:

> This sermon was lately attacked in a Letter,
> which some people think might have been somewhat better;
> be that as it will,
> he got a damned pill,
> which in vain he since thought to expel by his quill:
> O Synge, thou hast better by far held thy peace
> than thus to be slaved by the Vicar of Naas.[13]

The correspondence of Archbishop King of Dublin shows that that dignitary took a hand in attempting to bring the parish priest of Naas to heel, but apparently without success. In a lengthy letter dated 12 July 1727 to Archbishop Wake of Canterbury, King sets out the reasons why the religious provisions of the Penal Laws were to such a large extent left in abeyance, and mentions Radcliffe's experience with the parish priest of Naas as an example of the unwillingness of local magistrates to implement the laws, mainly because of fear of reprisals, in the form of attacks on the magistrates' persons or property, by an overwhelming Catholic majority. Even in Dublin city, with its Protestant majority, the possibility of being lynched by the Catholic mob was a very effective deterrent to anyone inclined to excessive zeal in the enforcement of the laws.[14]

The parish priest of Naas at this time was Father John Power. It is rather ironic that, at a time when the Protestant rector was giving him a hard time, Power in turn was being accused by the regular clergy of persecuting the Dominican community in Naas. The conduct of Father Power is detailed in the formal list of grievances drawn up by the regular clergy in 1728. (This protest by the regulars has been discussed at some length in Chapter 7.) In addition to being accused of hindering Father Francis Conmy and other Dominicans from questing for alms in the Naas area, Power was also accused of (a) prohibiting his parishioners from confessing their sins to regular clergy, (b) declaring from the altar that such confessions were sacrilegious and invalid, and (c) refusing Communion to anyone who was absolved by a regular priest.[15]

It was apparently following Radcliffe's second reply to Synge that Nary and his collaborator decided to intervene in the controversy. In their *Letter to Revd Stephen Radcliffe . . . vicar of Naas,* published in the spring of 1727, they naturally support Synge's proposals for toleration for Catholics. They begin in a rather taunting fashion when they state:

> It is hoped you [i.e. Radcliffe] are in a more calm and sedate temper than you were in the heat of your dispute, when you painted me and all my Brethren in the most odious and blackest colours; and endeavoured to exasperate the magistrates against us, without any provocation worthy a man of your cloth to take notice of; it being evident to the world that since the reduction at Limerick, that is, since we submitted to the present Government, we have demeaned ourselves quiet and peaceable under the benign influence of a connivance, which His Majesty, his Ministers and Magistrates, are pleased in their goodness to afford us. . . And as to my not subscribing my name to this letter, I shall only say that the virulence wherewith you have endeavoured to traduce me and my Brethren . . . gives me just cause to apprehend you would do me mischief, had you known my name and place of abode.[16]

Radcliffe had warned Synge that if he cherished such vipers (i.e. Catholics) in his bosom, 'they will never be satisfied until they suck out your blood, if the Court of Rome thinks fit to order it'. Nary and his collaborator make this comment:

> Here is a frightful idea of the Papists. 'Tis pity you did not preach this doctrine in Holland or Germany to caution the Protestants to beware of such vipers. In Germany the Lutheran and Roman priests do in some churches successively celebrate divine service upon the

169

same altar. The Papists there under Protestant princes bear civil and military employments without any other distinction than that of merit; have full liberty of conscience, intermarry with Protestants and enjoy all other benefits of human and civil society. In Holland the Papists have likewise full liberty of conscience. They are employed in all military affairs. They are Lieutenant Generals, Major Generals, Colonels, Captains, inferior officers and common soldiers. Nay, here in Ireland in King William's time, you yourself might have seen many Dutch officers and soldiers going to Mass, at the same time fighting for King William against King James and the Papists, and being frequently asked by such of the Irish officers as could speak French, why they, who were Catholics themselves, would fight against a Catholic Prince and Catholics? Their answer was that, though they were Catholics, their swords were Protestant, and that being employed and paid by a Protestant Prince, they could not, would not, betray their trust, nor forfeit their honour. Whence it is manifest that neither the German Protestant Princes, the States of Holland nor even King William himself had the notion of Papists which you are pleased to conceive of them.[17]

They go on:

Now, I dare answer for all the Catholics of Ireland and am sure that if the same toleration or liberty of conscience were given to them, and the same privileges in their civil rights and in the fruits of their industry, which Catholics under Protestant Princes enjoy in Germany and the States of Holland, they would be as zealous for their present Government and as true to it as either Germans or Dutchmen are to their respective Protestant Princes. Nay, and would fight tomorrow against the Pope himself should he come at the head of an army with a design to invade their country or their civil rights. And not only so, but even if they were more restrained in their civil rights than they are at present, it would be highly sinful in them to rebel, or to take up arms so long as they are protected by the Prince; because protection and allegiance are reciprocal.[18]

They point out that Synge and Radcliffe have very different notions of the Reformation, Synge believing that the Reformation can subsist of itself without Penal Laws to support it. They claim that Synge and Radcliffe have very different ideas as to how the Catholics might be won over to the Protestant faith:

You, Sir [i.e. Radcliffe], would compel them by all manner of force and violence (except death) to come in, and with an air of gravity tell us you are not for persecution in the strict and rigorous sense of the word, as if the loss of men's goods, or of their liberty, or of their being cast into dark and loathsome prisons among thieves, pickpockets and common harlots (as many of the Romish clergy have been until they ended their days) were not as grievous or as intolerable as present death, or rather more intolerable, a quick death being more eligible than a lingering one.[19]

Nary and his collaborator proceed to give some instances of the many fallacies and false reasonings contained in

170

Radcliffe's reply to Synge. They point out that Synge carefully distinguishes two different sorts of papist—one influenced by the pope's dispensing and deposing powers, the other not admitting or believing the pope to have such powers. While Synge believed that some benefit of a toleration could not be denied to the latter, he did not anywhere admit that the former were entitled to any sort of toleration. In opposing Synge's toleration proposals, Radcliffe had been careful to ignore the distinctions made by Synge.[20]

With regard to the pope's dispensing powers, they comment:

> If I believe the Pope can dispense me to take all the Oaths which the laws prescribe, and by which I am qualified to bear any civil or military employment, am I not a very great fool for not enjoying the liberty to enjoy such benefits of life as might render me easy in my circumstances in this world, when I might easily obtain such a dispensation had it been practised, or had it been part of my belief? And is this not the case of all the Catholics of Ireland? Of whom you will no doubt many are capable by their merits and parts to discharge offices of profit and advantage. Whereas by not taking such oaths, neither our gentlemen, nor lawyers, nor merchants, nor dealers, nor even tradesmen do now partake of the liberties or advantages, which the rest of their fellow subjects enjoy. Is it not then plain that we do not believe that the Pope, nor any power on earth, can dispense with or make it lawful to take any Oath, but what we intend and resolve to perform?[21]

With regard to Radcliffe's complaints about the parish priest in Naas, and in particular his charge that the parish priest had been baptising the children of Protestant parents, Nary's detailed local knowledge of the situation is apparent. The letter to Radcliffe claims that the fathers of the children in question were Catholics, who would not suffer their children to be christened but by a Catholic priest, and asks: 'How could then the said priest refuse to do his duty, when he was desired by the fathers, whom I hope you will allow to be the heads of their families, though the mothers should expressly forbid it and exhibit their complaints to you or to anybody else? What room was there then for your loud exclamation of being baffled by a Romish priest?'[22]

Radcliffe's references to Doctor Francis Martin of Louvain earn the derisive comment: 'Good Sir, I cannot but lament the uneasy situation you must needs be in. If the poor Parish Priest, at the request and desire of a father who is a Catholic, will christen his child, he is your open enemy, and if a learned Professor of Divinity who maintains your own opinion, should happen to succeed your priest, as you call him, he is your treacherous, seeming friend'.[23]

They heartily agree with Radcliffe when he says he thought it impossible that Doctor Martin should be translated to Naas as parish priest, in view of the fact that Doctor Martin 'spent every week of his life, since he commenced Professor of Divinity, more than your priest could get in a whole year, and you may rest satisfied he would not come to starve in the Naas'. They go on to point out that, in any event, Doctor Martin had died in Flanders in October 1722, some five years previously.[24]

Finally, in a blistering summing-up of Radcliffe's prowess as a controversialist, they pronounce: 'if the dispute betwixt you, Sir, and Mr Synge were to be managed by sharp, biting expressions, ridiculing scraps of poetry, long and boyish stories, clamorous appeals to the World, tedious and irksome citations of authors, not pertinent to the purpose, with many invidious reflections upon Mr Synge's person and parts: I should not stick to pronounce you had carried the Bell[25] . . . All the Podder you make is only a childish *Disputatio de nomine* '.[26]

Some other views expressed in this pamphlet deserve recording. There is fulsome praise for English law: 'Nor are they [the Catholics] so dull or ignorant as not to see that the English laws are the best for free-born men of any in the World, and most appositely calculated for the preservation of men's liberty and property. So that if they [Catholics] were allowed the benefits and privileges which the rest of their fellow subjects enjoy, they would be as zealous and sanguine in maintaining the said laws as any other men whatsoever'.[27]

And here are their views on good English: 'You say that however you may differ with Mr Synge in the controversy, the World will be so favourable as to believe you both know how to write good English. I shall not envy you the pleasure of believing you do so, but I humbly conceive it would be much more to your credit to write good sense. For good language at best is but the colouring of the piece; and there are many pictures dressed up in gay colours and fine drapery which have neither symmetry nor proportion, nor even true attitude in the placing of the figures; so we find in many writers round periods, a flowing style, luscious expressions and *Vox et Praeterea nihil* [a voice and nothing more]'.[28]

One other interesting snippet of information to emerge is that 'the ingenious Mr Sheridan, our famous schoolmaster of Dublin, has many Roman Catholic children repairing to his school for their education'.[29] This was Thomas Sheridan, the friend of Swift and grandfather of Richard Brinsley Sheridan; he kept a school in Capel Street in the 1720s and possibly earlier.

Later in the year 1727 Radcliffe issued a further pamphlet of 63 pages in which he summarised the points made in his two previous pamphlets and added an appendix of ten pages in reply to the letter dealt with above. He leaves little doubt that he is aware of the author's identity. He expresses a desire to meet him in public disputation but asks him to 'declare first who shall be judge between us, for unless I have reason to believe him competent and impartial, I shall never dare to enter the lists with such a formidable antagonist'.[30] At the same time he adverts to the very uncertain nature of the toleration which Catholics then enjoyed: 'You have reason to applaud and celebrate "the benign influence of the connivance which His late Majesty [George I], his ministers and magistrates (as you say) were pleased in their goodness to afford you". At least, till you find your mistake . . . .'.[31]

One wonders whether he had Nary specifically in mind when he remarks: ''Tis indeed a summary method you take to pick out a few instances on which you think you can talk most plausibly to the amusement of your deluded followers, who ought (if they duly considered) to blush that so great a person, whom they have chosen for their Champion, can say nothing in their defence more solid and substantial'. Later on the same page he refers perhaps to Nary as 'so considerable an advocate of their [Catholics'] own'.[32]

In answer to the boast 'I dare answer for all the Roman Catholics of Ireland', Radcliffe queries: 'But who are you, great Sir, that dare answer for all the Roman Catholics of Ireland? What security can you give? And quis custodiet ipsum custodem? I am sure it is worth the Government's while to find you out, at any rate, and bind you to your good behaviour, who professes to have such an absolute influence over all the Roman Catholics of Ireland'.[33]

Having thus far concentrated on the anti-Catholic side of Radcliffe, it has in fairness to be stated that, despite all his fulminations against popery, he disowned any personal animus against individual Catholics when he states: '. . . though I abhor the abominable errors and corruptions of popery, yet I have a most sincere affection and tender regard for the persons of all my Roman Catholic brethren and countrymen, who are in truth

173

a generous, hospitable and good-natured people, and have been in former ages famous for their piety and learning'.[34]

Although the authors of the letter to the vicar of Naas promised, in a projected second part, to expound their views further, there is no evidence that they ever did so. Nary was in any event by this time engaged in a lengthy controversy with Archbishop Synge, who was a much more civilised and important adversary than the rabid, cantankerous vicar of Naas.

The regular clergy, in their complaints to the nuncio, highlighted certain passages from the letter to the vicar of Naas as smacking of Gallicanism or downright disloyalty to the pope.[35] In citing and defending Synge's proposition that neither the governors of the Christian Church nor the civil magistrates had a right to use force to restrict or punish any opinions or practices in religion, the regulars claimed that, to the displeasure of the supreme pontiff and the bishops of the Church, the dogma of heretics was being asserted and defended by an alleged Catholic.

The regulars dubbed as most insolent and impious the claim that if the government treated Catholics fairly they would be so loyal to King George that 'they would fight against the Pope himself, should he come at the head of an army'.

The authors had not disagreed with Synge's view that Catholics could be divided into two classes—those who supported papal deposing and dispensing powers and who were *not* therefore deserving of toleration, and those who opposed such papal pretensions and should accordingly be allowed a toleration. The regulars here accused the authors of the letter of embroiling Catholics with one another and rousing the government against Catholics who supported the papal claims.

The condoning of Catholic children attending a Protestant school (Thomas Sheridan's in Capel Street, Dublin) the regulars termed scandalous ingratiation (with the Protestants), pernicious to Catholic affairs and contrary to the Council of Trent.

Notes

1. Ref. LL OO. 15. no. 3. The pamphlet is dated 'Dublin January the 12th 1726–7' (i.e. 1727 New Style).
2. Stephen Radcliffe, *A serious and humble enquiry* . . . (Dublin, 1727), 69.
3. Stephen Radcliffe, *A letter to the Revd. Mr Edward Synge . . . occasioned by a late sermon preached in St Andrew's Church Dublin* (Dublin, 1726), 17.

174

4. Stuart Papers, RA SP(M) vol. 108/80, British Library MFR 768.

5. Dublin diocesan archives, item 79, not paginated.

6. Stephen Radcliffe, *op. cit.* in note 3.

7. Edward Synge, *A vindication of a sermon preached before the Honourable House of Commons of Ireland* . . . . The question of an oath for Catholics is dealt with in Chapter 8.

8. Stephen Radcliffe, *A reply to the Revd. Edward Synge . . . wherein his sermon preached in St Andrew's Church, Dublin is further considered. . .* (Dublin, 1726), 71.

9. *Ibid.,* 81.

10. Stephen Radcliffe, *op. cit.* in note 5, 87.

11. R. M. Weaver, *A letter to the Revd. Radcliffe* . . . (Dublin, 1727), N.L.I. pamphlets 381. Radcliffe had failed in his efforts to be made dean of Kildare (see N.L.I. microfilm Pos. 1116.)

12. See entry for Radcliffe in *Alumni Dublinenses.*

13. Early Printed Books library, T.C.D., Press A.7.4. no. 22. F. Elrington Ball in his edition of Swift's poems attributes this ballad to Swift. A more recent editor, Harold Williams, disagrees with Ball, saying that 'it is well within the power of other pens'. It certainly is!

14. N.L.I. microfilm Pos. 1116, 231.

15. Dublin diocesan archives, item 79 (not paginated), in Latin.

16. Anon., *A letter to the Revd. Stephen Radcliffe . . . on the subject of his letter and reply to Mr Synge's sermon and vindication* (Dublin, 1727), 3.

17. *Ibid.,* 12. This may be to overstate the position of Catholics in King William's Dutch army. It will be seen from the following letter from William to the earl of Ossory in March 1675 (quoted in Nesca A. Robb, *William of Orange: a personal portrait* (London, Melbourne and Toronto, 1966), vol. 2, 49) that William had no great welcome for Catholics: 'I should always be glad to receive those who come to me through you and that without the least hesitation, if it were not that papists are not at all in favour in this country and that I have already got myself into a lot of nasty scrapes [*beaucoup de méchantes affaires*] for promoting some of them. So I beg you to send me some English officers who belong to the Religion, and that as soon as possible'.

18. Anon., *op. cit.* in note 16, 13.

19. *Ibid.,* 15.

20. *Ibid.,* 20.

21. *Ibid.,* 36.

22. *Ibid.,* 28.

23. *Ibid.,* 30.

24. *Ibid.,* 30.

25. *Ibid.,* 19.

26. *Ibid.,* 21.

27. *Ibid.,* 14.

28. *Ibid.,* 32–3.

29. *Ibid.,* 32.

175

30. Stephen Radcliffe, *A serious and humble enquiry* . . . (Dublin, 1727), 68.

31. *Ibid.,* 69.

32. *Ibid.,* 70. In this connection it is of interest that the historian Lecky describes Nary as 'probably the ablest catholic priest then living in Ireland' (William Lecky, *History of Ireland in the eighteenth century* (London, 1892–6), vol. 1, 159).

33. Radcliffe, *op. cit.* in note 30, 72.

34. Radcliffe, *op. cit.* in note 5, 128.

35. Dublin diocesan archives, item 79 (not paginated), in Latin.

Chapter 11

THE LONG CONTROVERSY WITH ARCHBISHOP SYNGE

ARCHBISHOP Edward Synge was a complex man. In his attitude to Catholics he was inclined to blow hot and cold, at one time proposing the sternest measures to drive the Catholic religion from Ireland, and but a few years later presenting himself as the soul of lenity and toleration. He could countenance, support and succour the renegade priest-hunter Garzia[1] while at the next turn engaging with Professor Martin of Louvain in a quite serious discussion about the possibility of Christian unity. While he could be indulgent to Catholics, he was less tolerant in the case of Protestant Dissenters, an attitude which he shared with his great contemporary Jonathan Swift.

Yet withal he was a man with a genuine interest and belief in the Christian religion, which was more than could be said for some of his colleagues on the Irish episcopal bench. He was not overly ambitious for preferment; at one stage he turned down a more lucrative post because it would mean leaving Cork, and his mother, who lived with him, had grown so accustomed to that city that she would not live anywhere else. A man of great charity, he gave away a large part of his income to the poorer clergy when he became archbishop. Nor was he in love with the trappings of office; when he first took over the diocese of Tuam, he did not consider it beneath his dignity during his sojourns there to live in a thatched house until such time as a suitable house was erected.[2] The son of a bishop and the nephew of another, himself an archbishop and the father of two bishops, he belonged to an episcopal dynasty which is probably unique in the Anglican Church.

He was born in April 1659 at Inishannon in County Cork, where his father, who was later to be bishop of Cork, was then vicar. He was educated at Oxford and at Trinity College, Dublin. Following ordination, his first parish was that of

Laracor, near Trim in County Meath, where he was to have the same experience with the Presbyterians of that quarter as Swift was to have some thirty years later. We find him in May 1683 reporting to his bishop that the Presbyterian minister had had the insufferable cheek to baptise a child. 'I know indeed', he states, 'that if either the parents of the child or the pastor be proceeded against, and anyway censured or punished for this action, it will presently raise a loud cry among the brethren, how we are more indulgent to papists and idolators than to them, though for my part, notwithstanding all the errors of the Church of Rome, I am satisfied that her priests are sufficiently qualified for the administering of Baptism, which I am in some doubt of concerning their presbyters.' His bishop, Dopping, who had 'a short and easy way with Dissenters', promptly ordered the Presbyterian minister to close down his chapel or suffer the consequences. It was to be only a temporary closure, for, as already mentioned, Swift was to encounter the same problem when he had charge of the same parish.[3]

After a few years in Laracor, Synge was appointed to Christ Church in Cork city, where he was to remain for twenty years. His next appointment was to the chancellorship of St Patrick's Cathedral, Dublin, and eight years later (in 1714) he was appointed bishop of Raphoe. It may be that appointment to the episcopal bench went to his head a little, for we find him in April 1715 writing to Archbishop Tenison of Canterbury about the best way to rid the country of popery. He was confident that 'if a way be found to remove those priests and place a competent number of Protestant preachers in their room, in twenty or thirty years the whole nation would become Protestant and past all danger of relapsing again into Popery'. Since they were already few in number and would eventually die out altogether, he proposed to take no action against priests registered under the act of 1704. In the case of unregistered priests (many of them regulars), however, he proposed that the grand jury in each county should make presentment of them, and that 'if such priests did not within a certain time depart the Kingdom, every man who should apprehend any one of them, and bring him before a Justice of the Peace, should be entitled to a certain reward, to be levied upon the Papists of the barony where such priest had his ordinary abode'.[4]

In 1716 Synge was appointed archbishop of Tuam, a post he retained until his death in July 1741, aged eighty-two years. By 1722 he had so altered his views about Catholics that he was busy devising an oath of fidelity to the king which Catholics could take instead of the Oath of Abjuration. (This matter is dealt with in Chapter 8.) But perhaps the most intriguing, as well as the most unlikely, facet of this many-faceted churchman was his correspondence with Professor Martin of Louvain, who has already figured briefly in several chapters of this biography. Synge was ready to concede (to the archbishop of Canterbury) that Martin had 'preserved something of freedom in his judgment, and to mean well at the bottom'. 'I most heartily wish', he wrote to Martin in June 1722, 'you would set about writing a treatise concerning the terms upon which an Union might be made of all the disagreeing parties of Christians. Some I know, look upon it as a thing impossible to be effected; but even that is no reason why it should not be attempted. He who is able to point the true way to Peace and Unity, I think ought to do it. If others will not walk in it, the fault is theirs: But I am persuaded that such a discourse from a person in your station, would be much taken notice of, and do a great deal of good, tho' perhaps not all that you desire.'[5]

Synge's unlikely proposition to Martin should, however, be viewed in the context of correspondence between Archbishop Wake of Canterbury and the Catholic Church in France in the period 1717–20 on the possibility of union. The French Church's disenchantment with Rome at this time derived from the high papal pretensions, unpalatable to many French churchmen, in the bull *Unigenitus*. But following the death of du Pin in 1719 negotiations with Canterbury made little further progress. Synge's overtures to Martin in June 1722 were also doomed to failure, for the sands of time were running out for Francis Martin, and he was to die a few months later in October 1722.

Such, then, was the man with whom Cornelius Nary began a controversy in 1727 which was to last for the rest of his life. One can only speculate as to how well these two knew each other. Synge never mentions Nary by name in his letters, although when he mentions in his private letters and published works that he has been speaking to popish priests it is a reasonable assumption that one of these was Nary. It is significant that at the end of his first reply to Nary in 1729 Synge signs himself 'Your affectionate friend, Edward Tuam'.[6] One can conclude from this that they were at the very least personally known to each other, but how close the friendship was is another matter.

The controversy had its beginning in Synge's *Charitable address to all who are of the communion of the Church of Rome,* a pamphlet of 71 pages published in 1727. In the course of the pamphlet Synge touches upon the main points at issue between the churches—the supremacy of the pope, papal infallibility, Transubstantiation, worshipping of the Host, Communion in two kinds, purgatory, indulgences, worshipping of images, confession and pilgrimages. He begins, however, with some cautionary words of a general nature to Catholics: 'The design of this Address being only to put you upon a serious and diligent enquiry into the truth and lawfulness of those several things which you profess and practise, and wherein other Christians differ from you; to the extent that you may fully satisfy your own consciences, either in retaining them, if, upon a full examination of them, you find them to be right, or in rejecting them in case they shall manifestly appear to be wrong'.[7]

He goes on to warn Catholics: 'Do not think it will excuse you before God at the Last Day, that your parents or friends brought you up in this religion which was professed by your forefathers. . . It is not good enough for a man to say (as I have heard some of you) "I am guided by my spiritual pastor; I believe as the Church believes and, if I am in error, the Church must answer for it". . . For every man must answer for himself to God'.[8]

Getting down to specific issues, Synge points out that when an adult is baptised in the Catholic Church, only very minimal beliefs (what is contained in the Creed and the Lord's Prayer) are required of him.

> In all this there is not the least word of the Pope or his supremacy, the pre-eminence of the Church of Rome above all other churches, the doctrine of Transubstantiation, the Sacrifice of the Mass, the worshiping of the Host, Communion under one kind, the doctrine of Purgatory, Indulgences. . . In the conversation which I have had with divers persons of your persuasion, finding them always to ground their religion upon the authority of the Church, which they say is an infallible guide that cannot err in matters of faith, I have often asked them what they mean by the Church. . . Not one that I have happened to meet with has given me that account of the Church which is set down in your own Catechism.[9]

By page 17 he is ready to throw down the gauntlet:

> Here then we are ready to put the whole controversy between you and us upon this fair and clear issue: Let your Church bring sufficient proof that she has received all the latter part of Pope Pius's Profession of Faith from God himself. And if she can do so (as it is

180

plain she never can) we shall be ready to join with her in the same Profession. But as long as this is not done . . . I beseech you in the name of God not to deceive yourselves, by embracing such things upon the bare authority of your Church, without enquiring further into the truth of them.

By reference to the Catholic catechism Synge seeks to prove that Pope Pius's Profession of Faith, published in 1564 following the Council of Trent, contains a number of new articles of faith that were not previously held by the Catholic Church.

Here then I beseech you all to read over these additions, and try them by the plain rule that I have laid down, whether they are to be looked upon as part of the Catholic or Universal Faith of the Catholic and Universal Church in all ages and places from the days of the Apostles to this present time[10] . . . Did the Apostles teach the Christian Church, under the penalty of damnation, to believe that in the Mass there is offered a true, proper and propitiatory Sacrifice? Or is there the least mention or intimation of such a Sacrifice as this in the whole of the New Testament?[11]

To the objection that belief in Transubstantiation is no more absurd than belief in the Trinity, Synge maintains that Transubstantiation is directly contrary to our reason but the mystery of the Trinity is altogether above it. He points out some practical difficulties in regard to Transubstantiation. If the bread be not made from wheat and the wine from grapes, Transubstantiation cannot occur. Neither can it occur if the celebrant priest has not been properly ordained. And the person receiving Communion will not be aware that these necessary conditions have been fulfilled.[12]

Synge mentions other additions made by Pope Pius in the Profession of Faith, i.e. Communion in one kind, the doctrine of purgatory and the worshipping of saints. He asks: 'And are you sure that every one of these doctrines were not only taught by the Apostles, but taught as a matter of Faith, the belief whereof is necessary to salvation? . . . Do not therefore swallow down whatever your Church proposes to you; but first examine and try it; lest instead of wholesome food you should take that which is noxious and poisonous'.[13]

Synge questions the doctrine of the infallibility of the pope and continues:

Consider then, I beseech you, what care is taken by the Governors of your Church to keep you all in a great degree of ignorance and to hinder you from seeking after more and more knowledge, even in matters of Faith which yet they say are necessary to be believed in order to salvation. . . And, therefore, the method which some of your learned men have taken, to avoid being pressed by such questions as these, is to advise you to enter into no debates about matters of Faith, but wholly to content yourselves with what is commonly called Fides Carbonaria, or the poor collier's Faith—'I believe what the Church believes; the Church believes what I believe'.[14]

Nary replied to Synge's *Charitable address* (referred to as A below) in a book of 236 pages (referred to as B below) published about May 1728. Whether he was deputed to do so by the archbishop (Murphy) or whether he had any consultations with any of his colleagues is not clear. The archbishop was by then an old and feeble man who died later that year and, as will be seen from Chapter 9, Nary was one of those who had opposed the archbishop's choice of a coadjutor. While Nary probably got the archbishop's agreement to publish an answer to Synge, it is likely that he acted on his own initiative as regards the precise terms of his reply. He begins by paying a tribute to Synge: 'I am very sensible and so are most of the Roman Catholics of this Kingdom of the many weighty obligations we have to Your Grace, from the repeated instances of your lenity and goodness, in matters of the last consequence to us'.[15] He then deals with the subjects in contention, devoting a chapter to each.

Synge replied to Nary in a 365-page book (referred to as C below) published in 1729. He says in the preface:

> The whole controversy between Doctor Nary and me is reducible to this single question: what does God require to be believed or done as of necessity to salvation? To which I cannot find he has given a direct answer throughout his whole book; except in the article on Purgatory, which he says is to be believed under pain of damnation. But touching all the other controverted articles, which he handles, he only endeavours to prove the truth of his Church's doctrine; but does not so much as attempt to show that God requires the belief of it as necessary to salvation. Indeed, the truth of the Romish doctrines can never be proved. But if it could, that would not make the belief of it as necessary to salvation; except it be further proved that God so requires it.[16]

Synge's tone throughout is quite conciliatory:

> But if an expression that is too sharp has unwarily dropped from me (which I have carefully endeavoured to avoid) it is by no means intended against Doctor Nary himself, but altogether against the error for which he pleads. Although the Doctor employs his wit and learning in defending a bad cause (for which by his education he seems to be strongly prejudiced), yet he has written against me with a just and becoming temper. And, therefore, ought by me to be treated with the same civility and good manners.[17]

It was Nary's turn now to reply further to Synge. This he did in 1730 in a book of 130 pages (referred to as D below). Again he expresses his appreciation of Synge: 'I own I want words to express the sense I have of Your Grace's goodness and civilities'.[18] He goes over again only some of the ground in this book. Subjects now omitted he considers to have been already adequately covered.

Synge made a further reply to Nary in a 192-page book (referred to as E below) published in 1731. In the introduction he puts forward an interesting theory: 'That men may live virtuously and holily in this life, and be eternally happy in the next, and that God may thereby be glorified in their salvation, is the only end and design of true religion'.[19] He praises the way in which Nary has conducted the controversy: 'The Doctor begins his rejoinder in a very civil and obliging manner and observes great temper through the whole. I wish all writers of controversy would herein imitate him: For it is our business in such cases to endeavour to convince men's understandings and not, by sharp expressions, to raise their passions'.[20]

Synge, however, dismisses Nary's two lengthy books as beside the question, when he states that 'his business must have been to have shown either that those additional articles of Pope Pius's Profession of Faith were taught by the Apostles as necessary to salvation (as the Church of Rome now teaches them to be) or else that the belief of some things, that were never so taught by the Apostles, is now necessary to salvation. If Doctor Nary had proved either of these things, so as to satisfy the conscience of a sober man, he had indeed given me an answer. But since in both his books he has not so much as attempted either of them, he must pardon me if I say that all he has written is quite beside the question'.[21]

It fell to Nary to have the last word in this contest. He finished in July 1737 what he calls an appendix to his two previous books. He died in March of the following year and this appendix of 38 pages was published after his death in 1738 by a friend ('A.N.') in the publishing business. He says in the introduction: 'Having now time and leisure and having withal, as I hope, stayed the stomachs of those who were most earnest for and desirous to see an Answer; I shall here insert by way of an Appendix some further proofs and reasonings to enforce and support the truth of the Real Presence and Transubstantiation, two points against which our adversaries level their keenest arrows'.[22]

In the final paragraph of this appendix Nary takes his leave as a controversialist with these words:

> Now this being in all likelihood the last time I shall ever put pen to paper to write either controversy or anything relating to Faith, I desire all mankind to take notice of this my solemn declaration: viz. That I do freely, heartily and cheerfully submit all that I ever writ or said on any subject relating to Faith or Religion, to the decision of the Holy Catholic Church, and to the Pope, the Vicar of Jesus Christ, and Supreme Head of his Church upon Earth: For, errare possum, sed haereticus nunquam ero.[23]

It will be seen from the foregoing that there were six different books or pamphlets published in this controversy between Synge and Nary, and that one could devote a whole book to a proper outline and analysis of the dispute. Although they both in their various books congratulated each other on the civilised, gentlemanly way in which the controversy was conducted, they could be quite sharp and unrelenting with each other on specific issues. In order to present a flavour of the controversy, I have extracted from the various books some of the more piquant exchanges and set them out in dialogue form below. These exchanges have been chosen as much for their human interest and local colour as for their theological content.

Worshipping of images

Synge, in his *Charitable address,* had maintained that St Paul's admonition to 'abhor idols, reject images' (in the Vulgate *'horrecce idola, respue simulacra'*) could hardly be reconciled with the practice of the Church of Rome (A, p. 51).

Nary maintained that the word *'simulacra'* was wrongly translated in the phrase mentioned, and that *'idola'* and *'simulacra'* should both be translated as 'idols'. St Paul's admonition applied, then, solely to idols and not to images or statues. No doubt with tongue in cheek, Nary explains the respect which Catholics pay to images of Christ and the saints as something akin to the respect paid to the statues of King George I and King William in Dublin: 'I hope, My Lord, your Grace would not call King George's statue[24] or image at Essex's Bridge "simulacrum", if you were to make it Latin. And as to the respect which we pay to Images of Christ and of the Saints, be pleased, My Lord, to call to mind that at the dedication (if I may be allowed to use that term) of this Statue, or when the canvas was taken off it, the Aldermen and Magistrates in their

Statue of King George I on Essex Bridge, from Brooking's map of Dublin, 1728. (Courtesy of the National Library of Ireland.)

robes and the Officers present at the ceremony, took off their hats and bowed their heads towards it, the soldiers in the meantime firing vollies of small shot. And if I may rely upon the word and honour of a very worthy Protestant gentleman (who averred he was eye witness of the fact) some officers of the Army, as they marched at the head of their men, did salute King William's Statue, when they passed it, with the usual form of turning their pikes down to the ground, as is commonly done to Kings and Princes when personally present . . . and I am pretty sure that if any man should presume to offer any violence to the said statues, the magistrates and judges of the land would, very justly, punish him for the same. . . The honour and respect we pay the Crucifix, and to the images of the Saints, is no more than what common sense and gratitude suggest to all men endued with right reason to practice in their respective degrees towards their benefactors in erecting monuments and statues to perpetuate their memory and communicate their benefits. . . The Catholic Church assembled in the Second Council of Nice, and the same Church assembled in Trent, has declared that due honour and veneration is to be given to the images of Christ, the Virgin Mary and the other saints, which implies no more than that the honour and veneration due them, is to be given to them' (B, pp 16–17).

185

Synge: 'If you would effectually vindicate your Church from the charge of idolatry, it is not enough to show that you do not worship Saints or images as gods (which is all you seem to aim at) but that the worship that you give them is a lawful worship. . . I never could hear any authentic and credible history of the life of St Gubinet. And yet I know that in the County Cork great devotion is paid to her and her image; in which I never could find that the poor, ignorant people were restrained, but rather always encouraged by their clergy. If the worship of true, real saints and their images could be defended (as it never can), yet the worship which is given to such fictitious saints and their images ought certainly to be suppressed. But it looks as if you were afraid to begin any such reformation, lest the eyes of the people should thereby be opened, and they should discover how they have hitherto been deluded' (C, p. 74).

Profession of faith at baptism

Synge in his *Charitable address* pointed out the contradiction between the minimal beliefs of the Catholic rite of baptism required when an adult is baptised and the many additional beliefs in Pope Pius's Profession of Faith which such a person is required to subscribe to.

Nary: 'I think, my Lord, it is plain by the doctrine of these holy and ancient Fathers of the Church, that though there be not a word nor the least intimation of the Pope or his supremacy in our rituals of Baptism, yet that both are very well founded in Scripture and antiquity' (B, p. 37). 'It is not, therefore, necessary we should require of infants or their sureties, nor of persons of age, to make at Baptism a distinct profession of all the articles and points of the Catholic Faith; since by professing the principal and chiefest articles . . . they profess to believe all the doctrine which the Catholic Church shall teach them' (B, p. 41).

Communion in one kind

Synge: 'It is confessed by the most learned of our Communion that the whole Church everywhere, for above a thousand years, gave the Sacrament in both kinds to all the people' (A, pp 45–6).

Nary: 'Your Grace then did not read the Bishop of Meaux's Treatise upon this subject, nor Bellarmine, nor Peron, nor an hundred other Controvertists' (B, p. 146). In support of the Catholic position on Communion in one kind (bread), Nary

186

adverts to St Paul's words 'whosoever shall eat this Bread *or* drink this Cup'. He continues: 'Your Grace will tell me it is in the English bibles with the Copulative "and" and not with the Disjunctive "or"—"whosoever shall eat this Bread *and* drink this Cup". I know, My Lord, it is so, but I cannot help it. But this I know also, that this translation is contrary to all the manuscripts, and ancient printed texts, of Saint Paul, whether in Greek or Latin, that ever I could find' (B, p. 147). Nary goes on to point out some practical difficulties in the way of making Communion under the form of wine generally available to the laity: 'And to go no further for an instance of all this than the Northern parts of our own country. How many of their priests to my certain knowledge, are so poor that many of them do scarce receive as much money in a year from their parishioners as would purchase wine enough to communicate their people under the species of Wine only, even at Easter. And must none of these receive the Sacrament in one Kind, because they cannot receive it in both?' (B, p. 149).

Synge suggests that, where wine is scarce (as in the example given by Nary), a large quantity of water be mixed with it to make it go further and so allow the laity to take Communion under that species. Synge goes on to air a long-standing grievance he has with Nary concerning allegations Nary had made many years before about Protestants in his book *Chief points in controversy between Roman Catholics and Protestants*. 'Upon this occasion', Synge writes, 'I think I ought to take notice of a passage in a book "A modest and true account of the chief points in controversy etc." In this book, page 195, the author, speaking of the horrid profanations which (he says) must inevitably attend the Communion in both kinds, in a degenerate age in which all piety and godliness are almost extinguished (nor does he here except the Church of Rome), he adds: "and whereof we have sad instances in our adversaries' practice; it being frequently boasted by many of their libertines that after hard drinking over-night, they come in the morning to receive the Communion, and drink off whole Communion Cups of Consecrated Wine, to quench their brutish thirst". Who can read these words and not be moved with indignation, to find such a horrid calumny published in print to the world, without the least ground for it? Here the author charges his adversaries with a most wicked and abominable practice, not only suffered, but by many boasted of; as if the thing were so common and well-known as that no doubt were to be made of it; whereas there is no man of the least sense, who has lived among the Protestants, as he for many years is supposed to have done, but may easily be convinced that what he here says is as false as it is scandalous. I think myself obliged, being now upon this subject, to take notice of this passage, which has for many years been published in a book very common (as I am told) in the hands of your Communion. And I beseech God to give the author grace to repent of his thus bearing false witness against his neighbours. Nor need I tell him that a man cannot truly repent of a public calumny, except he as publicly retracts it' (C, p. 283).

Nary: 'I assure your Grace it is my sincere opinion. The author [i.e. Nary himself] would not advance a thing so odious if he had not been well assured of the truth of it. Nor did he intend it as a reflection on the Church of England, but only to expose the abuse which some libertines make of Sacred Things; and of whom there are but too many in the Church of Rome, as well as in the Church of England' (D, p. 129).

The Mass, the Real Presence and Transubstantiation

Nary, in answer to Synge's queries in his *Charitable address* in regard to the Mass (A, p. 24), refers back to several of the early Fathers of the Church and to the liturgies of several Eastern Christian Churches to show that the Real Presence was a doctrine of the Church from the time of the Apostles. He also points out that several Anglican divines believed in the Real Presence and goes on: 'These quotations, borrowed from your own divines, My Lord, are so full and plain that they need no comment. I shall, therefore, beg leave to ask your Grace whether any Divine of the Church of Rome can teach the Real Presence . . . in more precise and express terms than these great and learned men of your own Church have done; or whether it is possible to find words that would explain the doctrine more fully or more plainly' (B, p. 118). Concerning certain difficulties in regard to Transubstantiation mentioned by Synge in his *Charitable address*—if the bread was not made from wheat nor the wine from grapes—Nary answers: 'Whether the apprehension of a failure in any of those things . . . be a sufficient reason not to worship the Host . . . I answer, that it is no reason at all; because a moral assurance is the most we can reasonably expect not only in this but also in every other weighty affair of human life. . . That other Sacraments and divine Ordinances are subject to the like defects as to their validity, and yet a moral assurance of their being duly performed is all that any rational man requires. A child is baptised. He grows up to man's estate, is ordained Deacon, Priest and Bishop. Neither he nor his parents have any other but a moral assurance that it was with Elementary, and not with some kind of those waters which gentlewomen usually distill in their homes, that he was baptised. . . And if it should happen that anything essential to the Sacrament of Baptism be wanting, either in the matter or the form, by the use of those distilled waters, or by any other defect, the man is not baptised, nor consequently Deacon, Priest or Bishop; nor are those whom he might happen to ordain, Deacons, Priests or Bishops; yet we see no scruple made in believing men to be truly baptised and truly ordained. In like manner, we need not scruple that the priest, who says Mass, does duly consecrate with the right matter and form, but may safely rely upon his integrity; and consequently worship the Host without any danger of idolatry' (B, pp 140–2).

Synge: 'It is very plain from the Scriptures and accordingly maintained by you and us that Jesus Christ, by His suffering and dying on the Cross, offered himself as a propitiatory Sacrifice for the sins of the whole world. About *this* Sacrifice, therefore, there is no dispute between us. But the question is only concerning the Sacrifice of the Mass, as it is commonly called; or that Sacrifice which your Church teaches to be made of Christ, in the Holy Sacrament of the Lord's Supper' (C, p. 195). 'All which has again and again been made clear partly by the Archbishop [Tillotson] himself, and more fully by other well-known Protestant writers; out of whom, as well as out of the Fathers themselves, it were easy to collect many quotations to this purpose, if in so plain a case it were necessary to do that which has already been so often done. The English reader may content himself with those the Archbishop has set down; and the Learned Reader knows where to find many more, as I have already told you' (C, p. 263). 'From whence as from many other arguments we unanswerably conclude that His Body, Blood and (human) Soul are not truly, really and substantially in the Holy Sacrament. And if this be your only sense of Real Presence, you may not only charge me, but all the Divines of the Church of England, and even those whom you quote in its favour, with denying or not believing it' (C, p. 265).

Authority of Church versus private interpretation

Nary (in answer to Synge's pleas in his *Charitable address* for private interpretation of the Scriptures): 'I ask your Grace whether the sense and meaning which the Catholic Church, which is guided by the Holy Ghost, gives it [i.e. the Scripture], is not more likely to be true than the sense which any private man, to whom no such Divine assistance is promised, puts upon it. You yourselves, My Lord, seem to give a like authority to your own Church, bateing that you add an exception or a proviso which, in my humble opinion, destroys all authority' (B, p. 51).

Synge (questioning papal supremacy): 'You ought in like manner to have proved that God requires every man to believe that Saint Peter was Bishop of Rome; of which I told in my Address, I do not find proof sufficient to ground an Article of Faith upon. And yet if this be not in such manner proved, the Pope's supremacy must fall to the ground. And here you should have solved the difficulty I there proposed, viz. how it could be that Saint Paul in his Epistle to the Romans, written at the time when Saint Peter (as is pretended) was their Bishop, should not so much as name him, or take the least notice of the great privilege, which on *his* account belonged to the Church, although he salutes no less than twenty-six persons by their proper names? But to all this you are silent' (C, p. 110). Synge maintains that St Peter was not given any power which the other Apostles were not also given. The existence of wicked popes (e.g. Alexander VI) he maintains is further proof against papal supremacy. How, he asks, could such a pope be called Vicar of Christ (C, p. 110)?

Nary (with regard to restraint on Catholics reading the Scriptures) admits as much and adds: 'And indeed, My Lord, I think it were to be wished that such a restraint had been observed by yourselves. For then we should not see so many new sects spring up constantly. Nor have room to lament the loss of the souls of so many thousand children of Quakers and Anabaptists, who die without Baptism' (B, p. 234).

Infallibility

Nary: 'It was the prerogative of the See of Rome to receive the appeals of all the Bishops in the Christian World, which is an evident sign of jurisdiction and power' (B, p. 198). 'Thus we see the many sacred testimonies, upon which the belief of an infallible Church is founded. I know very well that no text of Holy Scripture is so clear, but persons of wit may find interpretations to perplex it, or to set it in a false light' (B, p. 221). Referring to the early general councils of the Church, Nary states: 'These Councils did believe themselves to have a full and ample authority to pronounce sentence against Arius, Eunomius . . . and to condemn them as heretics, from which sentence they and all the Catholic Church for many ages did believe there was no appeal, no redress. They believed themselves to be entitled to pronounce after the model of the Apostles in the Council of Jerusalem—"it seemed good to the Holy Ghost and to us". They did then believe that they were assisted by the Holy Ghost, in giving their sentence, and, by consequence that they were infallible' (B, p. 222).

Synge: 'If the Council of Trent had really been persuaded that they had the assistance of the Holy Ghost to guide them into all truth, they would certainly have acted in a very different manner from what we find they did; and would have depended upon this assistance alone, which could never fail or mislead them, in the framing of all their decrees' (C, p. 30).

Nary (in answer to a query from Synge as to where to place the infallibility of the Church—whether in the pope singly, or in the pope and general council etc.): 'I answer, My Lord, we are agreed that infallibility is placed in the Pope and Council in conjunction' (B, p. 234).

The doctrine of purgatory

Nary: 'Consequently, if the Apostles taught the Christian Church this doctrine, they [Christians] are bound under pain of damnation to believe it. All that is incumbent on me then is to prove that the Apostles did teach this doctrine. . . Now that the Apostles did teach the Christian Church such a doctrine, we are as well assured as we are that they wrote the Epistles. We have for the truth of it the constant and uninterrupted tradition of all the Churches, whether Orthodox, Schismatical or Heretical, from the beginning of Christianity to that of the Sixteenth Century.' Although the early Christians did not use the word 'purgatory', Nary argues that since they prayed for their dead that God might forgive them their sins, this was tantamount to a belief in a third place between Heaven and Hell (B, p. 167).

Synge: 'Although the Apostles never taught this doctrine, nor anything like it, yet even upon a supposition that they had

191

taught it, a Christian who does not believe it may yet be saved, provided that his want of belief does not proceed from perverseness or obstinacy, but purely and only from the want of conviction' (C, p. 304). 'No footstep of the custom of praying for the dead appears to have been anywhere in the Christian Church, until very near two hundred years after the coming of Christ. The New Testament has not one syllable of any such practice' (C, p. 309). 'You have not offered one single word to prove that this trash was ever taught by the Apostles' (C, p. 317).

No salvation outside the Church of Rome?

Nary : 'It is frequently thrown in our dish as the greatest mark of our want of charity, that we do not allow salvation to any Heretics or Schismatics. Though we do not take upon us to judge of the state of any man after death, because we do not know but at the hour of death, or at some time before it, he might have renounced his errors, have returned to the Communion of the Church, repented of his sins and have obtained mercy from God' (B, p. 182).

Synge, in answer to the foregoing, makes the point that a very bad Catholic could make a deathbed repentance and be saved, whereas a good-living Protestant could never hope for salvation, if Nary's pronouncement were true. He goes on: 'Hereupon we justly charge your Church, firstly, with great uncharitableness and even injustice in that she would exclude those from salvation, who according to the terms of the Gospel, through the mercy of God and the merits of Christ are entitled to it; secondly, with great partiality to those of her own Communion . . . and thirdly, with giving great encouragement to a wicked life, there being very many who will run the venture of Purgatory, from whence they have assurance of being delivered by Masses and indulgences that are to be purchased for money' (C, p. 323).

Notes

1. Gilbert Library, Dublin, MS 28, 155.
2. *Ibid.,* 75.
3. John Healy, *History of the diocese of Meath* (Dublin, 1908), 313.
4. Gilbert Library, Dublin, MS 28, 23–6. Other biographical particulars have been taken from the *Dictionary of national biography* (London, 1895).
5. Gilbert Library, MS 28, 170–1.
6. Edward Synge, *The archbishop of Tuam's defence of his charitable address* (Dublin, 1729), 365.
7. Edward Synge, *Charitable address to all who are of the communion of the Church of Rome* (Dublin, 1727), 3.
8. *Ibid.,* 3.
9. *Ibid.,* 11–13.
10. *Ibid.,* 23.
11. *Ibid.,* 24.
12. *Ibid.,* 31.
13. *Ibid.,* 54.
14. *Ibid.,* 60.
15. Cornelius Nary, *Letter to his Grace Edward Lord Archbishop of Tuam in answer to his charitable address* (Dublin, 1728), 3.
16. Edward Synge, *op. cit.* in note 6, p. v of preface.
17. *Ibid.,* pp x–xi of preface.
18. Cornelius Nary, *A rejoinder to the reply to the answer to the charitable address* (Dublin, 1730), introduction.
19. Edward Synge, *The archbishop of Tuam's observations on Dr Nary's rejoinder* (Dublin, 1731), p. iii of introduction.
20. *Ibid.,* x.
21. *Ibid.,* ix–x.
22. Cornelius Nary, *An appendix to the letter and rejoinder in answer to the charitable address and reply . . .* (Dublin, 1738), 4.
23. *Ibid.,* 38.
24. The statue of George I was erected in 1722 at Essex Bridge, now officially Grattan Bridge, but generally known as Capel Street Bridge.

Chapter 12

'THE LAWS HAVE SLEPT': CORNELIUS NARY'S LATTER YEARS

WHEN Edward Synge *fils,* now bishop of Clonfert, preached in Christchurch Cathedral, Dublin, on 23 October 1731 a sermon to mark the anniversary of the alleged massacre of Protestants in 1641, he had some trenchant things to say about papists and the state of the popery laws. As regards the general effectiveness of the Penal Laws against Catholics, he had this to say: 'But have they [the popery laws] answered the good design with which they were framed? I answer, NO! They are all either evaded, or not executed. So that however severe or coercive the laws may have been in themselves, the real effects of them, upon the state of the Papists among us have been very inconsiderable, I had almost said none at all'.[1] And later in the course of a lengthy footnote to the same sermon, as published, he was to remark: 'The Laws in being have slept, as it were by a general consent of all Orders and Degrees of men. And the Legislature has not yet made any new ones'.[2]

He goes on in the same sermon to fulminate in well-rounded periods against popish infiltration:

> When their number [i.e. the Catholic clergy] is vastly greater than anyone can pretend to be necessary for these ends, so great as to be burthensome to the people themselves: When they are generally of the worst kind, Regulars, men under the more immediate influence of the Pope, and sworn to him: When they, as well as Religious of the other sex, are settled in Fraternities and Nunneries in the chief towns and villages: When besides these, there are Popish Archbishops and Bishops more in number, and as well known as the Protestant ones: When 'tis notorious they keep up a regular jurisdiction, have their appeals to Rome, and very probably at some seasons, a Nuncio or

Legate from thence to superintend their affairs: When the Roman Catholics affect to be open and public in the exercise of their religion, erect pompous mass-houses in the most conspicuous places of great cities and adorn them with all the expensive pageantry prescribed and countenanced by their absurd Superstition: When 'tis further observed that their wealth and power increase, that their influence is greatly felt in some parts of the Kingdom, and it begins to appear in others, where till of late 'twas hardly suspected: When this is the true present state of things, Who, who that has a just regard for the Protestant religion, for His Majesty's Person and Government, or for our present Happy Settlement under it, can at such a juncture avoid thinking a little seriously, whither all this tends, and what may possibly one day be the end thereof?[3]

But he had not quite forgotten the ideas on toleration for Catholics which he had propounded in a sermon on the same occasion in October 1725, for he concedes: 'The clearest principles of right reason and the Christian Religion establish this as an everlasting truth, that all subjects who have the misfortune to differ from the Established Religion, ought to be treated with as much lenity on account of their religious errors, whatever they be, as is consistant with the welfare and security of the Government'.[4]

Synge was apparently expressing the views of his colleagues in the Irish House of Lords, for only a week later, on 2 November 1731, a Lords' Committee 'on the present state of Popery' was appointed (a) to enquire into the present state of popery, and (b) to prepare heads of a bill to explain and amend the popery acts and 'to secure this Kingdom from all dangers from the great number of Papists in this nation'. On 4 November this committee ordered the lord mayor of Dublin and the ministers of the different parishes to lay before the committee by the following Tuesday morning an account of all the Mass-houses in the city and suburbs of Dublin, the number of priests who officiated in each Mass-house, and an account of all the private popish chapels, nunneries, friaries and popish schools.[5]

The very short notice given for the production of all this information can only mean that their lordships were working to a very tight deadline. By asking the lord mayor and the ministers of parishes for the same information a check on the accuracy of the figures presented was ensured.

Similar orders were made covering the rest of the country. The resulting *Report on popery 1731* is a most interesting and, for the historian, invaluable source of information on the Catholic Church in Ireland in the first half of the eighteenth century. The data collected confirmed only too well the fears expressed by Bishop Synge in his speech. Their lordships discovered to their horror that, for example, 'of the mass-houses returned to them, above 229 were found to have been erected since the reign of King George I, and that some of them appear to be large and pompous buildings, particularly one in Tipperary . . . one in Mullingar, one in the Parish of Saint Mary, Cork . . . which the Lords Committees find to be a large and expensive building, raised in one of the most conspicuous places of that great city'.[6]

But it is not our purpose to go into any detail on the state of popery in the country as a whole. It is proposed rather to concentrate on the parish of St Michan's and endeavour by reference to the *Report on popery* and other sources to discover how the Catholic Church there fared under Cornelius Nary's guidance in the 1720s and the 1730s.

When one considers the many diverse activities in which this man engaged—the author of several books, a very active apologist and controversialist in the realms of Catholic doctrine, spokesman for the archdiocese on the disabilities of Catholics—it is difficult to believe that he was at the same time engaged in administering very efficiently, under trying circumstances, a large parish. Yet such was the case. No doubt he had working under him a number of trusted lieutenants to whom he could delegate widely.

Knowing the kind of man he was, it is no surprise to find that in many respects he was a trail-blazer for the other parish priests in the archdiocese. For example, in the matter of parish records those for St Michan's are the earliest in the archdiocese and among the earliest in the country for Catholic parishes. Records of weddings and baptisms are available from 25 February 1726 and, although they are written in several hands, they are for the most part neat and very legible.[7] In the case of baptisms, in addition to the names of the child and the parents, the street where the parents lived and the names of the Godfather and Godmother are also given. Occasionally, when there were no ordinary sponsors present, someone with initials D.B. (perhaps Denis Byrne, Nary's right-hand man) was recorded as Godfather. It was rare for a christening to take place in the chapel in Mary's Lane; indeed, it appears that only 'people of the better sort' had their children baptised there. Normally, christenings took place in the homes of the parents, and this was a practice which continued for many years, even after the passing of the Emancipation Act, 1829. There were also occasions when the local public house was the venue. Christenings are on record as having taken place in the Rose and Crown, Ormond Market; the Red Cow, Church Street; the Black Lion, Pill Lane; the White Hart, Mary's Abbey; and the Punch Bowl, Old Abbey Street.

Since St Mary's had apparently not been established as a separate parish up to then, the registers up to mid-October 1729 are in respect of the combined parishes of St Michan's and St Mary's. If we take the period February–December 1726, it is interesting that Church Street, the principal thoroughfare in the area, had the highest number of christenings (36), even though only the east side of the street was in the parish. It says something for the general prosperity of Catholics at that time that christenings are also recorded in (then) up-market streets such as Capel Street (11), Liffey Street (12), the Strand, i.e. Upper Ormond Quay (7), Abbey Street (5), Britain Street, i.e. Parnell Street (3), Bolton Street (4), Henry Street (2) and Cow Lane (3)—the latter, in spite of its name, was favoured by professional people such as doctors and lawyers. Baptisms for the combined parish averaged about 400 per year and marriages about 70.

It appears to have been the custom also for weddings to take place in private houses, usually the bride's home. Here are a few examples from the Register:

> *October 24th, 1728* Ambrose Ferrall, Brewer, of Thomas Street was married to Ann Dillon, eldest Daughter of Mr Theobald Dillon and Christian White, alias Dillon, Merchant, on the Inns in the said Mr Dillon's house.
> *February 14th, 1727* Mr Garret Ailmer was married to Mrs Mary Moor, Mr Michael Moor, Mr Henry Dillon, Mr Edward Bellew, Mrs Moor, Mrs Eustace being present.
> *April 14th, 1729* Was married by me, John Linegar, with Dr Nary's leave, Mr Laurence Misset, County Kildare, to Mrs Mary Dillon of this parish, in presence of Counsellor Dillon, Mrs Dillon and Miss Dillon.
> *May 23rd, 1727* David Sheehan and Eleanor Heffernon married in Strand Street at Mr Leigh's, in presence of Cornelius Heffernan, Mr William Ferrall, John Butterfield and others.

Occasionally, however, the officiating priest failed to make a careful note of who was marrying whom, with the result that he had to record the marriage in the following less than satisfactory manner:

> *June 24th, 1733* Was married James Somebody to Catherine Kelly in Mr Morrice's house. I did not get ye witnesses but I remember ye

Widow Dalton on ye Apple Key and Mr Dickson of ye same were present.

The name Philip Morrice figures a good deal in the register as a witness at weddings, indicating that he was perhaps the parish clerk. He may have been the Mr Morrice in whose house James Somebody was married.

A perusal of the registers and some other sources shows that Father Nary had as parishioners quite a number of the Catholic nobility, as well as more than a fair proportion of the Catholic merchants, tradesmen, shopkeepers, doctors and surgeons. The following is a random selection of such people: Mr Maurice, linen draper, Pill Lane; Henry Dillon of Belgard with an address in Henry Street; Leonard MacNally, merchant, Mary's Lane— he was the grandfather of another Leonard MacNally, dramatist and notorious informer; Christopher Malpas of Rochestown, with an address at North Anne Street; George Usher, merchant, Church Street; Esquire Seagrave, Abbey Street; George Duany, the Surgeon's Arms, Strand Street; Gregory Duany, surgeon, opposite the Queen's Head, Charles Street; John Dowdall, the Surgeon's Arms, Church Street; Hugh McVeagh, surgeon, Ormond Mkt; Dr John Fitzpatrick; Anthony Hay, a prominent merchant; Ignatius Kelly, printer, Mary's Lane; Sir Patrick Bellew; Sir Andrew Aylmer; Lady Castlehaven. The earl of Fingall owned house property in Church Street, where Fingall House was also located.

Such a recital of the names of the more affluent should not obscure the fact that the majority of Nary's parishioners were poor, many of them homeless beggars. And, speaking of beggars, this is perhaps the place to record that on 17 August 1731 Hegball (alias Hackball), the King of the Beggars, was married in the Mary's Lane chapel. His real name was Patrick Carregan and his bride was Allice Lynch. And one of the 'rale quality', Dr John Fitzpatrick, did not consider it beneath his dignity to be cited as a witness to the happy event. Hegball must have been quite a well-known character in his time for there is extant a satirical pamphlet entitled *Hackball's address to the Court Party with some curious remarks on the beggars' feast.*[8]

I have not been able to discover the present whereabouts of this early register of St Michan's. The information given here is taken from the microfilm of the register in the National Library. An article in the *Irish Builder* (that improbable mine of information on local history) for 1892 describes this early register as 'perhaps one of the most interesting of Dr Nary's works',[9] a view which anyone acquainted with Nary's works would regard as quite unacceptable. The article goes on to describe the register as 'a small quarto volume, well bound in vellum'.[10] Since, as we have noted, christenings normally took place in the homes of the parents, a small register, which could easily be carried in the pocket of the officiating priest, was desirable.

Although the registers are given over to what they were intended to be (a record of baptisms and marriages), they do yield from time to time some interesting (at times tantalising) marginalia, the sacred and the profane sometimes curiously juxtapositioned. Thus on 19 May 1730 the profane world, in the shape of a rope-dancer, manifests itself, when someone scribbled over the entries for that date that 'Madam Violante is a rope-dancer in Dame Street in ye year one thousand seven hundred and thirty'.[11] But on the very next page we are back to reality with an account of payments made for altar wines, wafers and candles:

8 September, paid ye Bread		1s – 6d
Wine and candles	w.	3s – 0d
	can.	3s – 0d

Also listed are the addresses of various contacts in London, Brussels (important because the nuncio with responsibility for Ireland lived there), Paris and Rome, as well as some in Ireland.

Mary's Lane chapel

As we have seen in Chapter 3, this chapel was originally built by Nary in 1704. It must have been quite a solid structure for it did duty as a chapel until 1814 (when the present St Michan's, Halston Street, was opened), and it afterwards served as a school and later still as a tenement.[12] There is in fact extant a contemporary description of all the Catholic chapels in Dublin in 1749, and although St Michan's is stated in this document to have been repaired by Nary's successor, Fr Denis Byrne, this 1749 description can be taken as broadly indicating what it looked like in Nary's time:

> In Saint Mary's Lane is a parochial chapel, whose jurisdiction extends from one side of Boot Lane to one side of Church Street, inclusive. It was built by subscription obtained by solicitation of Dr Cornelius Nary, 'tis a large but irregular piece of building. The altar piece is a painting of the Annunciation of B. V. M. and on the Epistle side stands a large image of V. M. with Jesus in her arms, carved in wood, which statue before the Dissolution belonged to St Mary's Abbey. On the Gospel side stands the pulpit, and opposite it a choir enclosed, near to which is a large sacristy. There is another altar near

199

A statue of the Blessed Virgin which stood in Nary's chapel in Mary's Lane. It belonged to St Mary's Abbey before the Dissolution of the Monasteries, and now stands in the Carmelite Church, Whitefriars St. (Photo: John Kennedy, The Green Studio.)

the pulpit, over which is a large Painting of a Crucifix, and under it the picture of St Francis Xaverius; there are three galleries here, several pews and confessionals. The decorations of the altar are much the same as those mentioned in the chapel of Liffey Street. It has lately been repaired by the care of Mr Dennis Byrne, Titular Dean of St Patricks and parish priest of said chapel.[13]

The decorations of the altar of the chapel in Liffey Street, referred to in the foregoing, are described as follows: '. . . fore part of altar covered with gilt leather, and name of Jesus in glory in the midst. On the altar is a gilt tabernacle with six large gilt candlesticks, and as many nosegays of artificial flowers'.[14]

The statue of the Blessed Virgin mentioned above later found its way to an antique dealer's shop, whence it was retrieved in 1824 by Revd Dr Spratt, prior of the Calced Carmelites, and it now stands in the Carmelite Church, Whitefriars Street.[15] The holy water font which stood in the Mary's Lane chapel can now be seen in St Michan's Church, Halston Street, where there was until recently an ivory crucifix with the following note: 'This crucifix was brought from the Continent by the Reverend Doctor C. Nary, P.P. Saint Michan's (1699–1738) and stood over the High Altar in Saint Mary's Lane Chapel from 1700 till 1817 when it was removed to the present church. It is French art of the Seventeenth Century'. The painting of St Francis Xavier has not survived, but a copy, painted by John Keenan in 1817, may be seen in St Michan's Church, Halston Street.

In an examination given before a magistrate in 1751 the then parish priest, Father Patrick Fitzsimons, stated that he had five or six priests in St Michan's to assist him, and that the collection at the door provided for them. A share of the collection and some emoluments made up £50 to £60 per year, which was the parish priest's income. Exceedings on the chapel rent also went to him. Fr Fitzsimons described the parish as 'numerous but small', meaning presumably that it was small in area but with a large population. The situation was probably much the same in Nary's time. To put the emoluments of £50 to £60 a year in context, it should be remembered that at the same period there was many a curate and some ministers of the Established Church, with a wife and family, 'passing rich on £40 a year'.[16]

Apparently it was the practice in Dublin parishes to make a door-to-door collection for the chapel rent. In a poem *The fatigues of a faithful curate,* the poet-mathematician Laurence Whyte records the curate bemoaning his position:

201

About the parish twice a year I'm sent
in order to collect the chapel rent
and as Church Warden trudge from house to house
to stand the frown of some without a souse.[17]

The curate in question was evidently attached to the chapel in Rosemary Lane, just across the river from St Michan's parish.

As to the names of the other priests in the parish during the 1720s, apart from Nary, the most prominent was John Linegar (later archbishop), who appears on the list of priests for the parish in 1697. He was registered as parish priest of St Mary's in 1704 but may not have taken over that post canonically until 1729. Another priest serving in the parish at this time was Denis Byrne, who, as noted in Chapter 9, was appointed dean of the chapter in 1728. Donnelly was of the opinion that he spent his entire priestly career in the parish.[18] The Jesuits were also active in the parish, although they were probably confined for the most part to the sphere of education.

The priest-hunter Garzia, in his report (in Spanish), dated 2 February 1722, to Archbishop King on the priests in Dublin parishes, mentions by name only Nary and Linegar as attached to the Mary's Lane chapel. He states that two further unnamed priests were living at the sign of the Cock. Garzia's sources cannot have been all that reliable since he describes Nary as 'reputed Bishop of Meath'.[19]

With regard to the *Report on popery 1731,* it should be noted that the different Protestant ministers were not asked for the names of the priests in their parishes but only for the *number* of priests. On this latter point, Percival, the then minister of St Michan's, reported rather lamely: 'As to the number of priests who officiate in each or any of them [chapels], we have endeavoured to get information but can get none'.[20] He was in fact the only minister in Dublin not to give the number of priests per chapel in his parish. If the figures for St Audoen's are excluded (where a figure of 40 to 50 priests for two chapels is scarcely credible), the figures provided by the other ministers show that there was an average of six priests per chapel.

Predictably enough, the establishment of St Mary's as a separate parish in 1729 appears to have been the occasion of a dispute between Nary and Linegar as to the line of demarcation between the parishes. A committee of eight Dublin priests examined the matter and issued a statement as to the correct boundary of St Mary's parish, i.e. east side of Boot Lane (East

Arran Street), Bolton Street, Drumcondra Lane to Drumcondra Bridge (the bridge over the Tolka river).

The statement of the committee went on: 'And we do further declare to the parishioners or Catholic inhabitants within the said districts that they are to look upon the said Mr John Linegar as their only true and lawful pastor; and that no other priest whatsoever has, or ought to claim any right or title to the said parish of Saint Mary's or to any part thereof'.[21]

Population

In 1733 the number of houses in the three civil parishes on the north side of the city were: St Michan's, 1,248; St Mary's, 1,373; St Paul's, 482. It had been found (as mentioned in Chapter 3) by counting the number of houses and inhabitants in the parish of St Michan's in 1723 that the average number of persons per house was exactly twelve. While roughly the same average probably applied in St Paul's, in the largely Protestant and less congested St Mary's the average number per house was probably about ten.[22]

On this basis the populations of the three civil parishes could be estimated as follows: St Michan's, 15,000; St Mary's,

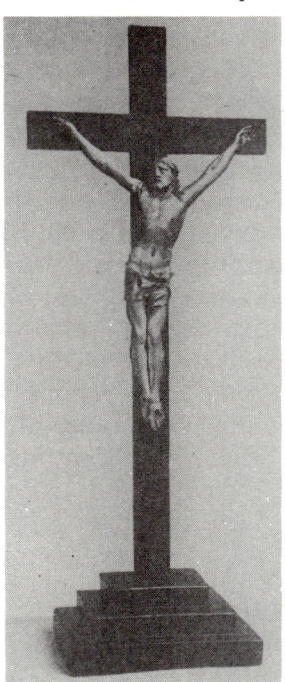

Ivory crucifix (until recently in St Michan's Church, Halston St.), which 'stood over the High Altar' in the Mary's Lane chapel from 1700 until 1817. (Photo: John Kennedy, The Green Studio.)

203

13,700; St Paul's, 5,800. It will be seen from Chapter 3 that around this time Catholics comprised about 60% of the population of St Michan's and St Paul's, and about 35% of St Mary's.

The population of the city and liberties continued to increase, reaching about 125,000 by 1733. The Catholic proportion had also improved and comprised about 40% of the population in 1733, as compared with about 30% in 1710.

Conferences between Catholics and Protestants

The Lords' Committees 'on the present state of Popery' also specifically ordered the ministers of the various Dublin parishes to lay before their lordships 'an account of what weekly conferences have been held within their respective parishes to carry on disputes upon points of controversy between the Protestants and the Papists'.[23] Since they made them the subject of a special order, it appears that the Lords' Committees were especially concerned that these conferences might succeed in converting some Protestants to the Catholic faith. The returns made show that conferences were most frequent in the parish of St Michan's. Indeed, there was only one other parish where conferences were currently being held, although there were a few parishes where conferences had been held in past years but where the practice had been discontinued.

Revd William Percival, minister of St Michan's, reported that 'there have been several conferences held in the said parish in order to pervert Protestants, viz. nine at the King's Head on the Inns, one at the Black Lion in Pill Lane, one at Mr Cannon's on Ormond Quay, all within a year and six months'.[24] With the possible exception of the one held in Mr Cannon's (which may have been in a private house), the venues for the conferences were inns or taverns. At first sight, these were hardly the most appropriate venues for religious disputation. However, the conferences were probably held in meeting rooms attached to these licensed premises.

Considered against the climate of the times, these conferences might be regarded as a most unexpected phenomenon. But when we take into account that the second half of the seventeenth century and the early years of the eighteenth was a period of great religious debate in these islands, it is perhaps not so surprising that Cornelius Nary, with his penchant for religious controversy, should have initiated debates between

Catholics and Protestants in his parish. Such disputation has, however, to be viewed in a context where the number of Catholics and Protestants in the city was by the 1730s moving in the direction of an equilibrium; the Protestants were still clearly in the majority, but it was a majority that was being whittled back year by year. It is easy to see how such a situation could generate tension between the rival faiths, and obviously the Church of Ireland minister in St Michan's parish believed that the purpose of the conferences in that parish was 'to pervert Protestants'. But at a time when it was Catholic Church policy to keep a low profile, it is difficult to believe that such was the purpose. There was perhaps the hope that participation in such conferences would result in an increase in knowledge of their faith on the part of Catholics. The conferences could perhaps also be viewed as a spin-off from the prolonged controversy at that time between Nary and Archbishop Synge.

Schools in the parish

The *Report on the state of popery 1731* gives the names of twelve Catholic schools in the civil parish of St Michan's, but since the boundaries of the civil and Catholic parishes did not correspond four of these are clearly in the Catholic parish of St Paul's. In addition, Donnelly was of the view that 'possibly one of the three that were to be found in Church Street' belonged to St Paul's—the difficulty about Church Street being that it was split down the middle between the two Catholic parishes. Assuming that all three schools in Church Street were in St Michan's, the *Report* listed eight schools in the parish, viz. one Latin school 'kept by Phill. Reily on the Inns' and seven English schools, kept by McGuire in Church Street, Lyons in Church Street, Kearnon in Church Street, Cullin in Pill Lane, Carty in Phrapper Lane, Ward in Mary's Lane, and Burke in Mary's Lane.[25]

It will be seen that Phill. Reily is the only one of these schoolmasters whose Christian name is given. This may be an indication that his Latin school on the Inns Quay was a well-known establishment. It seems likely that all the English schools were small and were conducted in the schoolmaster's own home. What role the Church had in setting up these schools is unclear. For the most part, they probably resulted from the initiative of the schoolmasters themselves, but in consultation with the parish priest. The Jesuits, who were active in the parish, probably also had some role.

The Charitable Infirmary

This hospital was originally established in Cook Street in 1718 but, following a short spell in Anderson's Court in St Michan's parish, was transferred to larger premises in Inns Quay, also in St Michan's parish. Since both the patients and the doctors and surgeons attached to it were in the early years mainly Catholics, it can be assumed that the priests in St Michan's parish had at least a spiritual involvement with it. When Archbishop Fagan died in 1733, his will disclosed that he had left £15 (equivalent to perhaps £3,000 today) to Dr Nary for passing on to the Infirmary, possibly indicating some personal involvement by Nary in its affairs. The finance for the running of the hospital was to a great extent provided by 'contributors', who chose annually twenty trustees, and these in turn oversaw the management of the hospital. While it is very likely that Nary was a contributor, he would have been prevented by the laws against Catholics from being a trustee.

A short account of the Infirmary, published in 1733, states in regard to its origin that 'about the year 1723 the Scheme appeared but did not take effect till 1725'.[26] The account goes on: 'The surgeons who attend this house, give their labour and skill gratis, without fee or reward; but meddle not with any that are deemed incurable, or such as labour under any venereal distempers'. In the previous twelve weeks the Infirmary had dealt with 250 out-patients. Inmates numbered 18 (13 men and 5 women) and 'distinct apartments were provided for each sex, and all proper conveniences'. The house could hold 30 inmates, if contributions sufficient to cater for that number could be obtained.

The account stresses the interdenominational aspect of the undertaking:

> Let it not be wondered at that Protestants and Papists join together in such an amicable manner to support the poor and miserable. The Principles of Christianity obliges us to lay aside all distinctions in this case. Indeed, the object of this charity being the poor in general, without distinction of party or religion, and the whole bounty being equally distributed with the most exact impartiality, it is not to be doubted but that persons of all denominations will contribute to it. And particularly we hope that the several able surgeons of this city, Protestants as well as Papists, will join in such a useful undertaking, where their apprentices may have an opportunity of seeing more cases in surgery and of learning more experience than can be expected in any Surgeon's family, let his business be never so extensive.

The account points out that 'at the same time we are thus doing good to the poor, we are providing for the benefit of the rich. For the labour of the poor is the wealth of the nation, and by preserving the limbs of a poor man, we enable him to be useful to the public, who would otherwise become a load and a burden to others'.

We can conclude that Nary's parish, as it had evolved in the 1720s, was in quite a prosperous condition and well organised to look after the spiritual and temporal needs of the parishioners, with several small schools and even a hospital. It was not unique in these respects. There were a number of parishes in the city in an equally prosperous condition. The parish of St Nicholas Without was rated, from the point of view of income of the clergy, as a better parish. The parish priest there at this time was Thomas Austin, a man with a great reputation for charity to the poor. He is on record as having given to charities for the poor £80 on two separate occasions— say, a total of £30,000 in today's money.[27]

But as long as the Penal Laws remained on the statute book, Catholics could have no grounds for complacency. There was the ever-present fear that the laws might at any time be activated against them. We have seen in Chapter 8 how such an activation had been averted in the 1724–6 period, mainly through the machinations of Vatican diplomacy, and how in the period 1731–2 the Irish parliament was again balked by London in its efforts to enact more stringent popery laws. In March 1732 the Lords' Committees resolved *inter alia* that 'it is absolutely necessary that the magistrates of this Kingdom, particularly those of the City of Dublin, do immediately enter upon a more steady and vigorous execution of the Laws against Popery; especially those against all Regulars and Persons exercising Ecclesiastical Jurisdiction, contrary to the Laws of this Kingdom'.[28] In the spring of 1734 further harsh measures were promulgated by the lord lieutenant at the instance of parliament. But again, owing mainly to lack of commitment by the local magistracy, these measures petered out after a few months. These kinds of threats were repeated periodically up to the 1750s, and while they all petered out after much the same fashion the general effect was to keep Catholics in a state of great unease and insecurity.

The last years (1730–8)

Cornelius Nary had long since attained the three-score-and-ten human ration of years spoken of by the psalmist. When he looked back over those years, conflict and controversy must have seemed their abiding characteristics—the several controversies with representatives of the Established Church, the not yet resolved conflict with the regular clergy of his own Church, the bickering on several occasions over the appointment of an archbishop, and the constant manoeuvring and conniving in the face of the ever-present threat of an activation of the laws against Catholics in general and against the Catholic clergy in particular. He had now reached an age when he could quite understandably have sat back and left it to younger men to carry on the fight he had engaged in so competently and with a degree of success for so many troublous years.

But there were still Protestant clerics who, like Clayton long ago, had an itch for controversy, and who were all too ready to beard the old papist lion in his den: men like John Maxwell, prebendary of Connor, for instance, who wrote to Nary on 3 April 1733:

> Having been lately in some company, where was a young gentle-woman of your Communion, a niece of ————, I happened to talk of the doctrine of Intention as maintained in the Church of Rome; by which doctrine it is asserted that in order to the validity of a Sacrament, it is required that the priest's intention, when he administers the Sacrament (which with you are seven), should concur with his outward actions; and that he should intend by those actions, what the Church intends by them. The Young Lady said that was not the doctrine of the Church of Rome; I asked her how she knew that. She told me she had indeed heard it before affirmed to be the doctrine of the Church of Rome by others, as then by me; that it startled her; and that she enquired of you about it, but you assured her it was not the doctrine of the Church of Rome; at which I was somewhat surprised and told her that I was then going out of town and that when I returned I would bring with me the Canons of the Council of Trent. . . Accordingly, I here send you transcribed the 11th Canon of 7th Session which is in these words: [here follows the canon in Latin]. Which I thus English for the benefit of the lady: 'If anyone affirms that the intention at least of doing what the Church does is not required in Ministers, when they perform and confer the Sacraments; let him be anathematised'. How then can you justify what you told the lady?[29]

Maxwell must have known the young lady quite well for it was she, he tells us, who took his letter to Nary. Nary is reported to have told her that she had mistaken him and that he had never denied the doctrine as set out in the canons of the Council of Trent. Far from putting an end to the matter, this gave Maxwell an excuse for a second and longer letter to Nary. Put briefly, Maxwell's argument was that, in view of the certainty that there were down the years priests and bishops who continued to administer sacraments long after they had lost their faith, how could the Catholic Church be certain that its chain of authority had not been breached and that, as Maxwell so eloquently put it, 'there is not so much as a Christian among you'.[30] He cites the notorious priest-hunter, Garzia, as an example: 'I suppose you remember the affair of Father Garcee, seven or eight years ago in this town; who was a priest among you, and all the while a Jew in his heart, according to his own declaration afterwards, during which time he celebrated Mass, and administered other Sacraments among you; but how validly according to your own doctrines, let anyone in the name of common sense determine'.[31]

But Nary, apparently, was not in the humour to be tempted to yet another controversy with the Anglican clergy. On this occasion he left the reply to one of his underlings, someone who signed himself 'A.B.'—initials often used as a cloak of anonymity. Perhaps it was his curate and protégé, and for some time now dean of the chapter, Denis Byrne, who wrote to Maxwell in reply: 'There came to my hands a letter directed to Dr Nary, who has neither health nor leisure to be employed in trifles, that don't touch the essentials of religion, which everyone can answer at a first view, who has even a superficial notion of our doctrine. Such quibbles may disturb weak heads, and seem to be designed towards that end, but not any man of learning or sense'.[32]

The effect of A.B.'s reply must have been to spread confusion further when he states: 'Your fundamental principle, from which you draw such wondrous and frightful consequences is so far from being an Article of our Church, that it is disputed by many divines, who tell you that no other intention is required in conferring any Sacrament but that of doing what the Church does, that is, of doing the outward action, for example, in Baptism, of washing the child and pronouncing the words. And this is all that you can prove from the Council of Trent Canons, for those above-mentioned are the very words'.[33]

A.B., however, goes on to defend in the remainder of his letter the other interpretation of the canon in question, that the right intention on the part of a priest is absolutely necessary for the valid performance of a Sacrament. He produces several arguments to show that even in that case the Roman Catholic Church has nothing to fear.

209

But it is not felt necessary to go any further into this controversy since Nary took no further part in it and, in any event, the doctrine of intention was one which Nary had a few years before discussed with Archbishop Synge.

With the appointment of Linegar as archbishop in 1734, Nary lost the position of vicar-general which he had held under Archbishop Fagan. Linegar appointed to that post Patrick Fitzsimons, a future archbishop of Dublin. However, Nary did not feel himself completely left out in the cold, for his legal talents are on record as having been availed of in these last years on at least two occasions. In 1736 there was a dispute between the archbishop of Armagh and the bishop of Meath concerning the right of presentation to the vicarage of Athboy. There is in the diocesan archives a document from the nuncio in Brussels, dated April 1736, nominating Cornelius Nary, John Clinch and the bishop of Kildare to proceed to a definitive judgement in the dispute.[34]

Another example of how Nary's legal qualifications were availed of may be found in the Shrewsbury Papers, where may be seen a letter dated 23 June 1737 from a James Roche of Denbighshire to the countess of Shrewsbury, in which he outlines how he lost his family's estates around Cork and Kinsale because he was not prepared to forsake the Catholic religion. It appears that the previous owner of the estates, Maurice Roche, died leaving no male heir. His nephew, the James Roche already mentioned, in these circumstances was entitled to the estates. However, Maurice Roche left an only daughter, who married a man named Francis Kearney. This Kearney forthwith possessed himself of the deeds of the estates, turned Protestant, and then as a Protestant discoverer under the popery acts sued James Roche for possession and recovered all the estates from him. In his letter to the countess James Roche appends a certificate signed by, among others, the archbishops of Dublin and Cashel; the bishop of Kildare; Patrick Fitzsimons, vicar-general; and C. Nary, L.L.D. This certificate outlines the facts of the case and states James Roche's moral entitlement to the estates in question.[35] The practical use to which such a certificate could be put is not apparent, in view of the then penal provisions in regard to Catholic ownership of landed property. Possibly all that was intended to be achieved was to put James Roche's case on record with a view to the certificate being of use if and when the law was amended.

Was Nary a friend of Swift?

Thomas R. England, in a note on Nary in his biography of Reverend Arthur O'Leary, published in 1812, claimed that Nary 'enjoyed the friendship and intimacy of Dean Swift to whom he was assimilated for various learning, ready wit and high conversational talents'.[36] This claim is repeated by Myles Ronan in an article in the *Irish Rosary,*[37] but Ronan's source is obviously England, since he repeats most of England's actual words. England (1790–1847) was a Cork priest and he was presumably repeating an oral tradition about Nary and Swift that was current in his time. It is a claim, then, that has to be taken seriously, although in all the lengthy correspondence of Swift there is no direct reference to Nary. There is one possible indirect reference in a letter from Swift to a Catholic friend in England, Martha (Patty) Blount: 'My greatest happiness would be to have you and Mr Pope condemned during my life to live in Ireland, he at the Deanery, and you for reputation's sake, just at next door. . . And you shall have Catholicity as much as you please, and the Catholic Dean of Saint Patrick's, old again as I, to your Confessor'.[38]

'The Catholic Dean of Saint Patrick's' may possibly have been Swift's playful way of referring to Nary, although Nary never enjoyed that title. But it is more likely that Swift is referring to Thomas Austin who was then parish priest of St Nicholas Without, Francis Street, only a stone's throw from St Patrick's Cathedral, although Austin held the office of archdeacon, not that of dean.

The fact that Swift never mentions Nary in his correspondence need not be taken as an overwhelming argument that they were not on friendly terms. Archbishop Synge, in his correspondence with the archbishop of Canterbury, mentions on a number of occasions that he has been in contact with Catholics, among whom Nary was probably numbered, but takes care not to mention any names. Other similar instances could be cited. In the circumstances of the times it was probably considered safer for all concerned not to mention names, in view of the possibility of such mention proving embarrassing or perhaps incriminating in the event of a reactivation of the Penal Laws. Indeed, the extent to which various people, including Nary, were intent on covering their tracks against the possibility of later incrimination is a frustrating aspect of research on Nary's life and times.

When Swift's library was auctioned in 1746[39] following his death, it is of some significance that none of Nary's books appeared on the catalogue, although three volumes by Archbishop Synge were included, one of which was his *Observations on Nary's rejoinder* (1731). If Swift and Nary had been friends, one would expect that Swift would have some works by Nary in his library.[40]

Given that they were both well-known writers living within half a mile or so of each other, it would have been difficult for Swift and Nary not to have known each other. But, on balance, it appears unlikely that there was any deep friendship between them. Let us consider for a moment their very opposite characters. On the one hand there was the bawdy, earthy, near-agnostic, wine-bibbing, *bon vivant* dean. On the other hand there was Nary, who, from what we know of him, must have been an abstemious, serious, frugal-living priest, totally committed to the defence of Catholic doctrines. We have to ask ourselves was it likely that two such opposites could have been close friends.

Portraits of Nary

A further indication of Nary's importance in his own time is the fact that two portraits of him have come down to us.[41] One of these is by a noted Dublin engraver of the time, John Brooks. It shows Nary in lay dress, with a curly wig, standing by a bookcase, holding a copy of his *New history of the world* in his right hand. The second portrait is by Andrew Millar, another noted engraver. It shows a bewigged Nary, wearing bands and surplice, with a book—perhaps his New Testament—in his right hand.

Nary's death

In an introduction, written in July 1737, to what was to be his last work of controversy, Nary begins with the words 'having now time and leisure . . . .'.[42] It appears from this that he may have retired from active work as a parish priest earlier in 1737. We gather from the letter from 'A. B.' to John Maxwell (above) that his health had already begun to deteriorate as early as 1733. Nevertheless, the end, when it came, appears to have been sudden, the cause of death probably apoplexy. The fatal attack probably happened on the morning of Friday 3 March 1738. His colleagues and relations soon found that no will had been made and there must have been a last-minute rush to remedy this while he had his faculties. Evidently he died that night, for the *Dublin Newsletter* of 4 March 1738 in a very brief announcement tells us: 'Last night died Dr Nary at his lodgings in Bull Lane in the 79th year of his age'. This would normally mean that he had not completed 79 years, but, as already argued in Chapter 1, note 2, it is evident that he was 79 years of age when he died.

His will, like so many other valuable documents, perished in the fire in the Public Records Office in 1922, but fortunately Donnelly had extracted the details some years before and published them in his *Short histories of Dublin parishes*.[43] His will directed that he 'be interred in the churchyard of Tipper, County Kildare, at the foot of an ash tree, South side of the churchyard, and where my father and mother were buried'. He furthermore directed that 'nothing costly be laid out on my funeral, but to have a plain coffin put into a hackney coach to carry my corpse to the grave; and, whereas most of my worldly substance consists of my library, and furniture of my room, clothes, and a few pieces of Church plate and other plate, I will, and my will is, that my Executors hereafter named do sell all the premises to answer the legacies herein after mentioned. I bequeath Mr Willes £5, and £5 to him that shall be my servant at my decease.[44] I devise £30 to be equally divided between my brother Walter, the children of my brother, Denis, of my sister Mary, my sister Joan, my sister Anne, share and share alike. And I do constitute Mr Dennis Byrne sole Executor and residuary legatee'. The will was made on 3 March 1738 and proved on 7 March 1738.

The brief announcement in the *Dublin Newsletter* is apparently the only public announcement of his passing. Its brevity need not surprise us when it is remembered that the Dublin newspapers at that time largely copied their news from the London papers, and added very little Irish news of their own. The absence of a lengthy obituary on the passing of such a well-known figure can therefore be readily understood.

There are, however, two contemporary tributes to be found elsewhere than in the newspapers, which should be mentioned. On the fly-leaf of the British Library copy of Nary's New Testament there is the following note: 'Dublin, March 7, 1738, Last Friday morning died, aged seventy-nine, Dr Nary, a Romish priest of this parish of Saint Michan's. He was a gentleman of great charity, piety and learning, and very much esteemed by Protestants as well as by those of his own religion'.

213

This was obviously written by a Protestant, perhaps by the then rector of St Michan's, John Antrobus. Nary could not have wished for a handsomer eulogy.

Included in *A new collection of poems on several occasions,* published in 1741, is a poem entitled *To the memory of Dr Nary* by an anonymous writer.[45] I have included it as an appendix to this chapter, not because it has any great value as verse but because it is the only detailed contemporary tribute to Nary which I have come across in the course of my research. Having seen Nary exposed in these pages, warts and all (as they say), some of the claims made for him in this poem must appear to us to be exaggerated. But then it is the kind of indiscriminate praise usually heaped upon the dead in such circumstances. The reference to Swift is interesting, though not very enlightening. But the fact that the writer mentions Swift at all in the same breath as Nary may be an indication of an acquaintance, if not of a friendship, between the two.

So ended the life of Cornelius Nary. It had been a very full life, a life filled with a high degree of insecurity and trepidation, but it could not be said to have been an unduly hard one. All the indications are that he lived in a degree of comfort in his lodgings in Bull Lane, with an income which was more than ample for the needs of a single man. The fact that he had a man-servant points to a certain degree of opulence.

It was a life of many achievements, and not a few failures. In the field of education, seven or eight schools had been set up in his parish, one of them a Latin school. There was also a Jesuit classical school for boys, and a boarding-school for the daughters of the Catholic gentry and wealthy classes had been set up just outside his parish in Channel Row. The parish had a sizeable chapel in Mary's Lane, which was adequate for all its needs. A system of records of births and marriages had been established well in advance of the other parishes in the archdiocese. A back-up staff of five or six curates ensured that all the varied work of a large parish was disposed of efficiently—Masses, confessions, christenings, marriages, funerals, attending the sick, catechising the young. The Charitable Infirmary on Inns Quay was doing great work for the sick poor.

Despite all the advantages to be gained by going over to the Established Church, very few of his parishioners had conformed. Indeed, during these early decades of the century,

The holy water font from Nary's chapel in Mary's Lane, now in St Michan's Church, Halston St. (Photo: John Kennedy, The Green Studio.)

very few had conformed in the country as a whole. Nary's long controversy with Archbishop Synge, which had been published in book form, must have done lasting good, not only through its exposition of Catholic doctrine but through the propaganda value of a Catholic priest doing battle with an archbishop of the Established Church on equal terms. In the public domain, *The*

215

case of the Roman Catholics of Ireland, while it may not have had any great impact on the authorities at the time of its first publication in 1724, would stand as a lasting reproof to Protestants for their treatment of Catholics.

Turning to the debit side, his translation of the New Testament was probably his most egregious failure. The conferences between Catholics and Protestants that he had initiated in his parish had not been allowed to continue, through the intervention of the authorities. His interventions in the appointment of an archbishop in Dublin had availed little, and only drew upon himself accusations of self-interest and self-aggrandisement. His efforts towards the formulation of an oath appropriate for Catholics had petered out in disillusionment and more bad odour with the Catholic Church establishment.

And yet this pernickety, cantankerous, controversial priest emerges as by far the most considerable Catholic figure in Ireland in the first half of the eighteenth century. That such a man could have lived through what are generally regarded as the darkest hours of the Penal night and at the same time could speak out so fearlessly and so trenchantly for Catholic rights and beliefs in itself says a lot about the reality, as opposed to the myth, of Catholic life in the Ireland of his time.

Appendix

From *A new collection of poems on several occasions* **(Dublin, 1741). Author's name not given**

To the memory of Doctor Nary

As that bright Orb, enlivener of the Day,
infuses Joy with ev'ry darting ray;
so Nary's learning, which shall never die,
in soaring lines and strongest energy.
Hail source of sense, thou honour to all schools,
obeying Heaven and its strictest rules;
thy bright example, who can imitate,
or shine like thee, peculiarly great;
thy practice Charity, thou pride of life,
unknown to Envy or to worldly strife;
laborious in thy office, just and great,
worthy our tears, and thy Celestial Fate:

216

With Joy, we know, thou with Archangels dwell,
thou scourge of vice, thou enemy of Hell;
strong balmy blessings from thy tongue did flow,
and swelling comforts from thy language grow:
Build marble pillars, and his deeds rehearse,
and Swift, immortal, write his living verse.
The Muses sigh, and Virtue's self doth mourn,
ethereal graces, weep about his Urn:
See distant lands give Nary's learning praise,
his works eternal monuments shall raise.

Notes

1. Edward Synge, *Sermon preached in Christchurch Cathedral, Dublin on Saturday 23 October 1731* . . . (Dublin, 1732), 17.

2. *Ibid.*, 17 (*recte* 21).

3. *Ibid.*, 19–20.

4. *Ibid.*, 17 (*recte* 21).

5. *Report on the state of popery in Ireland, 1731*, reprinted in *Archivium Hibernicum* 4 (1915), 136. See Chapter 8 in regard to heads of bills proposed in 1731.

6. *Journals of the Irish House of Lords,* vol. 3 (Dublin, 1784), 604.

7. National Library of Ireland, microfilm Pos. 8829.

8. Crofton collection of pamphlets in library of Trinity College, Dublin, ref. 82.11.

9. Anon. (believed to be Edward Evans), 'History of the Roman Catholic church and parish of St Michan', *The Irish Builder* 34 (1892), 175.

10. *Ibid.*, 176.

11. Madam Violante is best known as the discoverer of the great actress Peg Woffington.

12. *Op. cit.* in note 9, 201.

13. Nicholas Donnelly (ed.), *State and condition of the R.C. chapels in Dublin . . . 1749* (Egerton MS 1772) (Dublin, 1904), 12.

14. *Ibid.*, 11.

15. John Meagher, 'Glimpses of eighteenth century priests', *Reportorium Novum* 2, no. 1 (1958), 130.

16. W. P. Burke, *Irish priests in penal times* (Waterford, 1914), 307.

17. Laurence Whyte, *Original poems on various subjects* (Dublin, 1740), 176.

18. Nicholas Donnelly, *Short histories of Dublin parishes* (Dublin, issued in parts, various dates), part XI, 55.

19. Kevin McGrath, 'John Garzia, a noted priest-catcher and his activities, 1717–23', *Irish Ecclesiastical Record* 72 (July–Dec. 1949), 512. Garzia's original report in Spanish reads: 'dos más en la señal del Cok', literally 'two more in the sign of the Coke'. Admittedly, this is not a very probable sign for a house, and I note that Father McGrath has translated

this as 'two more at the sign of the Cook'. I believe, however, that what was intended was 'two more at the sign of the Cock'. The fact that there was a house with such a sign in Phrapper Lane nearby adds weight to this view. A memorial of a lease in respect of this house in favour of one Morgan Byrne and dated August 1738 can be found in the Registry of Deeds, Dublin (ref. 92–255).

20. *Op. cit.* in note 5, 141.
21. Anon. (believed to be Edward Evans), 'History of the Roman Catholic church and parish of St Michan', *The Irish Builder* 34 (1892), 17 ff.
22. Gilbert Library, Dublin, Monck Mason MS, part 3, 153–5. In 1733 there were ten Church of Ireland ministers in the three civil parishes, viz. St Michan's, 4; St Mary's, 4; St Paul's, 2.
23. *Op. cit.* in note 5, 142–3.
24. *Ibid.,* 146.
25. *Ibid.,* 141.
26. *Weekly Miscellany* of 28 December 1734 (available in King's Inns Library, Dublin).
27. *Op. cit.* in note 22, vol. 3, part 2, p. 236.
28. *Journals of the Irish House of Lords,* vol. 3 (Dublin, 1784), 10.
29. John Maxwell, *Two letters to Father Nary* (Dublin, 1734), 17. Available in King's Inns Library (ref. 355).
30. *Ibid.,* 19.
31. *Ibid.,* 22.
32. *Ibid.,* 23.
33. *Ibid.,* 23.
34. John Meagher, *op. cit.* in note 15, 135.
35. Historical Manuscripts Commission, *Report on manuscripts in various collections,* vol. 2 (1903), 313–15.
36. T. R. England, *The life of Revd Arthur O'Leary* (London, 1822), 22.
37. Myles Ronan, 'The story of a Dublin parish', *The Irish Rosary* 8 (April 1904), 255.
38. F. Elrington Ball (ed.), *The correspondence of Jonathan Swift* (London, 1910), vol. 4, 14–15.
39. Harold Williams, *Dean Swift's library* (Cambridge, 1932), *passim.*
40. It is also of interest that Nary is not mentioned among Swift's list of his friends, whom he categorised as grateful, ungrateful, indifferent and doubtful. (See Harold Williams (ed.), *The correspondence of Jonathan Swift* (Oxford, 1965), vol. 5, 270.)
41. Engravings of these portraits are in the National Library of Ireland. In the case of the portrait of Nary in lay dress, the title of one of the books on the shelf in the background can, with the aid of a magnifying glass, be deciphered as *Nary's answer,* i.e. Nary's answer to Archbishop Synge. Since Nary's first reply to Synge was dated 1728, it must follow that Nary was already seventy years of age when this portrait was made.
42. Cornelius Nary, *An appendix to the letter and rejoinder in answer to the charitable address and reply* . . . (Dublin, 1738), 4.
43. Nicholas Donnelly, *op. cit.* in note 18, 55.

44. The fact that Nary does not here name the servant should imply that the terms of the will had been drawn up some time before Nary's death, although the will was not executed until the day of his death. If the will was drawn up *and* executed on the day of his death, there should be no difficulty about naming the servant.

45. Anon., *A new collection of poems on several occasions* (Dublin, 1741), 14. This volume is available in the Gilbert Library, Dublin. There was nothing unusual at the time about a poetic tribute of this kind on the death of a Catholic cleric. D. F. Foxon, *English verse 1701–1750* (Cambridge, 1975), lists the titles of some still extant elegies on the deaths of Dublin priests printed in the 1720s and 1730s, viz. elegies on the deaths of Father Nicholas Dalton at his lodgings in Bridge Street, Father Sir Daniel Dowdall of St Paul's parish and Dr Francis Higgins at his lodgings in Mary Street.

INDEX